C++17 By Example

Practical projects to get you up and running with C++17

Stefan Björnander

BIRMINGHAM - MUMBAI

C++17 By Example

Copyright © 2018 Packt Publishing

Commissioning Editor: Merint Mathew
Acquisition Editor: Chaitanya Nair
Content Development Editor: Lawrence Veigas
Technical Editor: Adhithya Haridas
Copy Editor: Safis Editing
Project Coordinator: Prajakta Naik
Proofreader: Safis Editing
Indexer: Aishwarya Gangawane
Graphics: Jisha Chirayil
Production Coordinator: Deepika Naik

First published: February 2018

Production reference: 1220218

Published by Packt Publishing Ltd.
Livery Place
35 Livery Street
Birmingham
B3 2PB, UK.

ISBN 978-1-78839-181-8

www.packtpub.com

I dedicate this book to my parents, Ralf and Gunilla, my sister, Catharina, her husband, Magnus, and their sons, Emil and Rasmus.

mapt.io

Mapt is an online digital library that gives you full access to over 5,000 books and videos, as well as industry leading tools to help you plan your personal development and advance your career. For more information, please visit our website.

Why subscribe?

- Spend less time learning and more time coding with practical eBooks and Videos from over 4,000 industry professionals

- Improve your learning with Skill Plans built especially for you

- Get a free eBook or video every month

- Mapt is fully searchable

- Copy and paste, print, and bookmark content

PacktPub.com

Did you know that Packt offers eBook versions of every book published, with PDF and ePub files available? You can upgrade to the eBook version at www.PacktPub.com and as a print book customer, you are entitled to a discount on the eBook copy. Get in touch with us at service@packtpub.com for more details.

At www.PacktPub.com, you can also read a collection of free technical articles, sign up for a range of free newsletters, and receive exclusive discounts and offers on Packt books and eBooks.

Contributors

About the author

Stefan Björnander is the author of the books *Microsoft Windows C++* and *C++ Windows Programming*. He holds a Master of Engineering and a Licentiate in Computer Science. He has worked as a software developer and as a teacher in computer science and mathematics for many years.

About the reviewer

Mark Elston is a software architect for an automated test equipment company working primarily in the IC and mobile device test world. However, his 30 years of experience includes developing aircraft and missile simulations for the Air Force and Navy, hardware control systems for NASA, and tester operating systems for commercial products. He has also developed several Android applications for fun. His latest passion is delving into the world of functional programming and design.

> *I would like to thank my wife for her understanding when I had a chapter to finish reviewing. I would also like to thank the Pack team for giving me the opportunity to work with them on this project. It has been enlightening and entertaining. Finally, I would like to thank the author for taking even my smallest comments into account. It is a pleasure to be part of a project where your input is valued.*

Packt is searching for authors like you

If you're interested in becoming an author for Packt, please visit `authors.packtpub.com` and apply today. We have worked with thousands of developers and tech professionals, just like you, to help them share their insight with the global tech community. You can make a general application, apply for a specific hot topic that we are recruiting an author for, or submit your own idea.

Table of Contents

Preface

C++ is a general-purpose programming language built with a bias towards embedded programming and systems programming. Over the years, C++ has evolved and is used to develop software for many different sectors. Given its versatility and robustness, C++ is a wonderful language to start your coding journey with. This book covers exciting projects built in C++ that show how to implement the language in different scenarios. While developing these projects, you will not only learn the language constructs but also how you can use C++ to meet your software requirements.

In this book, you will study a set of applications written in C++, ranging from abstract datatypes to library management systems, graphical applications, games, and a Domain-Specific Language (DSL).

Who this book is for

This book is for developers who would like to develop software in C++. Basic programming experience would be an added advantage.

What this book covers

Chapter 1, *Getting Started with C++*, introduces you to Object-Oriented Programming (OOP) in C++. We start by looking into a simple program that rolls a dice. We write the code, compile, link, and execute the program. We then continue by constructing a simple object-oriented hierarchy, with pointers and dynamic binding. Finally, we create two simple abstract data types: stack and queue. The stack is a set of values ordered in a bottom-to-top manner, where only the top-most value is accessible, while the queue is a traditional queue where we inspect values at the front and add values at the rear.

Chapter 2, *Data Structures and Algorithms*, builds on what was learned in the previous chapter, especially the list and set abstract datatypes. We also introduce templates and operator overloading, and we look into linear and binary search algorithms and the insert, select, bubble, merge, and quicksort algorithms.

Chapter 3, *Building a Library Management System*, will help you develop a real-world system: a library management system that is made up of books and customers. The books keep track of the customers that have borrowed and reserved them, and the customers keep track of the books they have borrowed and reserved.

Chapter 4, *Library Management System with Pointers*, further develops the library management system. In the previous chapter, each book and customer were identified by integer numbers. In this chapter, however, we work with pointers. Each book holds pointers to the customers that have borrowed or reserved it, and each customer holds pointers to the books they have borrowed or reserved.

Chapter 5, *Qt Graphical Applications*, dives into three graphical applications that we develop with the Qt graphical library: an analog clock with hour, minute, and second hands, a drawing program that draws lines, rectangles, and ellipses in different colors, and an editor where the user can input and edit text. We will learn how to handle windows and widgets as well as menus and toolbars in the Qt Library. We will also learn how to draw figures and write text, and how to catch mouse and keyboard input.

Chapter 6, *Enhancing the Qt Graphical Applications*, further develops the three graphical applications: the analog clock, the drawing program, and the editor. We add digits to the clock dial, we add the possibility to move, modify, and cut-and-paste figures in the drawing program, and we add the possibility to change font and text alignment in the editor.

Chapter 7, *The Games*, introduces you to basic game development. In this chapter, we develop the games Othello, and Noughts and Crosses with the Qt library. In Othello, two players take turn adding marks, colored black and white, to the game grid in order to enclose the opponent's marks. In Noughts and Crosses, two players take turns adding noughts and crosses to a game grid in order to place five marks in a row.

Chapter 8, *The Computer Plays*, empowers the computer to play against a human player. In Othello, the computer tries to add marks that enclose as many as possible of the opponent's marks. In Nought and Crosses, the computer tries to add marks to obtain five marks in a row, and to prevent the opponent to get five marks in a row.

Chapter 9, *Domain–Specific Language*, teaches you to develop a Domain-Specific Language (DSL), which is a language intended for a specific domain. More specifically, we develop a language for writing graphical objects in a Qt widget. We start by formally defining our language with a grammar. We then write a scanner that recognizes meaningful sequences of characters, a parser that checks that the source code complies with the grammar, and a viewer that displays the graphical objects.

Chapter 10, *Advanced Domain–Specific Language*, improves on our Domain-Specific Language in several ways: we add selection and iteration that alter the flow of the program, we add variables that can be assigned to values during the program execution, and we add functions with parameters and a return value.

To get the most out of this book

This book is intended for every reader, from the beginner to the more proficient C++ programmer. However, some previous experience with C++ is useful.

The examples of this book are developed in Visual Studio and Qt Creator.

Download the example code files

You can download the example code files for this book from your account at `www.packtpub.com`. If you purchased this book elsewhere, you can visit `www.packtpub.com/support` and register to have the files emailed directly to you.

You can download the code files by following these steps:

1. Log in or register at `www.packtpub.com`.
2. Select the **SUPPORT** tab.
3. Click on **Code Downloads & Errata**.
4. Enter the name of the book in the **Search** box and follow the onscreen instructions.

Once the file is downloaded, please make sure that you unzip or extract the folder using the latest version of:

- WinRAR/7-Zip for Windows
- Zipeg/iZip/UnRarX for Mac
- 7-Zip/PeaZip for Linux

The code bundle for the book is also hosted on GitHub at `https://github.com/PacktPublishing/CPP17-By-Example`. We also have other code bundles from our rich catalog of books and videos available at `https://github.com/PacktPublishing/`. Check them out!

Download the color images

We also provide a PDF file that has color images of the screenshots/diagrams used in this book. You can download it here: `https://www.packtpub.com/sites/default/files/downloads/CPP17ByExample_ColorImages.pdf`.

Conventions used

There are a number of text conventions used throughout this book.

`CodeInText`: Indicates code words in text. For example; "Let's continue with a class hierarchy, where `Person` is the base class with `Student` and `Employee` as its sub classes:"

A block of code is set as follows:

```
class Person {
   public:
      Person(string name);
      virtual void print();
   private:
      string m_name;
};
```

When we wish to draw your attention to a particular part of a code block, the relevant lines or items are set in bold:

```
class Person {
   public:
      Person(string name);
      virtual void print();
   private:
      string m_name;
};
```

Bold: Indicates a new term, an important word, or words that you see onscreen. For example, words in menus or dialog boxes appear in the text like this. Here is an example: "In the first dialog we just press the **Next** button:"

Warnings or important notes appear like this.

Tips and tricks appear like this.

Get in touch

Feedback from our readers is always welcome.

General feedback: Email `feedback@packtpub.com` and mention the book title in the subject of your message. If you have questions about any aspect of this book, please email us at `questions@packtpub.com`.

Errata: Although we have taken every care to ensure the accuracy of our content, mistakes do happen. If you have found a mistake in this book, we would be grateful if you would report this to us. Please visit `www.packtpub.com/submit-errata`, selecting your book, clicking on the Errata Submission Form link, and entering the details.

Piracy: If you come across any illegal copies of our works in any form on the Internet, we would be grateful if you would provide us with the location address or website name. Please contact us at `copyright@packtpub.com` with a link to the material.

If you are interested in becoming an author: If there is a topic that you have expertise in and you are interested in either writing or contributing to a book, please visit `authors.packtpub.com`.

Reviews

Please leave a review. Once you have read and used this book, why not leave a review on the site that you purchased it from? Potential readers can then see and use your unbiased opinion to make purchase decisions, we at Packt can understand what you think about our products, and our authors can see your feedback on their book. Thank you!

For more information about Packt, please visit `packtpub.com`.

1
Getting Started with C++

This chapter provides an introduction to **Object-Oriented Programming (OOP)** in C++. We start by looking into a simple program that rolls a dice. We write the code and compile, link, and execute the program.

Then we continue by constructing a simple object-oriented hierarchy, involving the `Person` base class and its two subclasses, `Student` and `Employee`. We also look into pointers and dynamic binding.

Finally, we create two simple data types—stack and queue. A **stack** is constituted of a set of values ordered in a bottom-to-top manner, where we are interested in the top value only. A **queue** is a traditional queue of values, where we add values at the rear and inspect values at the front.

In this chapter, we will cover the following topics:

- We start by implementing a simple game: rolling the dice. Its main purpose is to provide an introduction to the environment and teach you how to set up the project, and how to compile, link, and execute the program.
- Then we start looking at object-oriented programming by writing a class hierarchy with `Person` as the base class and `Student` and `Employee` as subclasses. This provides an introduction to inheritance, encapsulation, and dynamic binding.
- Finally, we write classes for the abstract data types stack and queue. A stack is a structure where we both add and remove values at the top, while a queue is more like a traditional queue where we add values at the rear and remove them from the front.

Rolling the dice

As an introduction, we start by writing a program that rolls a dice. We use the built-in random generator to generate an integer value between one and six, inclusive:

Main.cpp

```
#include <CStdLib>
#include <CTime>
#include <IOStream>
using namespace std;
void main() {
  srand((int) time(nullptr));
  int dice = (rand() % 6 ) + 1;
  cout << "Dice: " << dice << endl;
}
```

In the preceding program, the initial `include` directives allow us to include header files, which mostly hold declarations of the standard library. We need the `CStdLib` header file to use the random generator, the `CTime` header file to initiate the random generator with the current time, and the `IOStream` header file to write the result.

The standard library is stored in a `namespace` called `std`. A `namespace` can be considered a container holding code. We gain access to the standard library with the `using namespace` directive.

Every C++ program holds exactly one `main` function. The execution of the program always starts in the `main` function. We use the `srand` and `time` standard functions to initialize the random generator, and `rand` to generate the actual random value. The percent (`%`) is the modulus operator, which divides two integers and gives the remainder of the division. In this way, the value of the `dice` integer variable is always at least one and at most six. Finally, we write the value of the `dice` variable with `cout`, which is an object used by the standard library to write text and values.

The programs of the first four chapters were written with Visual Studio, while the programs of the remaining chapters are written with Qt Creator.

The following are instructions on how to create a project, write the code, and execute the application. When we have started Visual Studio, we follow the following steps to create our project:

1. First, we select the New and Project items in the File menu, as shown in the following screenshot:

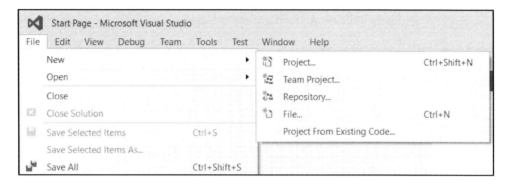

2. We choose the **Win32 Console Application** type, and name the project `Dice`:

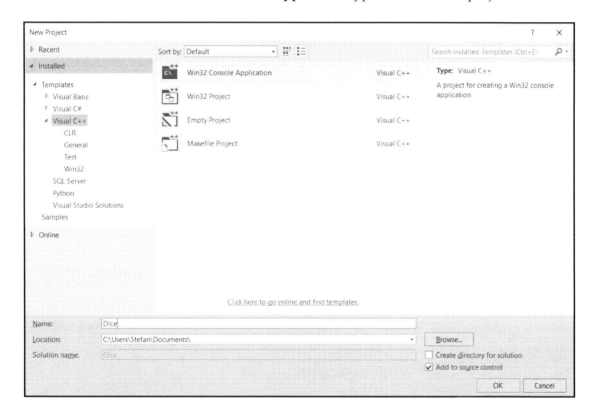

3. In the first dialog we just press the **Next** button:

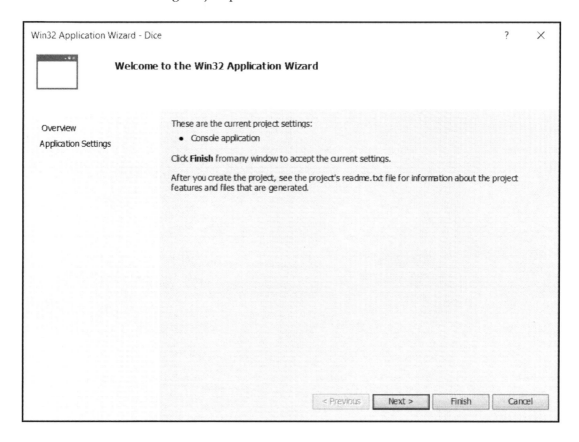

4. In the second dialog, we choose the **Empty project** checkbox and click on the **Finish** button. In this way, a project without files will be created:

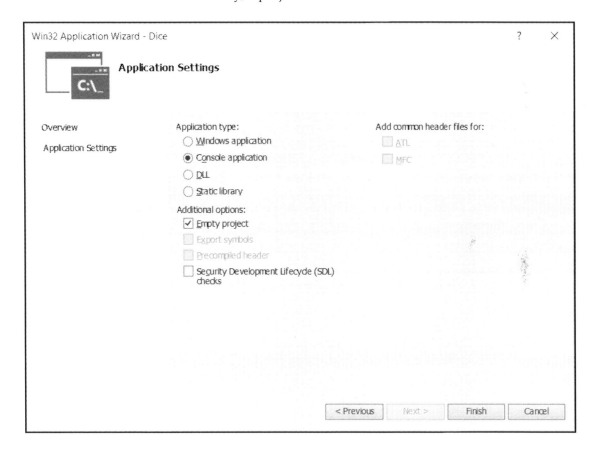

5. When we have created our project, we need to add a file:

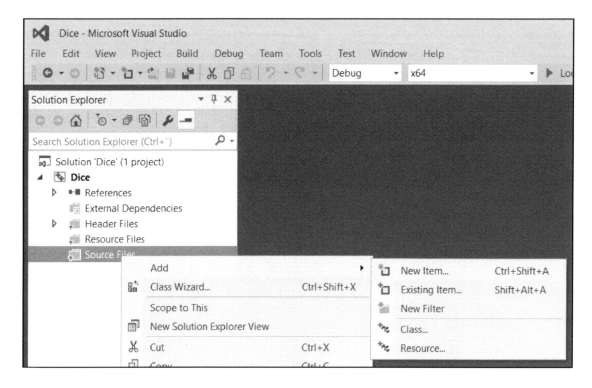

6. We choose a **C++ File(.cpp)** and name it `Main.cpp`:

7. Then, we input the code in the `Main.cpp` file:

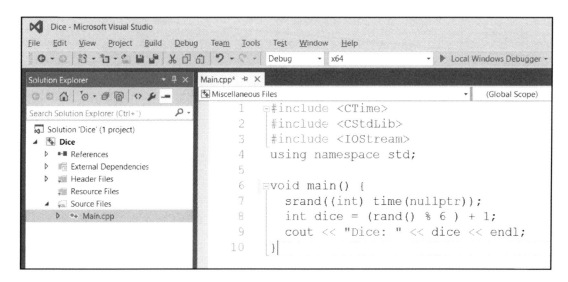

8. Finally, we execute the program. The easiest way to do this is to choose the **Start Debugging** or **Start Without Debugging** menu option. In this way, the program is compiled, linked, and executed:

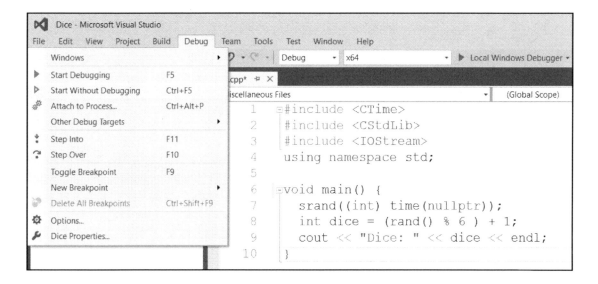

9. The output of the execution is displayed in a command window:

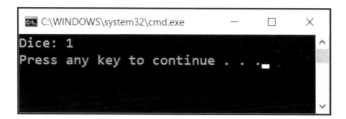

Understanding classes – the Car class

Let's continue by looking at a simple class that handles a car, including its speed and direction. A class is a very central feature in object-oriented languages. In C++, its specification is made up of two parts—its definition and implementation. The definition part is often placed in a header file (with the `.h` suffix), while the implementation part is placed in a file with the `.cpp` suffix, as in the `Car.h` and `Car.cpp` files. However, template classes, which are introduced in `Chapter 3`, *Building a Library Management System*, are stored in one file only.

A class is made up of its members, where a member is a field or a method. A **field** holds a value of a specific type. A **method** is a mathematical abstraction that may take input values and return a value. The input values of a method are called parameters. However, in C++ it is possible to define a function without parameters and without return types.

An object is an instance of the class; we can create many objects of one class. The methods can be divided into the following:

- **Constructor**: A constructor is called when the object is created
- **Inspector**: An inspector inspects the fields of the class
- **Modificator**: A modificator modifies the values of the fields
- **Destructor**: A destructor is called when the object is destroyed

Ideally, the methods of a class don't give direct access to the fields, as this would mean that the method names/types would have to change if the fields change. Instead, the methods should give access to a class property. These are the conceptual elements of a class that may not map to a single field. Each member of the class is public, protected, or private:

- A public member is accessible by all other parts of the program.
- A protected member is accessible only by its own members or members of its subclasses, which are introduced in the next section.
- A private member is accessible by its own members only. However, that is not completely true. A class can invite other classes to become its friends, in which case they are given access to its private and protected members. We will look into friends in the next chapter.

The following Car class definition has two constructors and one destructor. They always have the same name as the Car class in this case. The destructor is preceded by a tilde (~). A constructor without parameters is called the default constructor.

> More than one method can have the same name, as long as they have different parameter lists, which is called **overloading**. More specifically, it is called context-free overloading. There is also context-dependent overloading, in which case two methods have the same name and parameter list, but different return types. However, context-dependent overloading is not supported by C++.

Consequently, a class can hold several constructors, as long as they have different parameter lists. However, the destructor is not allowed to have parameters. Therefore, a class can hold only one destructor:

Car.h

```
class Car {
  public:
  Car();
  Car(int speed, int direction);
  ~Car();
```

The getSpeed and getDirection methods are inspectors returning the current speed and direction of the car. The return values hold the int type, which is short for integer. They are marked as constant with the const keyword since they do not change the fields of the class. However, a constructor or destructor cannot be constant:

```
  int getSpeed() const;
  int getDirection() const;
```

The `accelerate`, `decelerate`, `turnLeft`, and `turnRight` methods are modificators, setting the current speed and direction of the car. They cannot be marked as constant since they change the fields of the class:

```
void accelerate(int speed);
void decelerate(int speed);
void turnLeft(int degrees);
void turnRight(int degrees);
```

The `m_speed` and `m_direction` fields hold the current speed and direction of the car. The `-m prefix` indicates that they are members of a class, as opposed to fields local to a method:

```
private:
   int m_speed, m_direction;
};
```

In the implementation file, we must include the `Car.h` header file. The `#include` directive is part of the preprocessor and simply causes the content of the `Car.h` file to be included in the file. In the previous section, we included system files with the angle bracket characters (< and >). In this case, we include local files with quotes ("). The system include files (with angle brackets) include system code that are part of the language, while local include files (with quotes) include code that we write ourselves, as part of our project. Technically, the system include files are often included from a special directory in the file system, while the local include files are often included locally in the filesystem:

Car.cpp

```
#include "Car.h"
```

The default constructor initializes both `speed` and `direction` and set it to 0. The colon (`:`) notation is used to initialize the fields. The text between two slashes (`//`) and the end of the line is called a line comment and is ignored:

```
Car::Car()
 :m_speed(0),
  m_direction(0) {
  // Empty.
 }
```

The second constructor initializes both `speed` and `direction` to the given parameter values:

```
Car::Car(int speed, int direction)
 :m_speed(speed),
  m_direction(direction) {
  // Empty.
}
```

In the preceding constructors, it would be possible to use the assignment operator (=) instead of the class initialization notation, as in the following code. However, that is considered to be inefficient since the code may be optimized with the preceding initialization notation. Note that we use one equals sign (=) for assignments. For the comparison of two values, we use two equals signs (==), a method which is introduced in `Chapter 2`, *Data Structures and Algorithms*:

```
Car::Car() {
  m_speed = 0;
  m_direction = 0;
}
```

The destructor does nothing in this class; it is included only for the sake of completeness:

```
Car::~Car() {
  // Empty.
}
```

The `getSpeed` and `getDirection` methods simply return the current speed and direction of the car:

```
int Car::getSpeed() const {
  return m_speed;
}

int Car::getDirection() const {
  return m_direction;
}
```

A plus sign directly followed by an equals sign is called **compound assignment** and causes the right value to be added to the left value. In the same way, a minus sign directly followed by an equals sign causes the right value to be subtracted from the left value.

The text between a slash (/) directly followed by an asterisk (*), and an asterisk directly followed by a slash, is called a **block comment** and is ignored:

```
void Car::accelerate(int speed) {
  m_speed += speed; /* Same effect as: m_speed = m_speed + speed;
*/
}

void Car::decelerate(int speed) {
  m_speed -= speed;
}

void Car::turnLeft(int degrees) {
  m_direction -= degrees;
}

void Car::turnRight(int degrees) {
  m_direction += degrees;
}
```

Now it is time to test our class. To do so, we include the Car.h file, just as we did in the Car.cpp file. However, we also include the system IOStream header file. As in the previous section, the system headers are enclosed in arrow brackets (< and >). We also need to use the namespace std to use its functionality.

Main.cpp

```
#include <IOStream>
using namespace std;
#include "Car.h"
```

In C++, a function can be a part of a class or can be free-standing without a class. Functions of a class are often called methods. A function is a mathematical abstraction. It has input values, which are called parameters, and returns a value. However, in C++ a function is allowed to have zero parameters, and it may return the special type void, indicating that it does not return a value.

As mentioned in the previous section, the execution of the program always starts at the function named main, and every program must have exactly one function named main. Unlike some other languages, it is not necessary to name the file Main.

However, in this book, every file holding the `main` function is named `Main.cpp` out of convenience. The `void` keyword indicates that `main` does not return a value. Note that while constructors and destructors never return values, and are not marked with `void`, other methods and functions that do not return values must be marked with `void`:

```
void main() {
```

We create an object of the `Car` class that we call `redVolvo`. An object is an instance of the class; `redVolvo` is one of many cars:

```
Car redVolvo;
```

When writing information, we use the `cout` object (short for console output), which normally writes to a text window. The operator made up of two left arrow brackets (<<) is called the output stream operator. The `endl` directive makes the next output start at the beginning of the next line:

```
cout << "Red Volvo Speed: " << redVolvo.getSpeed()
     << " miles/hour" << ", Direction: "
     << redVolvo.getDirection() << " degrees" << endl;

redVolvo.accelerate(30);
redVolvo.turnRight(30);
cout << "Red Volvo Speed: " << redVolvo.getSpeed()
     << " miles/hour" << ", Direction: "
     << redVolvo.getDirection() << " degrees" << endl;

redVolvo.decelerate(10);
redVolvo.turnLeft(10);
cout << "Red Volvo Speed: " << redVolvo.getSpeed()
     << " miles/hour" << ", Direction: "
     << redVolvo.getDirection() << " degrees" << endl;
```

A `blueFiat` object is a constant object of the `Car` class. This means that it can only be initialized by one of the constructors and then inspected, but not modified. More specifically, only constant methods can be called on a constant object, and only methods that do not modify the fields of the object can be constant:

```
const Car blueFiat(100, 90);
cout << "Blue Fiat Speed: " << blueFiat.getSpeed()
     << " miles/hour" << ", Direction: "
     << blueFiat.getDirection() << " degrees" << endl;
}
```

When we execute the code, the output is displayed in a command window:

```
C:\WINDOWS\system32\cmd.exe                          —    □    ×
Red Volvo Speed: 0 miles/hour, Direction: 0 degrees
Red Volvo Speed: 30 miles/hour, Direction: 30 degrees
Red Volvo Speed: 20 miles/hour, Direction: 20 degrees
Blue Fiat Speed: 100 miles/hour, Direction: 90 degrees
Press any key to continue . . . _
```

Extending the Car class

In this section, we modify the `Car` class. In the earlier version, we initialized the fields in the constructors. An alternative way to initialize the fields is to initialize them directly in the class definition. However, this feature shall be used with care since it may result in unnecessary initializations. If the second constructor in the `Car` class is called, the fields are initialized twice, which is ineffective.

Car.h

```cpp
class Car {
  public:
    // ...

  private:
    int m_speed = 0, m_direction = 0;
};
```

While the `Car` class is defined in the `Car.h` file, its methods are defined in the `Car.cpp` file. Note that we begin by including the `Car.h` file, in order for the definitions of the methods to comply with their declaration in `Car.h`:

Car.cpp

```cpp
#include "Car.h"

Car::Car() {
  // Empty.
}
```

```
Car::Car(int speed, int direction)
 :m_speed(speed),
  m_direction(direction) {
  // Empty.
}
```

Moreover, the `Car` class of the previous section has some limitations:

- It is possible to accelerate the car indefinitely, and it is possible to decelerate the car to a negative speed
- It is possible to turn the car so that the direction is negative or more than 360 degrees

Let's start by setting the maximum speed of the car to 200 miles/hour. If the speed exceeds 200 miles per hour we set it to 200 miles/hour. We use the `if` statement, which takes a condition, and executes the following statement if the condition is true. In the case here, the statement (`m_speed = 200;`) is enclosed by brackets. This is not necessary since it is only one statement. However, it would be necessary in the case of more than one statement. In this book, we always use the brackets for clarity, regardless of the number of statements.

Car.cpp

```
void Car::accelerate(int speed) {
  m_speed += speed;

  if (m_speed > 200) {
    m_speed = 200;
  }
}
```

If the speed becomes negative, we change the sign of the speed to make it positive. Note that we cannot write `m_speed -= m_speed`. That would set the speed to zero since it would subtract the speed from itself.

Since the value is negative, it becomes positive when we change the sign. We also turn the car by 180 degrees to change its direction. Note that we also, in this case, must check that the car does not exceed the speed limit.

Also, note that we must check whether the direction is less than 180 degrees. If it is, we add 180 degrees; otherwise, we subtract 180 degrees to keep the direction in the interval 0 to 360 degrees. We use the `if...else` statement to do that. If the condition of the `if` statement is not true, the statement after the `else` keyword is executed:

```cpp
void Car::decelerate(int speed) {
  m_speed -= speed;

  if (m_speed < 0) {
    m_speed = -m_speed;
    if (m_speed > 200) {
      m_speed = 200;
    }

    if (m_direction < 180) {
      m_direction += 180;
    }
    else {
      m_direction -= 180;
    }
  }
}
```

When turning the car, we use the modulo (%), operator. When dividing by 360, the modulo operator gives the remainder of the division. For instance, when 370 is divided by 360 the remainder is 10:

```cpp
void Car::turnLeft(int degrees) {
  m_direction -= degrees;
  m_direction %= 360;

  if (m_direction < 0) {
    m_direction += 360;
  }
}

void Car::turnRight(int degrees) {
  m_direction += degrees;
  m_direction %= 360;
}
```

The `main` function creates one object of the `Car` class—`redVolvo`. We start by writing its speed and direction, then we accelerate and turn left and again write its speed and acceleration. Finally, we decelerate and turn right and write its speed and direction one last time:

Main.cpp

```
#include <IOStream>
using namespace std;
#include "Car.h"

void main() {
  Car redVolvo(20, 30);
  cout << "Red Volvo Speed: " << redVolvo.getSpeed()
       << " miles/hour" << ", Direction: "
       << redVolvo.getDirection() << " degrees" << endl;

  redVolvo.accelerate(30);
  redVolvo.turnLeft(60);
  cout << "Red Volvo Speed: " << redVolvo.getSpeed()
       << " miles/hour" << ", Direction: "
       << redVolvo.getDirection() << " degrees" << endl;

  redVolvo.decelerate(60);
  redVolvo.turnRight(50);
  cout << "Red Volvo Speed: " << redVolvo.getSpeed()
       << " miles/hour" << ", Direction: "
       << redVolvo.getDirection() << " degrees" << endl;
}
```

When we execute the code, the output is displayed in a command window as follows:

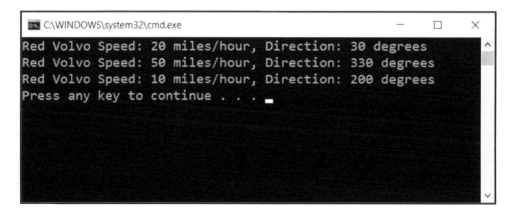

A class hierarchy – the Person, Student, and Employee classes

Let's continue with a class hierarchy, where Person is the base class with Student and Employee as its subclasses:

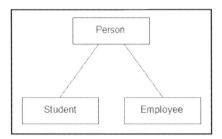

As a person has a name, we use the C++ standard class string to store the name. The virtual keyword marks that the print method is subject to dynamic binding, which we will look into later in this section:

Person.h

```
class Person {
  public:
    Person(string name);
    virtual void print();

  private:
    string m_name;
};
```

We include the String header, which allows us to use the string class:

Person.cpp

```
#include <String>
#include <IOStream>
using namespace std;

#include "Person.h"

Person::Person(string name)
 :m_name(name) {
   // Empty.
 }
```

```
void Person::print() {
  cout << "Person " << m_name << endl;
}
```

The `Student` and `Employee` classes are subclasses of `Person`, and they inherit `Person` publicly. Sometimes the term extension is used instead of inheritance. The inheritance can be `public`, `protected`, or `private`:

- With `public` inheritance, all members of the base class have the same access to the subclass
- With `protected` inheritance, all `public` members of the base class become protected in the subclass
- With `private` inheritance, all `public` and `protected` members of the base class become private in the subclass

The `Student` and `Employee` classes have the text fields `m_university` and `m_company`:

Student.h

```
class Student : public Person {
  public:
    Student(string name, string university);
    void print();

  private:
    string m_university;
};
```

The file `Student.cpp` defines the methods of the `Student` class:

Student.cpp

```
#include <String>
#include <IOStream>
using namespace std;

#include "Person.h"
#include "Student.h"
```

The subclass can call a constructor of the base class by stating its name with the colon notation (:). The constructor of Student calls the constructor of Person with the name as a parameter:

```
Student::Student(string name, string university)
 :Person(name),
  m_university(university) {
  // Empty.
}
```

We must state that we call print in Person rather than Student by using the double colon notation (::):

```
void Student::print() {
  Person::print();
  cout << "University " << m_university << endl;
}
```

The Employee class is similar to Student. However, it holds the field c_company instead of m_university.

Employee.h

```
class Employee : public Person {
  public:
    Employee(string name, string company);
    void print();

  private:
    string m_company;
};
```

The file Employee.cpp defines the methods of the Employee class.

Employee.cpp

```
#include <String>
#include <IOStream>
using namespace std;

#include "Person.h"
#include "Employee.h"
```

The constructor initializes the name of the person and the company they are employed by:

```
Employee::Employee(string name, string company)
:Person(name),
m_company(company) {
// Empty.
}
void Employee::print() {
Person::print();
cout << "Company " << m_company << endl;
}
```

Finally, the `main` function starts by including the system header files `String` and `IOStream`, which hold declarations about string handling and input and output streams. Since all standard headers are included in the standard namespace, we gain access to the system declaration with the `using` the `namespace` directive.

Main.cpp

```
#include <String>
#include <IOStream>
using namespace std;

#include "Person.h"
#include "Student.h"
#include "Employee.h"
```

We define the three objects, `Monica`, `Demi`, and `Charles`, and we call `print` on each of them. In all three cases the `print` method of the class `Person`, `Student`, and `Employee` is called:

```
void main() {
  Person monica("Monica");
  person.print();

  Student demi("Demi", "MIT");
  student.print();

  Employee charles("Charles", "Microsoft");
  employee.print();
```

The asterisk (*) marks that `personPtr` is a pointer to an object of `Person`, rather than an object of `Person`. A pointer to an object holds the memory address of the object, rather than the object itself. However, at the moment it does not hold any address at all. We will soon assign it to the address of an object:

```
Person *personPtr;
```

The ampersand (`&`) is an operator that provides the address of an object, which is assigned to the pointer `personPtr`. We assign `personPtr` in turn to the addresses of the `Person`, `Student`, and `Employee` objects and call `print` in each case. As `print` is marked as virtual in `Person`, `print`, in the class of the object the pointer currently points at, is called. Since `print` is marked as virtual in the base class `Person`, it is not necessary to mark `print` as virtual in the subclasses `Student` and `Employee`. When accessing a member of a pointer to an object, we use the arrow (`->`) operator instead of the point operator.

When `personPtr` points at an object of `Person`, print in `Person` is called:

```
personPtr = &person;
personPtr->print();
```

When `personPtr` points at an object of `Student`, `print` in `Student` is called:

```
personPtr = &student;
personPtr->print();
```

When `personPtr` points at an object of `Employee`, print `Employee` is called:

```
personPtr = &employee;
personPtr->print();
}
```

This process is called dynamic binding. If we omit the virtual marking in `Person`, static binding would occur and print in `Person` would be called in all cases.

The concept of object-oriented programming is built on the three cornerstones of encapsulation, inheritance, and dynamic binding. A language that does not support any of these features cannot be called object-oriented.

A simple data type – the stack

A **stack** is a simple data type where we add values to the top, remove the value on the top, and can only inspect the top value. In this section, we implement a stack of integers. In the next chapter, we look into template classes that can hold values of arbitrary types. We use a linked list, which is a construction where a pointer points at the first cell in the linked list, and each cell holds a pointer to the next cell in the linked list. Naturally, the linked list must end eventually. We use `nullptr` to mark the end of the linked list, which is a C++ standard pointer to a special null address.

To begin with, we need a class to hold each cell of the linked list. The cell holds an integer value and a pointer to the next cell in the list, or `nullptr` if it is the last cell of the list. In the following section, we will look into cell classes that hold pointers to both the previous and the next cell.

Cell.h

```
class Cell {
   public:
      Cell(int value, Cell *next);
```

It is possible to implement methods directly in the class definition; they are called inline methods. However, it is usually done for short methods only. A rule of thumb is that inline methods shall not exceed one line:

```
int value() const { return m_value; }
Cell *next() const { return m_next; }
```

Each cell holds a value and the address of the next cell in the linked list:

```
   private:
      int m_value;
      Cell *m_next;
};
```

Cell.h

```
#include "Cell.h"
```

A cell is initialized with a value and a pointer to the next cell in the linked list. Note that `m_next` has the value `nullptr` if the cell is the last cell in the linked list:

```
Cell::Cell(int value, Cell *next)
 :m_value(value),
  m_next(next) {
```

```
    // Empty.
  }
```

In a stack, we are in interested in its top value only. The default constructor initializes the stack to be empty. Push adds a value at the top of the stack, top returns the top value, pop removes the top value, size returns the number of values in the stack, and empty returns `true` if the stack is empty. The bool type is a logical type that can hold the values `true` or `false`.

Stack.h

```
class Stack {
  public:
    Stack();
    void push(int value);
    int top();
    void pop();
    int size() const;
    bool empty() const;
```

The `m_firstCellPtr` field is a pointer to the first cell of the linked list holding the values of the stack. When the stack is empty, `m_firstCellPtr` will hold the value `nullptr`. The `m_size` field holds the current size of the stack:

```
  private:
    Cell *m_firstCellPtr;
    int m_size;
};
```

The `CAssert` header is included for the assert macro, which is used to test whether certain conditions are true. A macro is part of the preprocessor that performs certain text replacements.

Stack.cpp

```
#include <CAssert>
using namespace std;

#include "Cell.h"
#include "Stack.h"
```

The default constructor sets the stack to empty by initializing the pointer to the first cell to `nullptr` and the size to zero:

```
Stack::Stack()
 :m_firstCellPtr(nullptr),
  m_size(0) {
  // Empty.
}
```

When pushing a new value at the top of the stack, we use the new operator to dynamically allocate the memory needed for the cell. If we run out of memory, `nullptr` is returned, which is tested by the assert macro. If `m_firstCellPtr` equals `nullptr`, the execution is aborted with an error message. The exclamation mark (!) followed by an equals sign (=) constitutes the not-equal operator. Two plus signs (++) constitute the increments operator, which means that the value is increased by one.

The increment operator actually comes in two versions—prefix (++`m_size`) and postfix (`m_size`++). In the prefix case, the value is first increased and then returned, while in the postfix case the value is increased but the original value is returned. However, in this case, it does not matter which version we use since we are only interested in the result—that the value of `m_size` is increased by one:

```
void Stack::push(int value) {
  m_firstCellPtr = new Cell(value, m_firstCellPtr);
  ++m_size;
}
```

When returning the top value of the stack, we must first check that the stack is not empty, since it would be illogical to return the top value of an empty stack. If the stack is empty, the execution is aborted with an error message. The single exclamation mark (!) is the logical `not` operator. We return the top value, which is stored in the first cell in the linked list:

```
int Stack::top() {
  assert(!empty());
  return m_firstCellPtr->getValue();
}
```

We must also check that the stack is not empty when popping the top value of the stack. We set the pointer to the first cell in the linked list to point at the next cell. However, before that, we must store the first pointer, `deleteCellPtr`, in order to deallocate the memory of the cell it points at.

We deallocate the memory with the `delete` operator:

```
void Stack::pop() {
  assert(!empty());
  Cell *deleteCellPtr = m_firstCellPtr;
  m_firstCellPtr = m_firstCellPtr->getNext();
  delete deleteCellPtr;
```

In the same way as the increment operator above, two minus signs (−−) constitutes the decrement operator, which decreases the value by one:

```
  --m_size;
}
```

The `size` method simply returns the value of the `m_size` field:

```
int Stack::size() const {
  return m_size;
}
```

A stack is empty if the pointer to the first cell pointer equals `nullptr`. Informally, we say that the pointer is null if it equals `nullptr`:

```
bool Stack::empty() const {
  return (m_firstCellPtr == nullptr);
}
```

We test the stack by pushing, topping, and popping some values.

Main.cpp

```
#include <String>
#include <IOStream>
using namespace std;

#include "Cell.h"
#include "Stack.h"

void main() {
  Stack s;
  s.push(1);
  s.push(2);
  s.push(3);
```

When printing a Boolean value, the `stream` operator does not print `true` or `false`, but rather one for `true` and zero for `false`. In order to really print `true` or `false` we use the `condition` operator. It takes three values, separated by a question mark (?) and a colon (:). If the first value is `true` the second value is returned. If the first value is `false` the third value is returned:

```
cout << "top " << s.top() << ", size " << s.size()
     << ", empty " << (s.empty() ? "true" : "false") << endl;

s.pop();
s.pop();
s.push(4);
cout << "top " << s.top() << ", size " << s.size()
     << ", empty " << (s.empty() ? "true" : "false") << endl;
}
```

A more advanced data type – the queue

A queue is a model of a traditional queue; we enter values at the rear, and inspect and remove values at the front. It is also possible to decide on the number of values it holds and whether it is empty.

Similar to the stack in the previous section, we implement the queue with a linked list. We reuse the `Cell` class; however, in the queue case, we need to set the next link of a cell. Therefore, we rename `next` to `getNext` and add the new `setNext` method:

Cell.h

```
class Cell {
  public:
    Cell(int value, Cell *next);
    int value() const {return m_value;}
    Cell *getNext() const { return m_next; }
    void setNext(Cell* next) { m_next = next; }

  private:
    int m_value;
    Cell *m_next;
};
```

We implement the queue with a linked list in a manner similar to the stack. The constructor initializes an empty queue, `enter` enters a value at the rear of the queue, `remove` removes the value at its front, `size` return the current size of the queue, and `empty` returns `true` if it is empty:

Queue.h

```
class Queue {
  public:
    Queue();
    void enter(int value);
    int first();
    void remove();
    int size() const;
    bool empty() const;
```

In the stack case, we were only interested in its top, which was stored at the beginning of the linked list. In the queue case, we are interested in both the front and rear, which means that we need to access both the first and last cell of the linked list. Therefore, we have the two pointers, `m_firstCellPtr` and `m_lastCellPtr`, pointing at the first and last cell in the linked list:

```
  private:
    Cell *m_firstCellPtr, *m_lastCellPtr;
    int m_size;
};
```

Queue.cpp

```
#include <CAssert>
using namespace std;

#include "Cell.h"
#include "Queue.h"
```

When the queue is created, it is empty; the pointers are null and the size is zero. Since there are no cells in the linked list, both the cell pointers points at `nullptr`:

```
Queue::Queue()
 :m_firstCellPtr(nullptr),
  m_lastCellPtr(nullptr),
  m_size(0) {
  // Empty.
}
```

When entering a new value at the rear of the queue, we check if the queue is empty. If it is empty, both the pointers are set to point at the new cell. If it is not empty, the last cell next-pointer is set to point at the new cell, and then the last cell pointer is set to be the new cell:

```
void Queue::enter(int value) {
  Cell *newCellPtr = new Cell(value, nullptr);

  if (empty()) {
    m_firstCellPtr = m_lastCellPtr = newCellPtr;
  }
  else {
    m_lastCellPtr->setNext(newCellPtr);
    m_lastCellPtr = newCellPtr;
  }

  ++m_size;
}
```

The first method simply returns the value of the first cell in the linked list:

```
int Queue::first() {
  assert(!empty());
  return m_firstCellPtr->value();
}
```

The `remove` method sets the first cell to point at the second cell. However, first we must store its address in order to deallocate its memory with the C++ standard `delete` operator:

```
void Queue::remove() {
  assert(!empty());
  Cell *deleteCellPtr = m_firstCellPtr;
  m_firstCellPtr = m_firstCellPtr->getNext();
  delete deleteCellPtr;
  --m_size;
}

int Queue::size() const {
  return m_size;
}

bool Queue::empty() const {
  return (m_firstCellPtr == nullptr);
}
```

We test the queue by entering and removing a few values. We enter the values one, two, and three, which are placed in the queue in that order. We then remove the first two values, and enter the value four. Then the queue holds the values three and four:

Main.cpp

```
#include <CMath>
#include <String>
#include <IOStream>
using namespace std;

#include "Cell.h"
#include "Queue.h"

void main() {
  Queue q;
  q.enter(1);
  q.enter(2);
  q.enter(3);
  cout << "first " << q.first() << ", size " << q.size()
       << ", empty " << (q.empty() ? "true" : "false") << endl;

  q.remove();
  q.remove();
  q.enter(4);
  cout << "first " << q.first() << ", size " << q.size()
       << ", empty " << (q.empty() ? "true" : "false") << endl;
}
```

Summary

In this chapter, we have looked into the basics of object-oriented programming. We have started by creating a project and executing a program for rolling a dice. We have also created a class hierarchy, including the base class Person and its two subclasses Student and Employee. By defining pointers to the objects, we have performed the dynamic binding.

Finally, we have created two data types—stack and queue. A stack is a structure where we are interested in the value at the top only. We can add values at the top, inspect the top value, and remove the top value. A queue is a traditional queue where we enter values at the rear while we inspect and remove values from the front.

In the next chapter, we will continue to create data types, and more advanced data types, such as lists and sets. We will also look into to more advanced features of C++.

2

Data Structures and Algorithms

In the previous chapter, we created classes for the `stack` and `queue` abstract datatypes. In this chapter, we will continue with the `list` and `set` abstract datatypes.

Similar to the stack and queue of the previous chapter, a list is an ordered structure with a beginning and an end. However, it is possible to add and remove values at any position in the list. It is also possible to iterate through the list.

A set, on the other hand, is an unordered structure of values. The only thing we can say about a set is whether a certain value is present. We cannot say that a value has any position in relation to any other value.

In this chapter, we will look at the following topics:

- We will start with a rather simple and ineffective version of the list and set classes. We will also look into basic algorithms for searching and sorting.
- Then we will continue by creating more advanced versions of the list and set classes, and look into more advanced searching and sorting algorithms. We will also introduce new concepts such as templates, operator overloading, exceptions, and reference overloading.

We will also look into the searching algorithms linear search, which works on every sequence, ordered and unordered, but is rather ineffective, and binary search, which is more effective but only works on ordered sequences.

Finally, we will study the rather simple sorting algorithms, insert sort, select sort, and bubble sort, as well as the more advanced and more effective merge sort and quick sort algorithms.

The List class

The `LinkedList` class is a more complicated abstract data type than the stack and the queue. It is possible to add and remove values at any location in the list. It is also possible to iterate through the list.

The Cell class

The cell of this section is an extension of the cell of the `stack` and `queue` sections. Similar to them, it holds a value and a pointer to the next cell. However, this version also holds a pointer to the previous cell, which makes the list of this section a double-linked list.

Note that the constructor is `private`, which means that the cell object can be created by its own methods only. However, there is a way to circumvent that limitation. We can define a class or a function to be a friend of `LinkedList`. In this way, we define `LinkedList` as a friend of `Cell`. This means that `LinkedList` has access to all private and protected members of `Cell`, including the constructor, and can thereby create `Cell` objects.

Cell.h:

```
class Cell {
  private:
    Cell(double value, Cell *previous, Cell *next);
    friend class LinkedList;

  public:
    double getValue() const { return m_value; }
    void setValue(double value) { m_value = value; }

    Cell *getPrevious() const { return m_previous; }
    void setPrevious(Cell *previous) { m_previous = previous; }

    Cell *getNext() const { return m_next; }
    void setNext(Cell *getNext) { m_next = getNext; }

  private:
    double m_value;
    Cell *m_previous, *m_next;
};
```

Cell.cpp:

```
#include "Cell.h"

Cell::Cell(double value, Cell *previous, Cell *next)
 :m_value(value),
  m_previous(previous),
  m_next(next) {
  // Empty.
}
```

The Iterator class

When going through a list, we need an iterator, which is initialized to the beginning of the list and step-wise moves to its end. Similar to the preceding cell, the constructor of `Iterator` is private, but we define `LinkedList` as a friend of `Iterator` too.

Iterator.h:

```
class Iterator {
  private:
     Iterator(Cell *cellPtr);
     friend class LinkedList;

  public:
     Iterator();
```

The third constructor is a `copy` constructor. It takes another iterator and then copies it. We cannot just accept the iterator as a parameter. Instead, we define a reference parameter. The ampersands (&) states that the parameter is a reference to an iterator object rather than an iterator object. In this way, the memory address of the iterator is sent as a parameter instead of the object itself. We also state that the object referred to is constant, so that it cannot be altered by the constructor.

In this case, it is necessary to use a reference parameter. If we had defined a simple iterator object as a parameter it would have caused indefinite circular initialization. However, in other cases, we use this technique for efficiency reasons. It takes less time and requires less memory to pass the address of the object than to copy the object itself as a parameter:

```
Iterator(const Iterator& iterator);

double getValue() { return m_cellPtr->getValue(); }
void setValue(double value) { m_cellPtr->setValue(value); }
```

The `hasNext` methods returns `true` if the iterator has not yet reached the end of the list, and `next` moves the iterator one step forwards, towards the end of the list, as shown in the following example:

```
bool hasNext() const { return (m_cellPtr != nullptr); }
void next() { m_cellPtr = m_cellPtr->getNext(); }
```

In the same way, the `hasPrevious` method returns `true` if the iterator has not yet reached the beginning of the list, and `previous` moves the iterator one step backward, to the beginning of the list:

```
bool hasPrevious() const { return (m_cellPtr != nullptr); }
void previous() { m_cellPtr = m_cellPtr->getPrevious(); }

  private:
    Cell *m_cellPtr;
};
```

Iterator.cpp:

```
#include "Cell.h"
#include "Iterator.h"

Iterator::Iterator(Cell *cellPtr)
 :m_cellPtr(cellPtr) {
   // Empty.
}

Iterator::Iterator()
 :m_cellPtr(nullptr) {
   // Empty.
}

Iterator::Iterator(const Iterator& iterator)
 :m_cellPtr(iterator.m_cellPtr) {
   // Empty.
}
```

The List class

The `LinkedList` class holds methods for finding, adding, inserting, and removing values, as well as comparing lists. Moreover, it also holds methods for reading and writing the list, and iterating through the list both forwards and backwards. The linked list is in fact a double-linked list. We can follow the links of the cells in both directions: from the beginning to the end as well as backwards from the end to the beginning.

LinkedList.h:

```
class LinkedList {
  public:
    LinkedList();
```

The `copy` constructor and the `assign` method both copies the given list:

```
    LinkedList(const LinkedList& list);
    void assign(const LinkedList& list);
```

The destructor deallocates all memory allocated for the cells in the linked list:

```
    ~LinkedList();

    int size() const {return m_size;}
    bool empty() const {return (m_size == 0);}
```

The `find` methods search for the `value`. If it finds the `value`, it returns `true` and sets `findIterator` to the position of the `value`:

```
    bool find(double value, Iterator& findIterator);
```

The `equal` and `notEqual` methods compare this linked list to the given linked list and return `true` if they are equal or not equal, respectively, as shown in the following code snippet:

```
    bool equal(const LinkedList& list) const;
    bool notEqual(const LinkedList& list) const;
```

What if we want to add a value or another list to an existing list? The `add` methods adds a value or another list at the end of this list, and `insert` inserts a value or a list at the position given by the iterator:

```
    void add(double value);
    void add(const LinkedList& list);

    void insert(const Iterator& insertPosition, double value);
```

```
void insert(const Iterator& insertPosition,
            const LinkedList& list);
```

The `erase` method erases the value at the given position, and `clear` erases every value in the list, as shown in the following example:

```
void erase(const Iterator& erasePosition);
void clear();
```

The `remove` method removes the values from the first iterator to the last iterator, inclusive. The second parameter is a default parameter. It means that the method can be called with one or two parameters. In case of one parameter, the second parameter is given the value in the declaration, which in this case is the `Iterator(nullptr)` that represents the position one step beyond the end of the list. This implies that when `remove` is called with one iterator, every value from that iterator, inclusive, to the end of the list are removed. The `nullptr` pointer is in fact a special pointer that is converted to the type it points at or is compared to. In this case, a pointer to `Cell`. Informally, we can say that a point is null when it holds the value `nullptr`:

```
void remove(const Iterator& firstPosition,
            const Iterator& lastPosition = Iterator(nullptr));
```

The `first` and `last` methods return iterators located at the first and last value of the list:

```
Iterator first() const { return Iterator(m_firstCellPtr); }
Iterator last() const { return Iterator(m_lastCellPtr); }
```

The `read` and `write` methods read the values of the list from an input file stream and write its values to an output file stream. A file stream is used to communicate with a file. Note that the `cin` and `cout` objects, which we have used in earlier sections, are in fact input and output stream objects:

```
void read(istream& inStream);
void write(ostream& outStream);
```

Similar to the queue of the earlier section, the list holds pointers to the first and last cell in the linked list:

```
private:
  int m_size;
  Cell *m_firstCellPtr, *m_lastCellPtr;
};
```

LinkedList.cpp:

```
#include <IOStream>
using namespace std;

#include "Cell.h"
#include "Iterator.h"
#include "List.h"

LinkedList::LinkedList()
 :m_size(0),
  m_firstCellPtr(nullptr),
  m_lastCellPtr(nullptr) {
  // Empty.
}
```

The copy constructor simply calls assign to copy the values of the list parameter:

```
LinkedList::LinkedList(const LinkedList& list) {
  assign(list);
}
```

The assign method copies the given list into its own linked list:

```
void LinkedList::assign(const LinkedList& list) {
  m_size = 0;
  m_firstCellPtr = nullptr;
  m_lastCellPtr = nullptr;
  Cell *listCellPtr = list.m_firstCellPtr;
  add(list);
}
```

The destructor simply calls clear to deallocate all the memory allocated by the cells of the linked list:

```
LinkedList::~LinkedList() {
  clear();
}
```

The clear method iterates through the linked list and deallocates every cell:

```
void LinkedList::clear() {
  Cell *currCellPtr = m_firstCellPtr;
```

For each cell in the linked list, we must first save its address in `deleteCellPtr`, move forward in the linked list, and deallocate the cell. If we would simply call `delete` on `currCellPtr`, the following call to `getNext` would not work since, in that case, we would call a method of a deallocated object:

```
while (currCellPtr != nullptr) {
  Cell *deleteCellPtr = currCellPtr;
  currCellPtr = currCellPtr->getNext();
  delete deleteCellPtr;
}
```

When the list has become empty, both cell pointers are null and the size is zero:

```
  m_firstCellPtr = nullptr;
  m_lastCellPtr = nullptr;
  m_size = 0;
}
```

The `find` method iterates through the linked list, sets `findIterator`, and returns `true` when it has found the value. If it does not find the value, `false` is returned and `findIterator` remains unaffected. In order for this to work, `findIterator` must be a reference to an `Iterator` object rather than an `Iterator` object itself. A pointer to an `Iterator` object would also work:

```
bool LinkedList::find(double value, Iterator& findIterator) {
  Iterator iterator = first();

  while (iterator.hasNext()) {
    if (value == iterator.getValue()) {
      findIterator = iterator;
      return true;
    }

    iterator.next();
  }

  return false;
}
```

If two lists have different sizes, they are not equal. Likewise, if they have the same size, but not the same values, they are not equal:

```
bool LinkedList::equal(const LinkedList& list) const {
  if (m_size != list.m_size) {
    return false;
  }
```

```
Iterator thisIterator = first(), listIterator = list.first();

while (thisIterator.hasNext()) {
  if (thisIterator.getValue() != listIterator.getValue()) {
    return false;
  }

  thisIterator.next();
  listIterator.next();
}
```

However, if the list holds the same size and the same values, they are equal:

```
  return true;
}
```

When we have to decide whether two lists are not equal, we simply call `equal`. The exclamation mark (`!`) is the logical `not` operator, as shown in the following example:

```
bool LinkedList::notEqual(const LinkedList& list) const {
  return !equal(list);
}
```

When adding a value to the list, we dynamically allocate a cell:

```
void LinkedList::add(double value) {
  Cell *newCellPtr = new Cell(value, m_lastCellPtr, nullptr);
```

If the first cell pointer is null, we set it to point at the new cell since the list is empty:

```
  if (m_firstCellPtr == nullptr) {
    m_firstCellPtr = newCellPtr;
  }
```

However, if the first cell pointer is not null, the list is not empty, and we set the next pointer of the last cell pointer to point at the new cell:

```
  else {
    m_lastCellPtr->setNext(newCellPtr);
  }
```

Either way, we set the last cell pointer to point at the new cell and increase the size of the list:

```
  m_lastCellPtr = newCellPtr;
  ++m_size;
}
```

Adding a list to an existing list

When adding a whole list to the list, we act the same way for each value in the list as when we added a single value in `add` previously. We dynamically allocate a new cell, if the first cell pointer is null, we assign it to point at the new cell. If it is not null, we assign the last cell pointer's next-pointer to point at the new cell. Either way, we set the last cell pointer to point at a new cell:

```
void LinkedList::add(const LinkedList& list) {
  Cell *listCellPtr = list.m_firstCellPtr;
```

The `while` statement repeats for as long as its condition is true. In this case, for as long as we have not reached the end of the list:

```
while (listCellPtr != nullptr) {
  double value = listCellPtr->getValue();
  Cell *newCellPtr = new Cell(value, m_lastCellPtr, nullptr);
```

If `m_firstList` is null, our linked list is still empty and `newCellPtr` points to the first cell of a new linked list. In that case, we let `m_firstList` point at the new cell:

```
if (m_firstCellPtr == nullptr) {
  m_firstCellPtr = newCellPtr;
}
```

If `m_firstList` is not null, our list is not empty and `m_firstList` shall not be modified. Instead, we set the next pointer of `m_lastCellPtr` to point at the new cell:

```
else {
  m_lastCellPtr->setNext(newCellPtr);
}
```

Either way, the last cell pointer is set to the new cell pointer:

```
m_lastCellPtr = newCellPtr;
```

Finally, the list cell pointer is set to point at its next cell pointer. Eventually, the list cell pointer will be null and the `while` statement is finished:

```
  listCellPtr = listCellPtr->getNext();
}

m_size += list.m_size;
}
```

When inserting a value at the position given by the iterator, we set its previous pointer to point at the cell before the position in the list (which is null if the position is the first one in the list). We then check whether the first cell pointer is null in the same way as in the preceding add methods:

```
void LinkedList::insert(const Iterator& insertPosition,
                        double value) {
  Cell *insertCellPtr = insertPosition.m_cellPtr;
  Cell *newCellPtr =
    new Cell(value, insertCellPtr->getPrevious(), insertCellPtr);
  insertCellPtr->setPrevious(newCellPtr);

  if (insertCellPtr == m_firstCellPtr) {
    m_firstCellPtr = newCellPtr;
  }
  else {
    newCellPtr->getPrevious()->setNext(newCellPtr);
  }

  ++m_size;
}
```

When inserting a list, we begin by checking whether the position represents the null pointer. In that case, the position is beyond the end of our list, and we just call add instead:

```
void LinkedList::insert(const Iterator& insertPosition,
                        const LinkedList& list) {
  Cell *insertCellPtr = insertPosition.m_cellPtr;

  if (insertCellPtr == nullptr) {
    add(list);
  }
  else {
    Cell *firstInsertCellPtr = nullptr,
         *lastInsertCellPtr = nullptr,
         *listCellPtr = list.m_firstCellPtr;

    while (listCellPtr != nullptr) {
      Cell *newCellPtr = new Cell(listCellPtr->getValue(),
                                  lastInsertCellPtr, nullptr);

      if (firstInsertCellPtr == nullptr) {
        firstInsertCellPtr = newCellPtr;
      }
      else {
        lastInsertCellPtr->setNext(newCellPtr);
      }
```

```
                    lastInsertCellPtr = newCellPtr;
                    listCellPtr = listCellPtr->getNext();
                }
```

We check whether the list to be inserted is empty by comparing
firstInsertCellPtr with nullptr. Since firstInsertCellPtr points at the first value
of the list, the list is empty if it is null:

```
            if (firstInsertCellPtr != nullptr) {
              if (insertCellPtr->getPrevious() != nullptr) {
                insertCellPtr->getPrevious()->setNext(firstInsertCellPtr);
                firstInsertCellPtr->
                  setPrevious(insertCellPtr->getPrevious());
              }
              else {
                m_firstCellPtr = firstInsertCellPtr;
              }
            }

            if (lastInsertCellPtr != nullptr) {
              lastInsertCellPtr->setNext(insertCellPtr);
              insertCellPtr->setPrevious(lastInsertCellPtr);
            }

            m_size += list.m_size;
          }
        }
```

Erasing a value from the list

The erase method simply calls remove with the given position as both its start and end
position:

```
        void LinkedList::erase(const Iterator& removePosition) {
          remove(removePosition, removePosition);
        }
```

When erasing a value from the list, we iterate through the list and deallocate the cell for
each value to be removed:

```
        void LinkedList::remove(const Iterator& firstPosition,
                const Iterator& lastPosition /*= Iterator(nullptr)*/) {
          Cell *firstCellPtr = firstPosition.m_cellPtr,
               *lastCellPtr = lastPosition.m_cellPtr;
          lastCellPtr = (lastCellPtr == nullptr)
                        ? m_lastCellPtr : lastCellPtr;
```

```
        Cell *previousCellPtr = firstCellPtr->getPrevious(),
            *nextCellPtr = lastCellPtr->getNext();

        Cell *currCellPtr = firstCellPtr;
        while (currCellPtr != nextCellPtr) {
          Cell *deleteCellPtr = currCellPtr;
          currCellPtr = currCellPtr->getNext();
          delete deleteCellPtr;
          --m_size;
        }
```

When we have to erase the cells, we have three cases to consider. If the last cell before the first removed cell is not null, meaning that there is a part of the list remaining before the remove position, we set its next pointer to point at the first cell after the removed position. If the last cell before the first removed cell is null, we set the first cell pointer to point at that cell:

```
        if (previousCellPtr != nullptr) {
          previousCellPtr->setNext(nextCellPtr);
        }
        else {
          m_firstCellPtr = nextCellPtr;
        }
```

We do the same thing with the position of the list remaining after the last cell to be removed. If there is a remaining part of the list left, we set its first cell's previous pointer to the last cell of the list remaining before the removed part:

```
        if (nextCellPtr != nullptr) {
          nextCellPtr->setPrevious(previousCellPtr);
        }
        else {
          m_lastCellPtr = previousCellPtr;
        }
      }
```

When reading a list, we first read its `size`. Then we read the values:

```
        void LinkedList::read(istream& inStream) {
          int size;
          inStream >> size;

          int count = 0;
          while (count < size) {
            double value;
            inStream >> value;
            add(value);
```

```
      ++count;
    }
  }
```

When writing a list, we write the values separated by commas and enclosed by brackets ("[" and "]"):

```
void LinkedList::write(ostream& outStream) {
  outStream << "[";
  bool firstValue = true;

  Iterator iterator = first();
  while (iterator.hasNext()) {
    outStream << (firstValue ? "" : ",") << iterator.getValue();
    firstValue = false;
    iterator.next();
  }

  outStream << "]";
}
```

We test the list by adding some values and iterate through them, forwards and backward.

Main.cpp:

```
#include <IOStream>
using namespace std;

#include "Cell.h"
#include "Iterator.h"
#include "List.h"

void main() {
  LinkedList list;
  list.add(1);
  list.add(2);
  list.add(3);
  list.add(4);
  list.add(5);
  list.write(cout);
  cout << endl;

  { Iterator iterator = list.first();
    while (iterator.hasNext()) {
      cout << iterator.getValue() << " ";
      iterator.next();
    }
    cout << endl;
```

```
      }

    { Iterator iterator = list.last();
      while (iterator.hasPrevious()) {
        cout << iterator.getValue() << " ";
        iterator.previous();
      }
      cout << endl;
    }
  }
```

When executing the code, the output is displayed in a command window:

The Set class

A set is an unordered structure without duplicates. The Set class is a subclass of
LinkedList. Note that the inheritance is private, causing all public and protected members
of LinkedList to be private in Set.

Set.h:

```
class Set : private LinkedList {
  public:
    Set();
    Set(double value);
    Set(const Set& set);
    void assign(const Set& set);
    ~Set();
```

The `equal` method returns `true` if the set has the values. Note that we do not care about any order in the set:

```
bool equal(const Set& set) const;
bool notEqual(const Set& set) const;
```

The `exists` method returns `true` if the given value, or each value in the given set, respectively, is present:

```
bool exists(double value) const;
bool exists(const Set& set) const;
```

The `insert` method inserts the given value or each value of the given set. It only inserts values not already present in the set, since a set holds no duplicates:

```
bool insert(double value);
bool insert(const Set& set);
```

The `remove` method removes the given value or each value of the given set, if present:

```
bool remove(double value);
bool remove(const Set& set);
```

The `size`, `empty`, and `first` methods simply call their counterparts in `LinkedList`. Since there is no order in a set it would be meaningless to also override `end` in `LinkedList`:

```
int size() const { return LinkedList::size(); }
bool empty() const { return LinkedList::empty(); }
Iterator first() const { return LinkedList::first(); }
```

The `unionSet`, `intersection`, and `difference` free-standing functions are friends to `Set`, which means that they have access to all private and protected members of `Set`.

 We cannot name the `unionSet` method `union` since it is a keyword in C++.

Note that when a method in a class is marked as a `friend`, it is in fact not a method of that class, but rather a function:

```
friend Set unionSet(const Set& leftSet, const Set& rightSet);
friend Set intersection(const Set& leftSet,
                        const Set& rightSet);
friend Set difference(const Set& leftSet,
                      const Set& rightSet);
```

The `read` and `write` methods read and write the set in the same way as their counterparts in `LinkedList`:

```
void read(istream& inStream);
void write(ostream& outStream);
};
```

The `unionSet`, `intersection`, and `difference` functions that were friends of `Set` are declared outside the class definition:

```
Set unionSet(const Set& leftSet, const Set& rightSet);
Set intersection(const Set& leftSet, const Set& rightSet);
Set difference(const Set& leftSet, const Set& rightSet);
```

Set.cpp:

```
#include <IOStream>
using namespace std;

#include "..\ListBasic\Cell.h"
#include "..\ListBasic\Iterator.h"
#include "..\ListBasic\List.h"
#include "Set.h"
```

The constructors call their counterparts in `LinkedList`. The default constructor (without parameters) calls, in fact, the default constructor of `LinkedList` implicitly:

```
Set::Set() {
  // Empty.
}

Set::Set(double value) {
  add(value);
}

Set::Set(const Set& set)
 :LinkedList(set) {
  // Empty.
}
```

The destructor calls implicitly its counterparts in `LinkedList`, which deallocates the memory associated with the values of the set. In this case, we could have omitted the destructor, and the destructor of `LinkedList` would still be called using the following code:

```
Set::~Set() {
  // Empty.
}
```

The `assign` method simply clears the set and adds the given set:

```
void Set::assign(const Set& set) {
  clear();
  add(set);
}
```

The sets are equal if they have the same `size`, and if every value of one set is present in the other set. In that case, every value of the other set must also be present in the first set:

```
bool Set::equal(const Set& set) const {
  if (size() != set.size()) {
    return false;
  }

  Iterator iterator = first();
  while (iterator.hasNext()) {
    if (!set.exists(iterator.getValue())) {
      return false;
    }

    iterator.next();
  }
  return true;
}

bool Set::notEqual(const Set& set) const {
  return !equal(set);
}
```

The `exists` method uses the iterator of `LinkedList` to iterate through the set. It returns `true` if it finds the value:

```
bool Set::exists(double value) const {
  Iterator iterator = first();

  while (iterator.hasNext()) {
    if (value == iterator.getValue()) {
```

```
        return true;
      }

      iterator.next();
    }

    return false;
  }
```

The second `exists` method iterates through the given set and returns `false` if any of its values are not present in the set. It returns `true` if all its values are present in the set:

```
bool Set::exists(const Set& set) const {
  Iterator iterator = set.first();

  while (iterator.hasNext()) {
    if (!exists(iterator.getValue())) {
      return false;
    }

    iterator.next();
  }

  return true;
}
```

The first `insert` method adds the value if it is not already present in the set:

```
bool Set::insert(double value) {
  if (!exists(value)) {
    add(value);
    return true;
  }

  return false;
}
```

The second `insert` method iterates through the given set and inserts every value by calling the first insert method. In this way, each value not already present in the set is inserted:

```
bool Set::insert(const Set& set) {
  bool inserted = false;
  Iterator iterator = set.first();

  while (iterator.hasNext()) {
    double value = iterator.getValue();
```

```
      if (insert(value)) {
        inserted = true;
      }

      iterator.next();
    }

    return inserted;
  }
```

The first `remove` method removes the value and returns `true` if it is present in the set. If it is not present, it returns `false`:

```
bool Set::remove(double value) {
  Iterator iterator;
  if (find(value, iterator)) {
    erase(iterator);
    return true;
  }

  return false;
}
```

The second `remove` method iterates through the given set and removes each of its values. It returns `true` if at least one value is removed:

```
bool Set::remove(const Set& set) {
  bool removed = false;
  Iterator iterator = set.first();

  while (iterator.hasNext()) {
    double value = iterator.getValue();

    if (remove(value)) {
      removed = true;
    }

    iterator.next();
  }

  return removed;
}
```

Union, intersection, and difference operations

The `unionSet` function creates a resulting set initialized with the left-hand set and then adds the right-hand set:

```
Set unionSet(const Set& leftSet, const Set& rightSet) {
  Set result(leftSet);
  result.insert(rightSet);
  return result;
}
```

The `intersection` method is a little bit more complicated than the `union` or `difference` methods. The intersection of two sets, A and B, can be defined as the difference between their union and their differences:

$$A \cap B = (A \cup B) - ((A-B)-(B-A))$$

```
Set intersection(const Set& leftSet, const Set& rightSet) {
  return difference(difference(unionSet(leftSet, rightSet),
                              difference(leftSet, rightSet)),
                    difference(rightSet, leftSet));
}
```

The `difference` method creates a result set with the left-hand set and then removes the right-hand set:

```
Set difference(const Set& leftSet, const Set& rightSet) {
  Set result(leftSet);
  result.remove(rightSet);
  return result;
}
```

The `read` method is similar to its counterpart in `LinkedList`. However, `insert` is called instead of `add`. In this way, no duplicates are inserted in the set:

```
void Set::read(istream& inStream) {
  int size;
  inStream >> size;

  int count = 0;
  while (count < size) {
    double value;
    inStream >> value;
    insert(value);
    ++count;
  }
```

```
        }
```

The `write` method is also similar to its counterpart in `LinkedList`. However, the set is enclosed in brackets ("{" and "}") instead of squares ("[" and "]"):

```
void Set::write(ostream& outStream) {
  outStream << "{";
  bool firstValue = true;
  Iterator iterator = first();

  while (iterator.hasNext()) {
    outStream << (firstValue ? "" : ",") << iterator.getValue();
    firstValue = false;
    iterator.next();
  }

  outStream << "}";
}
```

We test the set by letting the user input two sets and evaluate their union, intersection, and difference.

Main.cpp:

```
#include <IOStream>
using namespace std;

#include "..\ListBasic\Cell.h"
#include "..\ListBasic\Iterator.h"
#include "..\ListBasic\List.h"
#include "Set.h"

void main() {
  Set s, t;
  s.read(cin);
  t.read(cin);

  cout << endl << "s = ";
  s.write(cout);
  cout << endl;

  cout << endl << "t = ";
  t.write(cout);
  cout << endl << endl;

  cout << "union: ";
  unionSet(s, t).write(cout);
```

```
      cout << endl;

      cout << "intersection: ";
      unionSet(s, t).write(cout);
      cout << endl;

      cout << "difference: ";
      unionSet(s, t).write(cout);
      cout << endl;
    }
```

Basic searching and sorting

In this chapter, we will also study some searching and sorting algorithms. When searching for a value with linear search we simply go through the list from its beginning to its end. We return the zero-based index of the value, or minus one if it was not found.

Search.h:

```
      int linarySearch(double value, const LinkedList& list);
```

Search.cpp:

```
      #include <IOStream>
      using namespace std;

      #include "..\ListBasic\Cell.h"
      #include "..\ListBasic\Iterator.h"
      #include "..\ListBasic\List.h"
      #include "Search.h"

      int linarySearch(double value, const LinkedList& list) {
        int index = 0;
```

We use the `first` method of the list to obtain the iterator that we use to go through the list; `hasNext` returns `true` as long as there is another value in the list and `next` moves the iterator one step forward in the list:

```
      Iterator iterator = list.first();

      while (iterator.hasNext()) {
        if (iterator.getValue() == value) {
          return index;
        }
```

```
      ++index;
      iterator.next();
    }

    return -1;
  }
```

Now we study the select sort, insert sort, and bubble sort algorithms. Note that they take a reference to the list, not the list itself, a parameter in order for the list to become changed. Also note that the reference is not constant in these cases; if it was constant we would not be able to sort the list.

Sort.h:

```
void selectSort(LinkedList& list);
void insertSort(LinkedList& list);
void bubbleSort(LinkedList& list);
```

Sort.cpp:

```
#include <IOStream>
using namespace std;

#include "..\ListBasic\Cell.h"
#include "..\ListBasic\Iterator.h"
#include "..\ListBasic\List.h"
#include "Sort.h"

void insert(double value, LinkedList& list);
void swap(Iterator iterator1, Iterator iterator2);
```

The select sort algorithm

The select sort algorithm is quite simple, we iterate through the list repeatedly until it becomes empty. For each iteration, we found the smallest value, which we remove from the list and add to the resulting list. In this way, the resulting list will eventually be filled with the same values as the list. As the values were selected in order, the resulting list is sorted. Finally, we assign the resulting list to the original list:

```
void selectSort(LinkedList& list) {
  LinkedList result;

  while (!list.empty()) {
    Iterator minIterator = list.first();
    double minValue = minIterator.getValue();
```

```
        Iterator iterator = list.first();

        while (iterator.hasNext()) {
          if (iterator.getValue() < minValue) {
            minIterator = iterator;
            minValue = iterator.getValue();
          }

          iterator.next();
        }

        list.erase(minIterator);
        result.add(minValue);
      }

      list.assign(result);
    }
```

The insert sort algorithm

In the insert sort algorithm, we iterate through the list, and for each value we insert it at its appropriate location in the resulting list. Then we assign the resulting list to the original list:

```
        void insertSort(LinkedList& list) {
          LinkedList result;
          Iterator iterator = list.first();

          while (iterator.hasNext()) {
            insert(iterator.getValue(), result);
            iterator.next();
          }

          list.assign(result);
        }
```

The insert function takes a list and a value and places the value at its correct location in the list. It iterates through the list and places the value before the first value that it is less. If there is no such value in the list, the value is added at the end of the list:

```
        void insert(double value, LinkedList& list) {
          Iterator iterator = list.first();

          while (iterator.hasNext()) {
            if (value < iterator.getValue()) {
              list.insert(iterator, value);
              return;
```

```
      }

   iterator.next();
 }

 list.add(value);
}
```

The bubble sort algorithm

The bubble sort algorithm compares the values pairwise and lets them change place if they occur in the wrong order. After the first iteration, we know that the largest value is located at the end of the list. Therefore, we do not need to iterate through the whole list the second time, we can omit the last value. In this way, we iterate through the list at most the number of the values in the list minus one, because when all values except the first one is at it's correct location, the first one is also at its correct location. However, the list may be properly sorted before that. Therefore, we check after each iteration if any pair of values has been swapped. If they have not, the list has been properly sorted and we exit the algorithm:

```
void bubbleSort(LinkedList& list) {
  int listSize = list.size();

  if (listSize > 1) {
    int currSize = listSize - 1;
    int outerCount = 0;
    while (outerCount < (listSize - 1)) {
      Iterator currIterator = list.first();
      Iterator nextIterator = currIterator;
      nextIterator.next();
      bool changed = false;

      int innerCount = 0;
      while (innerCount < currSize) {
        if (currIterator.getValue() > nextIterator.getValue()) {
          swap(currIterator, nextIterator);
          changed = true;
        }

        ++innerCount;
        currIterator.next();
        nextIterator.next();
      }

      if (!changed) {
        break;
```

```
          }

        --currSize;
        ++outerCount;
      }
    }
  }
```

The `swap` function swaps the values at the locations given by the iterators:

```
void swap(Iterator iterator1, Iterator iterator2) {
  double tempValue = iterator1.getValue();
  iterator1.setValue(iterator2.getValue());
  iterator2.setValue(tempValue);
}
```

We test the algorithms by adding some values to a list, and then sort the list.

Main.cpp:

```
#include <IOStream>
#include <CStdLib>

using namespace std;

#include "..\ListBasic\Cell.h"
#include "..\ListBasic\Iterator.h"
#include "..\ListBasic\List.h"

#include "Search.h"
#include "Sort.h"

void main() {
  cout << "LinkedList" << endl;

  LinkedList list;
  list.add(9);
  list.add(7);
  list.add(5);
  list.add(3);
  list.add(1);

  list.write(cout);
  cout << endl;
```

We use the `iterator` class to go through the list and call `linarySearch` for each value in the list:

```
Iterator iterator = list.first();
while (iterator.hasNext()) {
  cout << "<" << iterator.getValue() << ","
       << linarySearch(iterator.getValue(), list) << "> ";
  iterator.next();
}
```

We also test the search algorithm for values not present in the list, their indexes will be minus one:

```
cout << "<0," << linarySearch(0, list) << "> ";
cout << "<6," << linarySearch(6, list) << "> ";
cout << "<10," << linarySearch(10, list) << ">"
     << endl;
```

We sort the list by the bubble sort, select sort, and insert sort algorithms:

```
cout << "Bubble Sort ";
bubbleSort(list);
list.write(cout);
cout << endl;

cout << "Select Sort ";
selectSort(list);
list.write(cout);
cout << endl;

cout << "Insert Sort ";
insertSort(list);
list.write(cout);
cout << endl;
}
```

One way to classify searching and sorting algorithms is to use the big O notation. Informally speaking, the notation focuses on the worst-case scenario. In the insert sort case, we iterate through the list once for each value, and for each value, we may have to iterate through the whole list to find its correct location. Likewise, in the select sort case we iterate through the list once for each value, and for each value, we may need to iterate through the whole list.

Finally, in the bubble sort case, we iterate through the list once for each value and we may have to iterate through the whole list for each value. In all three cases, we may have to perform n^2 operations on a list of n values. Therefore, the insert, select, and bubble sort algorithms have the big-O n^2, or O (n^2) with regards to their time efficiency. However, when it comes to their space efficiency, bubble sort is better since it operates on the same list, while insert and select sort demand an extra list for the resulting sorted list.

The extended List class

In this section, we will revisit the `LinkedList` class. However, we will expand it in several ways:

- The `Cell` class had a set of `set` and `get` methods. Instead, we will replace each pair with a pair of overloaded reference methods.
- The previous list could only store values of the type `double`. Now we will define the list to be `template`, which allows it to store values of arbitrary types.
- We will replace some of the methods with overloaded operators.
- `Cell` and `Iterator` were free-standing classes. Now we will let them be inner classes, defined inside `LinkedList`.

List.h:

```
class OutOfMemoryException : public exception {
  // Empty.
};
```

In the classes of the earlier sections, the list stored values of the type `double`. However, in these classes, instead of `double` we use the template type `T`, which is a generic type that can be instantiated by any arbitrary type. The `LinkedList` class of this section is `template`, with the generic type `T`:

```
template <class T>
class LinkedList {
  private:
    class Cell {
      private:
        Cell(const T& value, Cell* previous, Cell* next);
```

The `value` method is overloaded in two versions. The first version is constant and returns a constant value. The other version is not constant and returns a reference to the value. In this way, it is possible to assign values to the cell's value, as shown in the following example:

```
public:
  const T value() const { return m_value; }
  T& value() { return m_value; }
```

The `Cell*&` construct means that the methods return a reference to a pointer to a `Cell` object. That reference can then be used to assign a new value to the pointer:

```
      const Cell* previous() const { return m_previous; }
      Cell*& previous() { return m_previous; }

      const Cell* next() const { return m_next; }
      Cell*& next() { return m_next; }

      friend class LinkedList;

    private:
      T m_value;
      Cell *m_previous, *m_next;
  };

  public:
    class Iterator {
      public:
        Iterator();

      private:
        Iterator(Cell* cellPtr);

      public:
        Iterator(const Iterator& iterator);
        Iterator& operator=(const Iterator& iterator);
```

Instead of `equal` and `notEqual`, we overload the equal and not-equal operators:

```
      bool operator==(const Iterator& iterator);
      bool operator!=(const Iterator& iterator);
```

We also replace the increment and decrement methods with the increment (++) and decrement (−−) operators. They come in two versions each—prefix and postfix. The version without parameters is the prefix version (++i and −−i) and the version with an integer parameter is the postfix version (i++ and i−−). Note that we actually do not pass an integer parameter to the operator. The parameter is included only to distinguish between the two versions, and is ignored by the compiler:

```
bool operator++();    // prefix: ++i
bool operator++(int); // postfix: i++

bool operator--();    // prefix: --i
bool operator--(int); // postfix: i--
```

We replace the `getValue` and `setValue` methods with two overloaded dereference operators (*). They work in a way similar to the `value` methods in the preceding `Cell` class. The first version is constant and returns a value, while the second version is not constant and returns a reference to the value:

```
T operator*() const;
T& operator*();

friend class LinkedList;

private:
  Cell *m_cellPtr;
};
```

The ReverseIterator class

In order to iterate from the end to the beginning, as well as from the beginning to the end, we add `ReverseIterator`. It is nearly identical to `Iterator` used previously; the only difference is that the increment and decrement operators move in opposite directions:

```
class ReverseIterator {
  public:
    ReverseIterator();

  private:
    ReverseIterator(Cell* cellPtr);

  public:
    ReverseIterator(const ReverseIterator& iterator);
    const ReverseIterator&
        operator=(const ReverseIterator& iterator);
```

```
        bool operator==(const ReverseIterator& iterator);
        bool operator!=(const ReverseIterator& iterator);

        bool operator++();     // prefix: ++i
        bool operator++(int); // postfix: i++

        bool operator--();
        bool operator--(int);

        T operator*() const;
        T& operator*();

        friend class LinkedList;

      private:
        Cell *m_cellPtr;
  };

  public:
    LinkedList();
    LinkedList(const LinkedList& list);
    LinkedList& operator=(const LinkedList& list);
    ~LinkedList();
    void clear();

    int size() const {return m_size;}
    bool empty() const {return (m_size == 0);}

    bool operator==(const LinkedList& list) const;
    bool operator!=(const LinkedList& list) const;

    void add(const T& value);
    void add(const LinkedList& list);

    void insert(const Iterator& insertPosition, const T& value);
    void insert(const Iterator& insertPosition,
                const LinkedList& list);

    void erase(const Iterator& erasePosition);
    void remove(const Iterator& firstPosition,
                const Iterator& lastPosition = Iterator(nullptr));
```

In the earlier section, there was only the `first` and `last` methods, which return an iterator. In this section, the `begin` and `end` methods are used for forward iteration, while `rbegin` and `rend` (stands for reverse begin and reverse end) are used for backward iteration:

```
Iterator begin() const { return Iterator(m_firstCellPtr); }
Iterator end() const { return Iterator(nullptr); }
ReverseIterator rbegin() const
  {return ReverseIterator(m_lastCellPtr);}
ReverseIterator rend() const
  { return ReverseIterator(nullptr); }
```

We replace the `read` and `write` methods with overloaded input and output stream operators. Since they are functions rather than methods, they need their own template markings:

```
template <class U>
friend istream& operator>>(istream& outStream,
                           LinkedList<U>& list);

template <class U>
friend ostream& operator<<(ostream& outStream,
                           const LinkedList<U>& list);

private:
  int m_size;
  Cell *m_firstCellPtr, *m_lastCellPtr;
};
```

Note that when we implement the methods of a `template` class, we do so in the header file. Consequently, we do not need an implementation file when implementing a `template` class.

Similar to the class definitions, the method definitions must be preceded by the `template` keyword. Note that the class name `LinkedList` is followed by the type marker `<T>`:

```
template <class T>
LinkedList<T>::Cell::Cell(const T& value, Cell* previous,
                          Cell* next)
 :m_value(value),
  m_previous(previous),
  m_next(next) {
  // Empty.
}

template <class T>
LinkedList<T>::Iterator::Iterator()
```

```
        :m_cellPtr(nullptr) {
        // Empty.
    }
```

Note that when we implement a method of an inner class, we need to include both the names of the outer class (`LinkedList`) and inner class (`Cell`) in the implementation:

```
template <class T>
LinkedList<T>::Iterator::Iterator(Cell* cellPtr)
 :m_cellPtr(cellPtr) {
   // Empty.
}

template <class T>
LinkedList<T>::Iterator::Iterator(const Iterator& position)
 :m_cellPtr(position.m_cellPtr) {
   // Empty.
}
```

Since `LinkedList` is a `template` class, it is not known to the compiler that its inner class `Iterator` is, in fact, a class. As far as the compiler knows, the iterator could be a type, a value, or a class. Therefore, we need to inform the compiler by using the `typename` keyword:

```
template <class T>
typename LinkedList<T>::Iterator&
LinkedList<T>::Iterator::operator=(const Iterator& iterator) {
   m_cellPtr = iterator.m_cellPtr;
   return *this;
}
```

The following operator versions are implemented in the same way as its method counterparts in the previous version of `LinkedList`. That is, the `equal` method has been replaced by the equation operator (`operator==`), and the `notEqual` method has been replaced by the not-equal operator (`operator!=`):

```
template <class T>
bool LinkedList<T>::Iterator::operator==(const Iterator&position){
   return (m_cellPtr == position.m_cellPtr);
}

template <class T>
bool LinkedList<T>::Iterator::operator!=(const Iterator&position){
   return !(*this == position);
}
```

The increase operator has been replaced with both the prefix and postfix version of `operator++`. The difference between them is that the prefix version does not take any parameters, while the postfix version takes a single integer value as parameter. Note that the integer value is not used by the operator. Its value is undefined (however, it is usually set to zero) and is always ignored. It is present only to distinguish between the prefix and postfix cases:

```
template <class T>
bool LinkedList<T>::Iterator::operator++() {
  if (m_cellPtr != nullptr) {
    m_cellPtr = m_cellPtr->next();
    return true;
  }

  return false;
}

template <class T>
bool LinkedList<T>::Iterator::operator++(int) {
  if (m_cellPtr != nullptr) {
    m_cellPtr = m_cellPtr->next();
    return true;
  }

  return false;
}
```

The `decrease` operator also comes in a prefix and a postfix version, and works in a way similar to the `increase` operator:

```
template <class T>
bool LinkedList<T>::Iterator::operator--() {
  if (m_cellPtr != nullptr) {
    m_cellPtr = m_cellPtr->previous();
    return true;
  }

  return false;
}

template <class T>
bool LinkedList<T>::Iterator::operator--(int) {
  if (m_cellPtr != nullptr) {
    m_cellPtr = m_cellPtr->previous();
    return true;
  }
```

```
        return false;
    }
```

The dereference operator also comes in two versions. The first version is constant and returns a value. The second version is not constant and returns a reference to the value, instead of the value itself. In this way, the first version can be called on a constant object, in which case we are not allowed to change its value. The second version can be called on a non-constant object only, we can change the value by assigning a new value to the value returned by the method:

```
template <class T>
T LinkedList<T>::Iterator::operator*() const {
    return m_cellPtr->value();
}

template <class T>
T& LinkedList<T>::Iterator::operator*() {
    return m_cellPtr->value();
}
```

There are three constructors of the ReverseIterator class. The first constructor is a default constructor, the second constructor is initialized with a Cell pointer, and the third constructor is a copy constructor. It takes a reference to another ReverseIterator object, and initializes the Cell pointer:

```
template <class T>
LinkedList<T>::ReverseIterator::ReverseIterator()
 :m_cellPtr(nullptr) {
   // Empty.
}

template <class T>
LinkedList<T>::ReverseIterator::ReverseIterator(Cell* currCellPtr)
 :m_cellPtr(currCellPtr) {
   // Empty.
}

template <class T>
LinkedList<T>::ReverseIterator::ReverseIterator
                                (const ReverseIterator& position)
 :m_cellPtr(position.m_cellPtr) {
   // Empty.
}
```

The equality operator initializes the `Cell` pointer with the `Cell` pointer of the given `ReverseIterator` object reference:

```
template <class T>
const typename LinkedList<T>::ReverseIterator&
LinkedList<T>::ReverseIterator::operator=(const ReverseIterator&
position) {
  m_cellPtr = position.m_cellPtr;
  return *this;
}
```

Two reverse iterators are equal if their cell pointers point at the same cell:

```
template <class T>
bool LinkedList<T>::ReverseIterator::operator==
                             (const ReverseIterator& position) {
  return (m_cellPtr == position.m_cellPtr);
}

template <class T>
bool LinkedList<T>::ReverseIterator::operator!=
                             (const ReverseIterator& position) {
  return !(*this == position);
}
```

The difference between the increase and decrease operators of the `Iterator` and `ReverseIterator` classes is that in `Iterator` the increment operators calls next and the decrement operators call `previous` in `Cell`. In `ReverseIterator` it is the other way around: the increment operators call `previous` and the decrement operators call `next`. As the names implies: `Iterator` iterates forward, while `ReverseIterator` iterates backwards:

```
template <class T>
bool LinkedList<T>::ReverseIterator::operator++() {
  if (m_cellPtr != nullptr) {
    m_cellPtr = m_cellPtr->previous();
    return true;
  }

  return false;
}

template <class T>
bool LinkedList<T>::ReverseIterator::operator++(int) {
  if (m_cellPtr != nullptr) {
    m_cellPtr = m_cellPtr->previous();
```

```
      return true;
    }

    return false;
  }

  template <class T>
  bool LinkedList<T>::ReverseIterator::operator--() {
    if (m_cellPtr != nullptr) {
      m_cellPtr = m_cellPtr->next();
      return true;
    }

    return false;
  }

  template <class T>
  bool LinkedList<T>::ReverseIterator::operator--(int) {
    if (m_cellPtr != nullptr) {
      m_cellPtr = m_cellPtr->next();
      return true;
    }

    return false;
  }

  template <class T>
  T LinkedList<T>::ReverseIterator::operator*() const {
    return m_cellPtr->value();
  }

  template <class T>
  T& LinkedList<T>::ReverseIterator::operator*() {
    return m_cellPtr->value();
  }
```

The default constructor of `LinkedList` initializes the list to become empty, with the pointer to the first and last cell set to null:

```
  template <class T>
  LinkedList<T>::LinkedList()
   :m_size(0),
    m_firstCellPtr(nullptr),
    m_lastCellPtr(nullptr) {
    // Empty.
  }
```

```
template <class T>
LinkedList<T>::LinkedList(const LinkedList<T>& list) {
 *this = list;
}
```

The assignment operator copies the values of the given list, in the same way as the non-template method:

```
template <class T>
LinkedList<T>& LinkedList<T>::operator=(const LinkedList<T>&list){
  m_size = 0;
  m_firstCellPtr = nullptr;
  m_lastCellPtr = nullptr;

  if (list.m_size > 0) {
    for (Cell *listCellPtr = list.m_firstCellPtr,
              *nextCellPtr = list.m_lastCellPtr->next();
        listCellPtr != nextCellPtr;
        listCellPtr = listCellPtr->next()) {
      Cell *newCellPtr = new Cell(listCellPtr->value(),
                                  m_lastCellPtr, nullptr);
      if (m_firstCellPtr == nullptr) {
        m_firstCellPtr = newCellPtr;
      }
```

Note that we use the reference version of the next method, which allows us to assign values to the method call. Since next returns a reference to the next pointer of the cell, we can assign value of newCellPtr to that pointer:

```
      else {
        m_lastCellPtr->next() = newCellPtr;
      }

      m_lastCellPtr = newCellPtr;
      ++m_size;
    }
  }

  return *this;
}
```

The destructor simply calls the `clear` method, which goes through the linked list and deletes every cell:

```
template <class T>
LinkedList<T>::~LinkedList() {
  clear();
}

template <class T>
void LinkedList<T>::clear() {
  Cell *currCellPtr = m_firstCellPtr;

  while (currCellPtr != nullptr) {
    Cell *deleteCellPtr = currCellPtr;
    currCellPtr = currCellPtr->next();
    delete deleteCellPtr;
  }
```

When the cells are deleted, the pointer to the first and last cell is set to null:

```
  m_size = 0;
  m_firstCellPtr = nullptr;
  m_lastCellPtr = nullptr;
}
```

Two lists are equal if they have the same size, and if their cells hold the same values:

```
template <class T>
bool LinkedList<T>::operator==(const LinkedList<T>& list) const {
  if (m_size != list.m_size) {
    return false;
  }

  for (Iterator thisIterator = begin(),
                listIterator = list.begin();
       thisIterator != end(); ++thisIterator, ++listIterator) {
    if (*thisIterator != *listIterator) {
      return false;
    }
  }

  return true;
}

template <class T>
bool LinkedList<T>::operator!=(const LinkedList<T>& list) const {
  return !(*this == list);
}
```

The add method adds a cell with a new value at the end of the list, as shown in the following example:

```
template <class T>
void LinkedList<T>::add(const T& value) {
  Cell *newCellPtr = new Cell(value, m_lastCellPtr, nullptr);

  if (m_lastCellPtr == nullptr) {
    m_firstCellPtr = newCellPtr;
    m_lastCellPtr = newCellPtr;
  }
  else {
    m_lastCellPtr->next() = newCellPtr;
    m_lastCellPtr = newCellPtr;
  }

  ++m_size;
}
```

The second version of add adds the given list at the end of the list, as shown in the following example:

```
template <class T>
void LinkedList<T>::add(const LinkedList<T>& list) {
  for (Cell *listCellPtr = list.m_firstCellPtr;
       listCellPtr != nullptr; listCellPtr = listCellPtr->next()){
    const T& value = listCellPtr->value();
    Cell *newCellPtr = new Cell(value, m_lastCellPtr, nullptr);

    if (m_lastCellPtr == nullptr) {
      m_firstCellPtr = newCellPtr;
    }
    else {
      m_lastCellPtr->next() = newCellPtr;
    }

    m_lastCellPtr = newCellPtr;
  }

  m_size += list.m_size;
}
```

The `insert` method adds a value or a list at the given position:

```
template <class T>
void LinkedList<T>::insert(const Iterator& insertPosition,
                           const T& value) {
  if (insertPosition.m_cellPtr == nullptr) {
    add(value);
  }
  else {
    Cell *insertCellPtr = insertPosition.m_cellPtr;
    Cell *newCellPtr =
      new Cell(value, insertCellPtr->previous(), insertCellPtr);
    insertCellPtr->previous() = newCellPtr;

    if (insertCellPtr == m_firstCellPtr) {
      m_firstCellPtr = newCellPtr;
    }
    else {
      newCellPtr->previous()->next() = newCellPtr;
    }

    ++m_size;
  }
}

template <class T>
void LinkedList<T>::insert(const Iterator& insertPosition,
                           const LinkedList<T>& list) {
  if (insertPosition.m_cellPtr == nullptr) {
    add(list);
  }
  else {
    Cell *insertCellPtr = insertPosition.m_cellPtr;

    Cell *firstInsertCellPtr = nullptr,
         lastInsertCellPtr = nullptr;
    for (Cell *listCellPtr = list.m_firstCellPtr;
         listCellPtr != nullptr;listCellPtr=listCellPtr->next()) {
      double value = listCellPtr->value();
      Cell *newCellPtr =
        new Cell(value, lastInsertCellPtr, nullptr);

      if (firstInsertCellPtr == nullptr) {
        firstInsertCellPtr = newCellPtr;
      }
      else {
        lastInsertCellPtr->next() = newCellPtr;
```

```
      }

    lastInsertCellPtr = newCellPtr;
  }

  if (firstInsertCellPtr != nullptr) {
    if (insertCellPtr->previous() != nullptr) {
      insertCellPtr->previous()->next() = firstInsertCellPtr;
      firstInsertCellPtr->previous() =
        insertCellPtr->previous();
    }
    else {
      m_firstCellPtr = firstInsertCellPtr;
    }
  }

  if (lastInsertCellPtr != nullptr) {
    lastInsertCellPtr->next() = insertCellPtr;
    insertCellPtr->previous() = lastInsertCellPtr;
  }

  m_size += list.m_size;
  }
}
```

The erase and remove methods remove a value of a sub-list from the list:

```
template <class T>
void LinkedList<T>::erase(const Iterator& removePosition) {
  remove(removePosition, removePosition);
}

template <class T>
void LinkedList<T>::remove(const Iterator& firstPosition,
        const Iterator& lastPosition /*= Iterator(nullptr)*/) {
  Cell *firstCellPtr = firstPosition.m_cellPtr,
      *lastCellPtr = lastPosition.m_cellPtr;
  lastCellPtr = (lastCellPtr == nullptr)
                ? m_lastCellPtr : lastCellPtr;

  Cell *previousCellPtr = firstCellPtr->previous(),
      *nextCellPtr = lastCellPtr->next();

  Cell *currCellPtr = firstCellPtr;
  while (currCellPtr != nextCellPtr) {
    Cell *deleteCellPtr = currCellPtr;
    currCellPtr = currCellPtr->next();
    delete deleteCellPtr;
```

```
      --m_size;
    }

    if (previousCellPtr != nullptr) {
      previousCellPtr->next() = nextCellPtr;
    }
    else {
      m_firstCellPtr = nextCellPtr;
    }

    if (nextCellPtr != nullptr) {
      nextCellPtr->previous() = previousCellPtr;
    }
    else {
      m_lastCellPtr = previousCellPtr;
    }
  }
```

The input stream operator first reads the `size` of the list, and then the values themselves:

```
template <class T>
istream& operator>>(istream& inStream, LinkedList<T>& list) {
  int size;
  inStream >> size;

  for (int count = 0; count < size; ++count) {
    T value;
    inStream >> value;
    list.add(value);
  }

  return inStream;
}
```

The output stream operator writes the list on the given stream, surrounded by brackets and with the values separated by commas:

```
template <class T>
ostream& operator<<(ostream& outStream,const LinkedList<T>& list){
  outStream << "[";

  bool first = true;
  for (const T& value : list) {
    outStream << (first ? "" : ",") << value;
    first = false;
  }

  outStream << "]";
```

```
        return outStream;
    }
```

We test the `LinkedList` class by letting the user input a list that we iterate automatically with the `for` statement, as well as manually with forward and backward iterators.

Main.cpp:

```
#include <IOStream>
#include <Exception>
using namespace std;

#include "List.h"

void main() {
  LinkedList<double> list;
  cin >> list;
  cout << list <&amp;lt; endl;
```

Note that it is possible to use the `for` statement directly on the list since the extended list holds the `begin` method, which returns an iterator with the prefix increment (++) and dereference (*) operators:

```
for (double value : list) {
  cout << value << " ";
}
cout << endl;
```

We can also iterate through the list manually with the `begin` and `end` methods of the `Iterator` class:

```
for (LinkedList<double>::Iterator iterator = list.begin();
     iterator != list.end(); ++iterator) {
  cout << *iterator << " ";
}
cout << endl;
```

With the `rbegin` and `rend` methods and the `ReverseIterator` class we iterate from its end to its beginning. Note that we still use increment (++) rather than decrement (−−), even though we iterate through the list backwards:

```
for (LinkedList<double>::ReverseIterator iterator =
     list.rbegin(); iterator != list.rend(); ++iterator) {
  cout << *iterator << " ";
}
cout << endl;
}
```

The extended Set class

The Set class of this section has been extended in three ways compared to the version of the earlier section:

- The set is stored as an ordered list, which makes some of the methods more efficient
- The class is a template; it may store values of arbitrary types as long as those types support ordering
- The class has operator overloading, which (hopefully) makes it easier and more intuitive to use

In C++ it is possible to define our own types with the typedef keyword. We define Iterator of Set to be the same iterator as in LinkedList. In the earlier section, Iterator was a free-standing class that we could reuse when working with sets. However, in this section, Iterator is an inner class. Otherwise, LinkedList could not be accessed when handling sets since Set inherits LinkedList privately. Remember that when we inherit privately, all methods and fields of the base class become private in the subclass.

Set.h:

```
template <class T>
class Set : private LinkedList<T> {
  public:
    typedef LinkedList<T>::Iterator Iterator;

    Set();
    Set(const T& value);
    Set(const Set& set);
    Set& operator=(const Set& set);
    ~Set();
```

We replace the equal and notEqual methods with overloaded operators for comparison. In this way, it is possible to compare two sets in the same way as when comparing, for instance, two integers:

```
    bool operator==(const Set& set) const;
    bool operator!=(const Set& set) const;

    int size() const { return LinkedList<T>::size(); }
    bool empty() const { return LinkedList<T>::empty(); }
    Iterator begin() const { return LinkedList<T>::begin(); }
```

We replace the `unionSet`, `intersection`, and `difference` methods with the operators for addition, multiplication, and subtraction:

```
Set operator+(const Set& set) const;
Set operator*(const Set& set) const;
Set operator-(const Set& set) const;
```

The `merge` function is called by the set methods to perform efficient merging of sets. Since it is a function rather than a method, it must have its own template marking:

```
private:
  template <class U>
  friend Set<U>
    merge(const Set<U>& leftSet, const Set<U>& rightSet,
          bool addLeft, bool addEqual, bool addRight);

public:
  Set& operator+=(const Set& set);
  Set& operator*=(const Set& set);
  Set& operator-=(const Set& set);
```

Similar to the preceding `LinkedList` class, we replace the `read` and `write` methods with overloaded stream operators. Since they also are functions rather than methods, they also need their own template markings:

```
  template <class U>
  friend istream& operator>>(istream& inStream, Set<U>& set);

  template <class U>
  friend ostream& operator<<(ostream& outStream,
                             const Set<U>& set);
};
```

The constructors look pretty much the same, compared to the non-template versions:

```
template <class T>
Set<T>::Set() {
  // Empty.
}

template <class T>
Set<T>::Set(const T& value) {
  add(value);
}

template <class T>
Set<T>::Set(const Set& set)
```

```
    :LinkedList(set) {
      // Empty.
    }

    template <class T>
    Set<T>::~Set() {
      // Empty.
    }

    template <class T>
    Set<T>& Set<T>::operator=(const Set& set) {
      clear();
      add(set);
      return *this;
    }
```

When testing whether two sets are equal, we can just simply call the equality operator in `LinkedList` since the sets of this section are ordered:

```
    template <class T>
    bool Set<T>::operator==(const Set& set) const {
      return LinkedList::operator==(set);
    }
```

Similar to the earlier classes, we test whether two sets are not equal by calling `equal`. However, in this class, we use the equality operator explicitly by comparing the own object (by using the `this` pointer) with the given set:

```
    template <class T>
    bool Set<T>::operator!=(const Set& set) const {
      return !(*this == set);
    }
```

Union, intersection, and difference

We replace the `unionSet`, `intersection`, and `difference` methods with the addition, subtraction, and multiplication operators. They all call `merge`, with the sets and different values for the `addLeft`, `addEqual`, and `addRight` parameters. In case of union, all three of them are `true`, which means that values present in the left-hand set only, or in both sets, or in the right-hand set only shall be included in the union set:

```
    template <class T>
    Set<T> Set<T>::operator+(const Set& set) const {
      return merge(*this, set, true, true, true);
    }
```

In case of intersection, only `addEqual` is `true`, which means that the values present in both sets, but not values present in only one of the sets, shall be included in the intersection set. Take a look at the following example:

```
template <class T>
Set<T> Set<T>::operator*(const Set& set) const {
    return merge(*this, set, false, true, false);
}
```

In case of difference, only `addLeft` is true, which means that only the values present in the left-hand set, but not in both the sets or the right-hand set only, shall be included in the difference set:

```
template <class T>
Set<T> Set<T>::operator-(const Set& set) const {
    return merge(*this, set, true, false, false);
}
```

The `merge` method takes two sets and the three Boolean values `addLeft`, `addEqual`, and `addRight`. If `addLeft` is true, values present in the left-hand set only are added to the resulting set, if `addEqual` is true, values present in both sets are added, and if `rightAdd` is `true`, values present in the right-hand set only are added:

```
template <class T>
Set<T> merge(const Set<T>& leftSet, const Set<T>& rightSet,
            bool addLeft, bool addEqual, bool addRight) {
    Set<T> result;
    Set<T>::Iterator leftIterator = leftSet.begin(),
                    rightIterator = rightSet.begin();
```

The `while` statement keeps iterating while there are values left in both the left-hand set and right-hand set:

```
    while ((leftIterator != leftSet.end()) &&
          (rightIterator != rightSet.end())) {
```

If the left-hand value is smaller, it is added to the resulting set if `addLeft` is `true`. Then the iterator for the left-hand set is incremented:

```
        if (*leftIterator < *rightIterator) {
            if (addLeft) {
                result.add(*leftIterator);
            }

            ++leftIterator;
        }
```

If the right-hand value is smaller, it is added to the resulting set if addRight is true. Then the iterator for the right-hand set is incremented:

```
else if (*leftIterator > *rightIterator) {
  if (addRight) {
    result.add(*rightIterator);
  }

  ++rightIterator;
}
```

Finally, if the values are equal, one of them (but not both, since there are no duplicates in a set) is added and both iterators are incremented:

```
else {
  if (addEqual) {
    result.add(*leftIterator);
  }

  ++leftIterator;
  ++rightIterator;
  }
}
```

If addLeft is true, all remaining values of the left-hand set, if any, are added to the resulting set:

```
if (addLeft) {
  while (leftIterator != leftSet.end()) {
    result.add(*leftIterator);
    ++leftIterator;
  }
}
```

If addRight is true, all remaining values of the right-hand set, if any, are added to the resulting set:

```
if (addRight) {
  while (rightIterator != rightSet.end()) {
    result.add(*rightIterator);
    ++rightIterator;
  }
}
```

Finally, the resulting set is returned using the following:

```
        return result;
    }
```

When performing the union operator to this set and another set, we simply call the addition operator. Note that we return our own object by using the `this` pointer:

```
    template <class T>
    Set<T>& Set<T>::operator+=(const Set& set) {
     *this = *this + set;
      return *this;
    }
```

In the same way, we call the multiplication and subtraction operators when performing intersection and difference on this set and another set. Look at the following example:

```
    template <class T>
    Set<T>& Set<T>::operator*=(const Set& set) {
     *this = *this * set;
      return *this;
    }

    template <class T>
    Set<T>& Set<T>::operator-=(const Set& set) {
     *this = *this - set;
      return *this;
    }
```

When reading a set, the number of values of the set is input, and then the values themselves are input. This function is very similar to its counterpart in the `LinkedList` class. However, in order to avoid duplicates, we call the compound addition operator (+=) instead of the `add` method:

```
    template <class T>
    istream& operator>>(istream& inStream, Set<T>& set) {
      int size;
      inStream >> size;

      for (int count = 0; count < size; ++count) {
        T value;
        inStream >> value;
        set += value;
      }

      return inStream;
    }
```

When writing a set we enclose the value in brackets ("{" and "}") instead of squares ("[" and "]"), as in the list case:

```
template <class T>
ostream& operator<<(ostream& outStream, const Set<T>& set) {
  outStream << "{";
  bool first = true;

  for (const T& value : set) {
    outStream << (first ? "" : ",") << value;
    first = false;
  }

  outStream << "}";
  return outStream;
}
```

We test the set by letting the user input two sets, which we iterate manually with iterators and automatically with the `for` statement. We also evaluate the union, intersection, and difference between the sets.

Main.cpp:

```
#include <IOStream>
using namespace std;

#include "..\ListAdvanced\List.h"
#include "Set.h"

void main() {
  Set<double> s, t;
  cin >> s >> t;

  cout << endl << "s: " << s << endl;
  cout << "t: " << t << endl;

  cout << endl << "s: ";
  for (double value : s) {
    cout << value << " ";
  }

  cout << endl << "t: ";
  for (Set<double>::Iterator iterator = t.begin();
       iterator != t.end(); ++iterator) {
    cout << *iterator << " ";
  }
```

```
    cout << endl << endl << "union: " << (s + t) << endl;
    cout << "intersection: " << (s *t) << endl;
    cout << "difference: " << (s - t) << endl << endl;
}
```

When we execute the program, the output is displayed in a command window:

Advanced searching and sorting

We looked at linear search in the earlier section. In this section, we will look at binary search. The binary search algorithm looks for the value in the middle of the list, and then performs the search with half of the list. In this way, it has $O(log_2 n)$ since it splits the list in half in each iteration.

Search.h:

```
template <class ListType, class ValueType>
int binarySearch(const ValueType& value, const ListType& list) {
  ListType::Iterator* positionBuffer =
    new ListType::Iterator[list.size()];

  int index = 0;
  for (ListType::Iterator position = list.begin();
       position != list.end(); ++position) {
    positionBuffer[index++] = position;
```

```
    }

    int minIndex = 0, maxIndex = list.size() - 1;

    while (minIndex <= maxIndex) {
      int middleIndex = (maxIndex + minIndex) / 2;
      ListType::Iterator iterator = positionBuffer[middleIndex];
      const ValueType& middleValue = *iterator;

      if (value == middleValue) {
        return middleIndex;
      }
      else if (value < middleValue) {
        maxIndex = middleIndex - 1;
      }
      else {
        minIndex = middleIndex + 1;
      }
    }

    return -1;
}
```

The merge sort algorithm

The merge sort algorithm divides the list into two equal sublists, sorts the sublists by recursive calls (a recursive call occurs when a method or function calls itself), and then merges the sorted sublist in a way similar to the `merge` method of the extended version of the `Set` class in the earlier section.

Sort.h:

```
template <class ListType, class ValueType>
void mergeSort(ListType& list) {
  int size = list.size();

  if (size > 1) {
    int middle = list.size() / 2;
    ListType::Iterator iterator = list.begin();

    ListType leftList;
    for (int count = 0; count < middle; ++count) {
      leftList.add(*iterator);
      ++iterator;
    }
```

```
      ListType rightList;
      for (; iterator != list.end(); ++iterator) {
        rightList.add(*iterator);
      }

      mergeSort<ListType, ValueType>(leftList);
      mergeSort<ListType,ValueType>(rightList);

      ListType resultList;
      merge<ListType,ValueType>(leftList, rightList, resultList);
      list = resultList;
    }
  }
```

The merge method of this section is reusing the idea of merge in the extended Set class earlier in this chapter:

```
template <class ListType, class ValueType>
void merge(ListType& leftList, ListType& rightList,
          ListType& result) {
  ListType::Iterator leftPosition = leftList.begin();
  ListType::Iterator rightPosition = rightList.begin();

  while ((leftPosition != leftList.end()) &&
         (rightPosition != rightList.end())) {
    if (*leftPosition < *rightPosition) {
      result.add(*leftPosition);
      ++leftPosition;
    }
    else {
      result.add(*rightPosition);
      ++rightPosition;
    }
  }

  while (leftPosition != leftList.end()) {
    result.add(*leftPosition);
    ++leftPosition;
  }

  while (rightPosition != rightList.end()) {
    result.add(*rightPosition);
    ++rightPosition;
  }
}
```

The quick sort algorithm

The quick sort algorithm selects the first value (called the **pivot value**) and then places all values less than the pivot value in the smaller sublist, and all values greater or equal to the pivot value in the larger sublist. Then the two lists are sorted by recursive calls and then just concatenated together. Let's look at the following example:

```
template <class ListType, class ValueType>
void quickSort(ListType& list) {
  if (list.size() > 1) {
    ListType smaller, larger;
    ValueType pivotValue = *list.begin();

    ListType::Iterator position = list.begin();
    ++position;

    for (;position != list.end(); ++position) {
      if (*position < pivotValue) {
        smaller.add(*position);
      }
      else {
        larger.add(*position);
      }
    }

    quickSort<ListType,ValueType>(smaller);
    quickSort<ListType,ValueType>(larger);
    list = smaller;
    list.add(pivotValue);
    list.add(larger);
  }
}
```

The merge sort algorithm is balanced in a way that it always divides the list into two equal parts and sorts them. The algorithm must iterate through the list once to divide them into two sublists and sorts the sublists. Given a list of values, it must iterate through its *n* values and divide the list log_2n times. Therefore, merge sort $O(n\ log_2n)$.

The quick sort algorithm, on the other hand, is, in the worst case (if the list is already sorted), no better than insert, select, or bubble sort: $O(n^2)$. However, it is fast in the average case.

Summary

In this chapter, we have created classes for the abstract datatypes list and set. A list is an ordered structure with a beginning and an end, while a set is an unordered structure.

We started off with rather simple versions where the list had separate classes for the cell and iterator. Then we created a more advanced version where we used templates and operator overloading. We also placed the cell and iterator classes inside the list class. Finally, we introduced overloaded reference methods.

In the same way, we started by creating a rather simple and ineffective version of the set class. Then we created a more advanced version with templates and operator overloading, where we stored the values in order to be able to perform the union, intersection, and difference operations in a more effective way.

Moreover, we have implemented the linear and binary search algorithms. The linear search works on every unordered sequence, but it is rather ineffective. The binary search is more effective, but it only works on ordered sequences.

Finally, we looked into sorting algorithms. We started with the simple but rather ineffective insert, select, and bubble sort algorithms. Then we continued with the more advanced and effective merge and quick sort algorithms.

In the next chapter, we will start to build a library management system.

3

Building a Library Management System

In this chapter, we study a system for the management of a library. We continue to develop C++ classes, as in the previous chapters. However, in this chapter, we develop a more real-world system. The library system of this chapter can be used by a real library.

The library is made up of sets of books and customers. The books keep track of which customers have borrowed or reserved them. The customers keep track of which books they have borrowed and reserved.

The main idea is that the library holds a set of books and a set of customers. Each book is marked as borrowed or unborrowed. If it is borrowed, the identity number of the customer that borrowed the book is stored. Moreover, a book can also be reserved by one or several customers. Therefore, each book also holds a list of identity numbers for the customers that have reserved the book. It must be a list rather than a set, since the book shall be loaned to the customers in the order that they reserved the book.

Each customer holds two sets with the identity numbers of the book they have borrowed and reserved. In both cases, we use sets rather than lists since the order they have borrowed or reserved the books does not matter.

In this chapter, we will cover the following topics:

- Working with classes for books and customers that constitute a small database with integer numbers as keys.
- Working with standard input and output streams, where we write information about the books and customers, and prompt the user for input.

- Working with file handling and streams. The books and customers are written and read with standard C++ file streams.
- Finally, we work with the generic classes `set` and `list` from the C++ standard library.

The Book class

We have three classes: `Book`, `Customer`, and `Library`:

- The `Book` class keeps track of a book. Each book has an author and a title, and a unique identity number.
- The `Customer` class keeps track of a customer. Each customer has a name and an address, and a unique identity number.
- The `Library` class keeps track of the library operations, such as adding and removing books and customers, borrowing, returning, and reserving books, as well as listing books and customers.
- The `main` function simply creates an object of the `Library` class.

Moreover, each book holds information on whether it is borrowed at the moment. If it is borrowed, the identity number of the customer who has borrowed the book is also stored. Each book also holds a list of reservations. In the same way, each customer holds sets of books currently borrowed and reserved.

The `Book` class holds two constructors. The first constructor is a default constructor and is used when reading books from a file. The second constructor is used when adding a new book to the library. It takes the name of the author and the title of the book as parameters.

Book.h

```
class Book {
  public:
    Book(void);
    Book(const string& author, const string& title);
```

The `author` and `title` methods simply return the author and title of the book:

```
const string& author(void) const { return m_author; }
const string& title(void) const { return m_title; }
```

The books of the library can be read from and written to a file:

```
void read(ifstream& inStream);
void write(ofstream& outStream) const;
```

A book can be borrowed, reserved, or returned. A reservation can also be removed. Note that when a book is borrowed or reserved, we need to provide the identity number of the customer. However, that is not necessary when returning a book, since the Book class keeps track of the customer that has currently borrowed the book:

```
void borrowBook(int customerId);
int reserveBook(int customerId);
void unreserveBookation(int customerId);
void returnBook();
```

When the book is borrowed, the customer's identity number is stored, which is returned by bookId:

```
int bookId(void) const { return m_bookId; }
```

The borrowed method returns true if the book is borrowed at the moment. In that case, customerId returns the identity number of the customer who has borrowed the book:

```
bool borrowed(void) const { return m_borrowed; }
int customerId(void) const { return m_customerId; }
```

A book can be reserved by a list of customers, and reservationList returns that list:

```
list<int>& reservationList(void) { return m_reservationList; }
```

The MaxBookId field is static, which means that it is common to all objects of the class:

```
static int MaxBookId;
```

The output stream operator writes the information of the book:

```
friend ostream& operator<<(ostream& outStream,
                           const Book& book);
```

The m_borrowed field is true when the book is borrowed. The identity of the book and potential borrower are stored in m_bookId and m_customerId:

```
private:
  bool m_borrowed = false;
  int m_bookId, m_customerId;
```

The name of the author and the title of the book are stored in `m_author` and `m_title`:

```
string m_author, m_title;
```

More than one customer can reserve a book. When they do, their identities are stored in `m_reservationList`. It is a list rather than a set because the reservations are stored in order. When a book is returned, the next customer, in reservation order, borrows the book:

```
list<int> m_reservationList;
};
```

In this chapter, we use the generic `set`, `map`, and `list` classes from the C++ standard library. Their specifications are stored in the `Set`, `Map`, and `List` header files. The `set` and `list` classes hold a set and a list similar to our set and list classes in the previous chapter. A map is a structure where each value is identified by a unique key in order to provide fast access.

Book.cpp

```
#include <Set>
#include <Map>
#include <List>
#include <String>
#include <FStream>
using namespace std;

#include "Book.h"
#include "Customer.h"
#include "Library.h"
```

Since `MaxBookId` is static, we initialize it with the double colon (`::`) notation. Every static field needs to be initialized outside the class definition:

```
int Book::MaxBookId = 0;
```

The default constructor does nothing. It is used when reading from a file. Nevertheless, we still must have a default constructor to create objects of the `Book` class:

```
Book::Book(void) {
  // Empty.
}
```

When a new book is created, it is assigned a unique identity number. The identity number is stored in `MaxBookId`, which is increased for each new `Book` object:

```
Book::Book(const string& author, const string& title)
 :m_bookId(++MaxBookId),
  m_author(author),
  m_title(title) {
  // Empty.
}
```

Writing the book

A book is written to a stream in a similar manner. However, instead of `read` we use `write`. They work in a similar manner:

```
void Book::write(ofstream& outStream) const {
  outStream.write((char*) &m_bookId, sizeof m_bookId);
```

When reading a string we use `getline` instead of the stream operator, since the stream operator reads one word only, while `getline` reads several words. When writing to a stream, however, we can use the stream operator. It does not matter whether the name and title are made up of one or several words:

```
outStream << m_author << endl;
outStream << m_title << endl;

outStream.write((char*) &m_borrowed, sizeof m_borrowed);
outStream.write((char*) &m_customerId, sizeof m_customerId);
```

Similar to the reading case here, we first write the number of reservations in the list. Then we write the reservation identities themselves:

```
{ int reservationListSize = m_reservationList.size();
  outStream.write((char*) &reservationListSize,
            sizeof reservationListSize);

  for (int customerId : m_reservationList) {
    outStream.write((char*) &customerId, sizeof customerId);
  }
}
}
```

Reading the book

When reading any kind of value (except strings) from a file, we use the read method, which reads a fixed number of bytes. The sizeof operator gives us the size, in bytes, of the m_bookId field. The sizeof operator can also be used to find the size of a type. For instance, sizeof (int) gives us the size in bytes of a value of the type int. The type must be enclosed in parentheses:

```
void Book::read(ifstream& inStream) {
  inStream.read((char*) &m_bookId, sizeof m_bookId);
```

When reading string values from a file, we use the C++ standard function getline to read the name of the author and the title of the book. It would not work to use the input stream operator if the name is made up of more than one word. If the author or title is made up of more than one word, only the first word would be read. The remaining words would not be read:

```
getline(inStream, m_author);
getline(inStream, m_title);
```

Note that we use the read method to read the value of the m_borrowed field, too, even though it holds the bool type rather than int:

```
inStream.read((char*) &m_borrowed, sizeof m_borrowed);
inStream.read((char*) &m_customerId, sizeof m_customerId);
```

When reading the reservation list, we first read the number of reservations in the list. Then we read the reservation identity numbers themselves:

```
{ int reservationListSize;
  inStream.read((char*) &reservationListSize,
            sizeof reservationListSize);
  for (int count = 0; count < reservationListSize; ++count) {
    int customerId;
    inStream.read((char*) &customerId, sizeof customerId);
    m_reservationList.push_back(customerId);
  }
}
}
```

Borrowing and reserving the book

When the book is borrowed, m_borrowed becomes true and m_customerId is set to the identity number of the customer that borrowed the book:

```
void Book::borrowBook(int customerId) {
  m_borrowed = true;
  m_customerId = customerId;
}
```

It is a little bit different when the book is reserved. While a book can be borrowed by one customer only, it can be reserved by more than one customer. The identity number of the customer is added to m_reservationList. The size of the list is returned for the caller to know their position in the reservation list:

```
int Book::reserveBook(int customerId) {
  m_reservationList.push_back(customerId);
  return m_reservationList.size();
}
```

When the book is returned, we just set m_borrowed to false. We do not need to set m_customerId to anything specific. It is not relevant as long as the book is not borrowed:

```
void Book::returnBook() {
  m_borrowed = false;
}
```

A customer can remove themselves from the reservation list. In that case, we call remove on m_reservationList:

```
void Book::unreserveBookation(int customerId) {
  m_reservationList.remove(customerId);
}
```

Displaying the book

The output stream operator writes the title and author of the book. If the book is borrowed, the customer's name is written, and if the reservation list is full, the reservation customers' names are written:

```
ostream& operator<<(ostream& outStream, const Book& book) {
  outStream << """ << book.m_title << "" by " << book.m_author;
```

We use the double-colon notation (::) when accessing a static field, such as
`s_customerMap` in `Library`:

```cpp
  if (book.m_borrowed) {
    outStream << endl << "  Borrowed by: "
              << Library::s_customerMap[book.m_customerId].name()
              << ".";
  }

  if (!book.m_reservationList.empty()) {
    outStream << endl << "  Reserved by: ";
    bool first = true;
    for (int customerId : book.m_reservationList) {
      outStream << (first ? "" : ",")
                << Library::s_customerMap[customerId].name();
      first = false;
    }

    outStream << ".";
  }

  return outStream;
}
```

The Customer class

The `Customer` class keeps track of a customer. It holds sets of the books the customer
currently has borrowed and reserved.

Customer.h

```cpp
class Customer {
  public:
    Customer(void);
    Customer(const string& name, const string& address);

    void read(ifstream& inStream);
    void write(ofstream& outStream) const;

    void borrowBook(int bookId);
    void reserveBook(int bookId);
    void returnBook(int bookId);
    void unreserveBook(int bookId);
```

The `hasBorrowed` method returns true if the customer has at least one book borrowed at the moment. In the `Library` class in the next section, it is not possible to remove a customer who currently has borrowed books:

```
bool hasBorrowed(void) const { return !m_loanSet.empty(); }

const string& name(void) const {return m_name;}
const string& address(void) const {return m_address;}
int id(void) const {return m_customerId;}
```

In the same way, as in the `Book` class, which was used previously, we use the static field `MaxCustomerId` to count the identity number of the customers. We also use the output stream operator to write information about the customer:

```
static int MaxCustomerId;
friend ostream& operator<<(ostream& outStream,
                          const Customer& customer);
```

Each customer has a name, address, and unique identity number. The sets `m_loanSet` and `m_reservationSet` hold the identity numbers of the books currently borrowed and reserved by the customer. Note that we use sets instead of lists, since the order of the books borrowed and reserved does not matter:

```
private:
  int m_customerId;
  string m_name, m_address;
  set<int> m_loanSet, m_reservationSet;
};
```

Customer.cpp

```
#include <Set>
#include <Map>
#include <List>
#include <String>
#include <FStream>
using namespace std;

#include "Book.h"
#include "Customer.h"
#include "Library.h"
```

Since `MaxCustomerId` is a static field, it needs to be defined outside the class:

```
int Customer::MaxCustomerId;
```

The default constructor is used when loading objects from a file only. Therefore, there is no need to initialize the fields:

```
Customer::Customer(void) {
  // Empty.
}
```

The second constructor is used when creating new book objects. We use the `MaxCustomerId` field to initialize the identity number of the customer; we also initialize their `name` and `address`:

```
Customer::Customer(const string& name, const string& address)
 :m_customerId(++MaxCustomerId),
  m_name(name),
  m_address(address) {
  // Empty.
}
```

Reading the customer from a file

The `read` method reads the information on a customer from the file stream:

```
void Customer::read(ifstream& inStream) {
 inStream.read((char*) &m_customerId, sizeof m_customerId);
```

In the same way, as in the `read` method of the `Book` class, we have to use the `getline` function instead of the input stream operator, since the input stream operator would read one word only:

```
getline(inStream, m_name);
getline(inStream, m_address);

{ int loanSetSize;
  inStream.read((char*) &loanSetSize, sizeof loanSetSize);

  for (int count = 0; count < loanSetSize; ++count) {
    int bookId;
    inStream.read((char*) &bookId, sizeof bookId);
    m_loanSet.insert(bookId);
  }
}
```

```
{ int reservationListSize;
  inStream.read((char*) &reservationListSize,
            sizeof reservationListSize);

  for (int count = 0; count < reservationListSize; ++count) {
    int bookId;
    inStream.read((char*) &bookId, sizeof bookId);
    m_loanSet.insert(bookId);
  }
 }
}
```

Writing the customer to a file

The write method writes information on the customer to the stream in the same way as in
the Book class previously:

```
void Customer::write(ofstream& outStream) const {
  outStream.write((char*) &m_customerId, sizeof m_customerId);
  outStream << m_name << endl;
  outStream << m_address << endl;
```

When writing a set, we first write the size of the set, and then the individual values of the
set:

```
{ int loanSetSize = m_loanSet.size();
  outStream.write((char*) &loanSetSize, sizeof loanSetSize);

  for (int bookId : m_loanSet) {
    outStream.write((char*) &bookId, sizeof bookId);
  }
 }

{ int reservationListSize = m_reservationSet.size();
  outStream.write((char*) &reservationListSize,
            sizeof reservationListSize);

  for (int bookId : m_reservationSet) {
    outStream.write((char*) &bookId, sizeof bookId);
  }
 }
}
```

Borrowing and reserving a book

When a customer borrows a book, it is inserted into the loan set of the customer:

```
void Customer::borrowBook(int bookId) {
  m_loanSet.insert(bookId);
}
```

In the same way, when a customer reserves a book, it is inserted into the reservation set of the customer:

```
void Customer::reserveBook(int bookId) {
  m_reservationSet.insert(bookId);
}
```

When a customer returns or unreserves a book, it is removed from the loan set or reservation set:

```
void Customer::returnBook(int bookId) {
  m_loanSet.erase(bookId);
}

void Customer::unreserveBook(int bookId) {
  m_reservationSet.erase(bookId);
}
```

Displaying the customer

The output stream operator writes the name and address of the customer. If the customer has borrowed or reserved books, they are written too:

```
ostream& operator<<(ostream& outStream, const Customer& customer){
  outStream << customer.m_customerId << ". " << customer.m_name
            << ", " << customer.m_address << ".";

  if (!customer.m_loanSet.empty()) {
    outStream << endl << "  Borrowed books: ";

    bool first = true;
    for (int bookId : customer.m_loanSet) {
      outStream << (first ? "" : ",")
                << Library::s_bookMap[bookId].author();
      first = false;
    }
  }
```

```
    if (!customer.m_reservationSet.empty()) {
      outStream << endl << "  Reserved books: ";
      bool first = true;
      for (int bookId : customer.m_reservationSet) {
        outStream << (first ? "" : ",")
                  << Library::s_bookMap[bookId].title();
        first = false;
      }
    }

    return outStream;
  }
```

The Library class

Finally, the `Library` class handles the library itself. It performs a set of tasks regarding borrowing and returning books.

Library.h

```
    class Library {
      public:
        Library();

      private:
        static string s_binaryPath;
```

The `lookupBook` method looks up a book by the author and title. It returns true if the book is found. If it is found, its information (an object of the `Book` class) is copied into the object pointed at by `bookPtr`:

```
    bool lookupBook(const string& author, const string& title,
              Book* bookPtr = nullptr);
```

In the same way, `lookupCustomer` looks up a customer by the name and address. If the customer is found, true is returned, and the information is copied into the object pointed at by `customerPtr`:

```
    bool lookupCustomer(const string& name, const string& address,
              Customer* customerPtr = nullptr);
```

The application of this chapter revolves around the following methods. They perform the tasks of the library system. Each of the methods will prompt the user for input and then perform a task, such as borrowing or returning a book.

The following methods perform one task each, which are looking up the information about a book or a customer, adding or deleting a book, listing the books, adding and deleting books from the library, and borrowing, reserving, and returning books:

```
void addBook(void);
void deleteBook(void);
void listBooks(void);
void addCustomer(void);
void deleteCustomer(void);
void listCustomers(void);
void borrowBook(void);
void reserveBook(void);
void returnBook(void);
```

The `load` and `save` methods are called at the beginning and the end of the execution:

```
void load();
void save();
```

There are two maps holding the books and the customers of the library. As mentioned previously, a map is a structure where each value is identified by a unique key in order to provide fast access. The unique identity numbers of the books and customers are the keys:

```
public:
    static map<int,Book> s_bookMap;
    static map<int,Customer> s_customerMap;
};
```

Library.cpp

```
#include <Set>
#include <Map>
#include <List>
#include <String>
#include <FStream>
#include <IOStream>
#include <Algorithm>
using namespace std;

#include "Book.h"
#include "Customer.h"
#include "Library.h"

map<int,Book> Library::s_bookMap;
map<int,Customer> Library::s_customerMap;
```

Between executions, the library information is stored in the `Library.bin` file on the hard drive. Note that we use two backslashes to represent one backslash in the `string`. The first backslash indicates that the character is a special character, and the second backslash states that it is a backslash:

```
string Library::s_binaryPath("Library.bin");
```

The constructor loads the library, presents a menu, and iterates until the user quits. Before the execution is finished, the library is saved:

```
Library::Library(void) {
```

Before the menu is presented, the library information (books, customers, loans, and reservations) is loaded from the file:

```
load();
```

The while statement continues as long as `quit` is true. It remains false until the user chooses the **Quit** option from the menu:

```
bool quit = false;
while (!quit) {
  cout << "1. Add Book" << endl
       << "2. Delete Book" << endl
       << "3. List Books" << endl
       << "4. Add Customer" << endl
       << "5. Delete Customer" << endl
       << "6. List Customers" << endl
       << "7. Borrow Book" << endl
       << "8. Reserve Book" << endl
       << "9. Return Book" << endl
       << "0. Quit" << endl
       << ": ";
```

The user inputs an integer value from the console input stream (`cin`), which is stored in `choice`:

```
int choice;
cin >> choice;
```

We use a `switch` statement to perform the requested task:

```
switch (choice) {
  case 1:
    addBook();
    break;
```

```
        case 2:
          deleteBook();
          break;

        case 3:
          listBooks();
          break;

        case 4:
          addCustomer();
          break;

        case 5:
          deleteCustomer();
          break;

        case 6:
          listCustomers();
          break;

        case 7:
          borrowBook();
          break;

        case 8:
          reserveBook();
          break;

        case 9:
          returnBook();
          break;

        case 0:
          quit = true;
          break;
      }

    cout << endl;
  }
```

Before the program is finished, the library information is saved:

```
      save();
    }
```

Looking up books and customers

The `lookupBook` method iterates through the book map. It returns true if a book with the author and title exists. If the book exists, its information is copied to the object pointed at by the `bookPtr` parameter and true is returned, as long as the pointer is not null. If the book does not exist, false is returned, and no information is copied into the object:

```
bool Library::lookupBook(const string& author,
    const string& title, Book* bookPtr /* = nullptr*/) {
  for (const pair<int,Book>& entry : s_bookMap) {
    const Book& book = entry.second;
```

Note that `bookPtr` may be `nullptr`. In that case, only true is returned, and no information is written to the object pointed at by `bookPtr`:

```
    if ((book.author() == author) && (book.title() == title)) {
      if (bookPtr != nullptr) {
        *bookPtr = book;
      }

      return true;
    }
  }

  return false;
}
```

In the same way, `lookupCustomer` iterates through the customer map and returns true, as well as copies the customer information to a `Customer` object if a customer with the name exists:

```
bool Library::lookupCustomer(const string& name,
    const string& address, Customer* customerPtr /*=nullptr*/){
  for (const pair<int,Customer>& entry : s_customerMap) {
    const Customer& customer = entry.second;
```

Also, in this case, `customerPtr` may be `nullptr`. In that case, only true is returned. When adding a new customer, we would like to know if there already is a customer with the same name and address:

```
    if ((customer.name() == name) &&
        (customer.address() == address)) {
      if (customerPtr != nullptr) {
        *customerPtr = customer;
      }
```

```
            return true;
        }
    }

    return false;
}
```

Adding a book

The addBook method prompts the user for the name and title of the new book:

```
void Library::addBook(void) {
  string author;
  cout << "Author: ";
  cin >> author;

  string title;
  cout << "Title: ";
  cin >> title;
```

If a book with the author and title already exists, an error message is displayed:

```
  if (lookupBook(author, title)) {
    cout << endl << "The book "" <<  title << "" by "
         << author << " already exists." << endl;
    return;
  }
```

If the book does not already exist, we create a new Book object that we add to the book map:

```
  Book book(author, title);
  s_bookMap[book.bookId()] = book;
  cout << endl << "Added: " << book << endl;
}
```

Deleting a book

The deleteBook method prompts the user for the author and title of the book, and deletes it if it exists:

```
void Library::deleteBook() {
  string author;
  cout << "Author: ";
```

```
cin >> author;

string title;
cout << "Title: ";
cin >> title;
```

If the book does not exist, an error message is displayed:

```
Book book;
if (!lookupBook(author, title, &book)) {
   cout << endl << "There is no book "" << title << "" by "
        << "author " << author << "." << endl;
   return;
}
```

When a book is being deleted, we iterate through all customers and, for each customer, return, and unreserve the book. We do that for every book just in case the book has been borrowed or reserved by customers. In the next chapter, we will work with pointers, which allow us to return and unreserve books in a more effective manner.

Note that when we iterate through a map and obtain each Customer object, we need to put it back in the map after we have modified the values of its fields:

```
for (pair<int,Customer> entry : s_customerMap) {
   Customer& customer = entry.second;
   customer.returnBook(book.bookId());
   customer.unreserveBook(book.bookId());
   s_customerMap[customer.id()] = customer;
}
```

Finally, when we have made sure the book exists, and when we have returned and unreserved it, we remove it from the book map:

```
s_bookMap.erase(book.bookId());
cout << endl << "Deleted." << endl;
}
```

Listing the books

The listBook method is quite simple. First, we check if the book map is empty. If it is empty, we write "No books." If the book map is not empty, we iterate through it, and for each book, we write its information to the console output stream (cout):

```
void Library::listBooks(void) {
   if (s_bookMap.empty()) {
```

```
    cout << "No books." << endl;
    return;
  }

  for (const pair<int,Book>& entry : s_bookMap) {
    const Book& book = entry.second;
    cout << book << endl;
  }
}
```

Adding a customer

The addCustomer method prompts the user for the name and address of the new customer:

```
void Library::addCustomer(void) {
  string name;
  cout << "Name: ";
  cin >> name;

  string address;
  cout << "Address: ";
  cin >> address;
```

If a customer with the same name and address already exists, an error message is displayed:

```
  if (lookupCustomer(name, address)) {
    cout << endl << "A customer with name " << name
         << " and address " << address << " already exists."
         << endl;
    return;
  }
```

Finally, we create a new Customer object that we add to the customer map:

```
  Customer customer(name, address);
  s_customerMap[customer.id()] = customer;
  cout << endl << "Added." << endl;
}
```

Deleting a customer

The `deleteCustomer` method deletes the customer if they exist:

```
void Library::deleteCustomer(void) {
  string name;
  cout << "Name: ";
  cin >> name;

  string address;
  cout << "Address: ";
  cin >> address;
  Customer customer;
  if (!lookupCustomer(name, address, &customer)) {
    cout << endl << "There is no customer with name " << name
         << " and address " << address << "." << endl;
    return;
  }
```

If the customer has borrowed at least one book, it must be returned before the customer can be removed:

```
if (customer.hasBorrowed()) {
  cout << "Customer " << name << " has borrowed at least "
       << "one book and cannot be deleted." << endl;
  return;
}
```

However, if the customer has reserved books, we just unreserve them before removing the customer:

```
for (pair<int,Book> entry : s_bookMap) {
  Book& book = entry.second;
  book.unreserveBookation(customer.id());
  s_bookMap[book.bookId()] = book;
}

cout << endl << "Deleted." << endl;
s_customerMap.erase(customer.id());
}
```

Listing the customers

The listCustomer method works in a way similar to listBooks. If there are no customers, we write "No Customers." If there are customers, we write them to the console output stream (cout):

```
void Library::listCustomers(void) {
  if (s_customerMap.empty()) {
    cout << "No customers." << endl;
    return;
  }
  for (const pair<int,Customer>& entry : s_customerMap) {
    const Customer& customer = entry.second;
    cout << customer << endl;
  }
}
```

Borrowing a book

The borrowBook method prompts the user for the author and title of the book:

```
void Library::borrowBook(void) {
  string author;
  cout << "Author: ";
  cin >> author;

  string title;
  cout << "Title: ";
  cin >> title;
```

If a book with the author and title does not exist, an error message is displayed:

```
Book book;
if (!lookupBook(author, title, &book)) {
  cout << endl << "There is no book "" << title << "" by "
       << "author " << author << "." << endl;
  return;
}
```

Also, if the `book` is already borrowed, an error message is displayed:

```
if (book.borrowed()) {
  cout << endl << "The book "" << title << "" by " << author
       << " has already been borrowed." << endl;
  return;
}
```

Then we prompt the user for the customer's `name` and `address`:

```
string name;
cout << "Customer name: ";
cin >> name;

string address;
cout << "Adddress: ";
cin >> address;
```

If there is no `customer` with the `name` and `address`, an error message is displayed:

```
Customer customer;
if (!lookupCustomer(name, address, &customer)) {
  cout << endl << "There is no customer with name " << name
       << " and address " << address << "." << endl;
  return;
}
```

However, if the book exists and is not already borrowed, and the customer exists, we add the book to the loan set of the customer and mark the book as to be borrowed by the customer:

```
book.borrowBook(customer.id());
customer.borrowBook(book.bookId());
```

Note that we have to put the `Book` and `Customer` objects back into their maps after we have altered them. In the next chapter, we will work with a more direct approach to pointers:

```
s_bookMap[book.bookId()] = book;
s_customerMap[customer.id()] = customer;
cout << endl << "Borrowed." << endl;
}
```

Reserving a book

The `reserveBook` method works in the same way as `borrowBook`. It prompts the user for the `author` and `title` of the book:

```
void Library::reserveBook(void) {
  string author;
  cout << "Author: ";
  cin >> author;

  string title;
  cout << "Title: ";
  cin >> title;
```

Similar to the `borrowBook` case, we check that the book with the `author` and `title` exists:

```
Book book;
if (!lookupBook(author, title, &book)) {
  cout << endl << "There is no book "" << title << "" by "
       << "author " << author << "." << endl;
  return;
}
```

However, one difference compared to `borrowBook` is that the book must have been borrowed in order to be reserved. If it has not been borrowed, there is no point reserving it. In that case, the user should borrow the book instead:

```
if (!book.borrowed()) {
  cout << endl << "The book with author " << author
       << " and title "" << title << "" has not been "
       << "borrowed. Please borrow the book instead." << endl;
  return;
}
```

If the book exists and has not been borrowed, we prompt the user for the `name` and `address` of the customer:

```
string name;
cout << "Customer name: ";
cin >> name;

string address;
cout << "Address: ";
cin >> address;
```

If the customer does not exist, an error message is displayed:

```
Customer customer;
if (!lookupCustomer(name, address, &customer)) {
   cout << endl << "No customer with name " << name
        << " and address " << address << " exists." << endl;
   return;
}
```

Moreover, if a book has already been borrowed by the customer, we display an error message:

```
if (book.customerId() == customer.id()) {
   cout << endl << "The book has already been borrowed by "
        << name << "." << endl;
   return;
}
```

If the book exists and has been borrowed, but not by the customer, we add the customer to the reservation list for the book and the book to the reservation set of the customer:

```
customer.reserveBook(book.bookId());
int position = book.reserveBook(customer.id());
```

Also, in this case, we have to put the `Book` and `Customer` objects back into their maps:

```
s_bookMap[book.bookId()] = book;
s_customerMap[customer.id()] = customer;
```

Finally, we write the position of the customer in the reservation list:

```
   cout << endl << position << "nd reserve." << endl;
}
```

Returning a Book

The `returnBook` method prompts the user for the author and title of the book:

```
void Library::returnBook(void) {
   string author;
   cout << "Author: ";
   cin >> author;

   string title;
   cout << "Title: ";
   cin >> title;
```

If the book does not exist, an error message is displayed:

```
Book book;
if (!lookupBook(author, title, &book)) {
  cout << endl << "No book "" << title
       << "" by " << author << " exists." << endl;
  return;
}
```

If the book has not been borrowed, an error message is displayed:

```
if (!book.borrowed()) {
  cout << endl << "The book "" << title
       << "" by " << author
       << "" has not been borrowed." << endl;
  return;
}
```

Unlike the methods described previously, in this case, we do not ask for the customer. Instead, we return the book and look up the book in the reservation list of each customer:

```
book.returnBook();
cout << endl << "Returned." << endl;

Customer customer = s_customerMap[book.customerId()];
customer.returnBook(book.bookId());
s_customerMap[customer.id()] = customer;
```

If the book has been reserved, we look up the first customer in the reservation list, remove them from the reservation list, and let them borrow the book:

```
list<int>& reservationList = book.reservationList();

if (!reservationList.empty()) {
  int newCustomerId = reservationList.front();
  reservationList.erase(reservationList.begin());
  book.borrowBook(newCustomerId);

  Customer newCustomer = s_customerMap[newCustomerId];
  newCustomer.borrowBook(book.bookId());

  s_customerMap[newCustomerId] = newCustomer;
  cout << endl << "Borrowed by " << newCustomer.name() << endl;
}

s_bookMap[book.bookId()] = book;
}
```

Saving the library information to a file

When saving the library information, we first open the file:

```
void Library::save() {
    ofstream outStream(s_binaryPath);
```

If the file was correctly opened, first we write the number of books, and then we write the information for each book by calling `write` on the `Book` objects:

```
if (outStream) {
    int numberOfBooks = s_bookMap.size();
    outStream.write((char*) &numberOfBooks, sizeof numberOfBooks);

    for (const pair<int,Book>& entry : s_bookMap) {
        const Book& book = entry.second;
        book.write(outStream);
    }
```

In the same way, we write the number of customers, and then the information of each customer, by calling `write`:

```
    int numberOfCustomers = s_customerMap.size();
    outStream.write((char*) &numberOfCustomers,
                    sizeof numberOfCustomers);

    for (const pair<int,Customer>& entry : s_customerMap) {
        const Customer& customer = entry.second;
        customer.write(outStream);
    }
}
}
```

Loading the library information from a file

When loading the library information from a file, we use the same method we would for `read`. We start by opening the file:

```
void Library::load() {
    ifstream inStream(s_binaryPath);
```

We read the number of books and then the information of each book:

```
if (inStream) {
    int numberOfBooks;
    inStream.read((char*) &numberOfBooks, sizeof numberOfBooks);
```

For each book, we create a new `Book` object, read its information by calling `read`, and add it to the book map. We also calculate the new value of the `MaxBookId` static field by assigning it the maximum value of itself and the identity number of the book:

```
for (int count = 0; count < numberOfBooks; ++count) {
  Book book;
  book.read(inStream);
  s_bookMap[book.bookId()] = book;
  Book::MaxBookId = max(Book::MaxBookId, book.bookId());
}
```

In the same way, we read the number of customers and then the information of each customer by calling `read`:

```
int numberOfCustomers;
inStream.read((char*) &numberOfCustomers,
              sizeof numberOfCustomers);
```

For each customer, we create a `Customer` object, read its information from the file, add it to the customer map, and calculate a new value for the `MaxCustomerId` static field:

```
for (int count = 0; count < numberOfCustomers; ++count) {
  Customer customer;
  customer.read(inStream);
  s_customerMap[customer.id()] = customer;
  Customer::MaxCustomerId =
    max(Customer::MaxCustomerId, customer.id());
}
}
}
```

The main function

Finally, we write the `main` function, which executes the library. It is quite easy; the only thing to do is to instantiate an object of the `Library` class. Then the constructor displays the main menu:

Main.cpp

```
#include <Set>
#include <Map>
#include <List>
#include <String>
#include <FStream>
```

```
#include <IOStream>
using namespace std;

#include "Book.h"
#include "Customer.h"
#include "Library.h"

void main(void) {
  Library();
}
```

Summary

In this chapter, we built a library management system made up of the classes Book, Customer, and Library.

The Book class holds information about a book. Each Book object holds a unique identity number. It also keeps track of the borrower (if the book is borrowed) and a list of reservations. In the same way, the Customer class holds information about a customer. Similar to the book, each customer holds a unique identity number. Each Customer object also holds a set of borrowed and reserved books. Finally, the Library class provides a set of services, such as adding and removing books and customers, borrowing, returning, and reserving books, as well as displaying lists of books and customers.

In this chapter, each book and customer have a unique identity number. In the next chapter, we will look into to the library system again. However, we will omit the identity numbers and work with pointers instead.

4

Library Management System with Pointers

In this chapter, we will continue to study a system for the management of a library. Similar to `Chapter 3`, *Building a Library Management System*, we have three classes—`Book`, `Customer`, and `Library`. However, there is one large difference: we do not work with identity numbers. Instead, we work with pointers; each `Book` object holds a pointer to the customer (an object of the `Customer` class) that has borrowed the book as well as a list of pointers to the customers that have reserved the book. In the same way, each customer holds sets of pointers for the books (objects of the `Book` class) they have borrowed and reserved.

However, this approach gives rise to a problem; we cannot store the values of pointers directly in the file. Instead, when we save the file we need to convert from pointers to indexes in the book and customer lists, and when we load the file we need to transform the indexes back to pointers. This process is called **marshmallowing**.

In this chapter, we are going to dive deeper into the following topics:

- Just as in `Chapter 3`, *Building a Library Management System*, we will work with classes for books and customers that constitute a small database. However, in this chapter, we will work directly with pointers instead of integer numbers.
- As we work with pointers instead of integer numbers, the file handling becomes more complicated. We need to perform a process called marshmallowing.
- Finally, we will work with the generic standard C++ classes, `set` and `list`. However, in this chapter they hold pointers to book and customer objects instead of objects.

The Book class

Similar to the system of the previous chapter, we have three classes: Book, Customer, and Library. The Book class keeps track of a book, where each book has an author and a title. The Customer class keeps track of a customer, where each customer has a name and an address. The Library class keeps track of the library operations, such as borrowing, returning, and reserving. Finally, the main function simply creates an object of the Library class.

The Book class is similar to the Book class of Chapter 3, *Building a Library Management System*. The only real difference is that there are no identity numbers, only pointers.

Book.h:

```
class Customer;

class Book {
  public:
  Book();
  Book(const string& author, const string& title);

  const string& author() const { return m_author; }
  const string& title() const { return m_title; }
  void read(ifstream& inStream);
  void write(ofstream& outStream) const;

  int reserveBook(Customer* customerPtr);
  void removeReservation(Customer* customerPtr);
  void returnBook();
```

We do not have a method returning the identity number of the book, since the books in this chapter do not use identity numbers.

The borrowedPtr method returns the address of the customer who has borrowed the book, or nullptr if the book is not borrowed at the moment. It comes in two versions, where the first version returns a reference to a pointer to a Customer object. In that way, we can assign a new value of the pointer to the customer. The second version is constant, which means that we can call it on constant objects:

```
Customer*& borrowerPtr() { return m_borrowerPtr; }
const Customer* borrowerPtr() const { return m_borrowerPtr; }
```

Note that we do not have a borrowed method in this chapter. We do not need it since borrowerPtr returns nullptr if the book is not borrowed at the moment.

In this chapter, `reservationPtrList` returns a list of customer pointers instead of integer values. It comes in two versions, where the first version returns a reference to the list. In that way, we can add and remove pointers from the list. The second version is constant and returns a constant list, which means it can be called on constant `Book` objects and returns a list that cannot be changed:

```
list<Customer*>& reservationPtrList()
                { return m_reservationPtrList; }
const list<Customer*> reservationPtrList() const
                { return m_reservationPtrList; }
```

The output stream operator works in the same way as in Chapter 3, *Building a Library Management System*:

```
friend ostream& operator<<(ostream& outStream,
    const Book& book);
```

The `m_author` and `m_title` fields are strings similar to Chapter 3, *Building a Library Management System*:

```
private:
  string m_author, m_title;
```

However, we have omitted the `m_bookId` field, since we do not use identity numbers in this chapter. We have also replaced the `m_borrowedId` and `m_customerId` fields with `m_borrowerPtr`, which is initialized to `nullptr` since the book is not borrowed from the beginning:

```
Customer* m_borrowerPtr = nullptr;
```

The `m_reservationPtrList` field holds a list of pointers to the customers that have reserved the book, rather than a list of integer identity numbers of Chapter 3, *Building a Library Management System*:

```
list<Customer*> m_reservationPtrList;
  };
```

Book.cpp:

```
#include <Set>
#include <Map>
#include <String>
#include <FStream>
#include <Algorithm>
using namespace std;
```

```
#include "Book.h"
#include "Customer.h"
#include "Library.h"
```

The default constructor is similar to the constructor of Chapter 3, *Building a Library Management System*:

```
Book::Book() {
  // Empty.
}
```

The second constructor is also similar to the constructor of Chapter 3, *Building a Library Management System*. However, there is no m_bookId field to initialize:

```
Book::Book(const string& author, const string& title)
:m_author(author),
m_title(title) {
  // Empty.
}
```

Reading and writing the book

The read and write methods have been shortened in this chapter. They only read and write the author and title of the book. The potential loan and reservation lists are read and written by the save and write methods of the Library class:

```
void Book::read(ifstream& inStream) {
  getline(inStream, m_author);
  getline(inStream, m_title);
}

void Book::write(ofstream& outStream) const {
  outStream << m_author << endl;
  outStream << m_title << endl;
}
```

Borrowing and reserving the book

When a customer reserves a book, the pointer to the `Customer` object is added to the reservation pointer list of the book. The size of the list is returned for the customer to be notified of their position in the reservation list:

```
int Book::reserveBook(Customer* borrowerPtr) {
  m_reservationPtrList.push_back(borrowerPtr);
  return m_reservationPtrList.size();
}
```

When a customer returns a book, we simply set `m_borrowerPtr` to `nullptr`, which indicates that the book is no longer borrowed:

```
void Book::returnBook() {
  m_borrowerPtr = nullptr;
}
```

The `removeReservation` method simply removes the customer pointer from the reservation list:

```
void Book::removeReservation(Customer* customerPtr) {
  m_reservationPtrList.remove(customerPtr);
}
```

Displaying the book

The output stream operator writes the title and author, the customer that has borrowed the book (if any), and the customers that have reserved the book (if any):

```
ostream& operator<<(ostream& outStream, const Book& book) {
 outStream << """ << book.m_title << "" by " << book.m_author;
```

If the book is borrowed, we write the borrower to the stream:

```
if (book.m_borrowerPtr != nullptr) {
    outStream << endl << "  Borrowed by: "
        << book.m_borrowerPtr->name() << ".";
}
```

If the reservation list of the book is not empty, we iterate through it, and for each reservation, we write the customer:

```
if (!book.m_reservationPtrList.empty()) {
  outStream << endl << "  Reserved by: ";
```

```
          bool first = true;
          for (Customer* customerPtr : book.m_reservationPtrList) {
            outStream << (first ? "" : ",") << customerPtr->name();
            first = false;
          }

          outStream << ".";
        }

        return outStream;
```

The Customer class

The Customer class of this chapter is similar to the Customer class of Chapter 3, *Building a Library Management System*. Again, in this case, the difference is that we work with pointers instead of integer identity numbers.

Customer.h:

```
        class Customer {
          public:
            Customer();
            Customer(const string& name, const string& address);

            const string& name() const { return m_name; }
            const string& address() const { return m_address; }

            void read(ifstream& inStream);
            void write(ofstream& outStream) const;
```

The borrowBook, returnBook, reserveBook, and unreserveBook take a pointer to a Book object as the parameter:

```
        void borrowBook(Book* bookPtr);
        void returnBook(Book* bookPtr);
        void reserveBook(Book* bookPtr);
        void unreserveBook(Book* bookPtr);
```

The loadPtrSet and reservationPtrSet methods return sets of Book pointers, rather than sets of integer identity numbers:

```
        set<Book*>& loanPtrSet() { return m_loanPtrSet; }
        const set<Book*> loanPtrSet() const { return m_loanPtrSet; }

        set<Book*>& reservationPtrSet(){ return m_reservationPtrSet; }
```

```
const set<Book*> reservationPtrSet() const
                { return m_reservationPtrSet; }
```

The output stream operator is unchanged, compared to Chapter 3, *Building a Library Management System*:

```
friend ostream& operator<<(ostream& outStream,
                           const Customer& customer);
```

The m_name and m_address fields store the name and address of the customer, just as in Chapter 3, *Building a Library Management System*:

```
private:
    string m_name, m_address;
```

The m_loanPtrSet and m_reservationPtrSet fields hold pointers to Book objects, rather than integer identity numbers:

```
set<Book*> m_loanPtrSet, m_reservationPtrSet;
   };
```

Customer.cpp:

```
#include <Set>
#include <Map>
#include <String>
#include <FStream>
using namespace std;

#include "Book.h"
#include "Customer.h"
#include "Library.h"
```

The constructors are similar to the constructors of Chapter 3, *Building a Library Management System*. The first constructor does nothing and is called when the customer list is loaded from a file:

```
Customer::Customer() {
  // Empty.
}
```

The second constructor initializes the name and address of the customer. However, compared to the constructor of Chapter 3, *Building a Library Management System*, there is no m_customerId field to initialize:

```
Customer::Customer(const string& name, const string& address)
:m_name(name),
```

```
m_address(address) {
    // Empty.
}
```

Reading and writing the customer

Similar to the preceding `Book` case, the `read` and `write` methods have been shortened. They only read and write the name and address. The loan and reservation sets are read and written in the `Library` class, shown as follows:

```
void Customer::read(ifstream& inStream) {
  getline(inStream, m_name);
  getline(inStream, m_address);
}

void Customer::write(ofstream& outStream) const {
 outStream << m_name << endl;
 outStream << m_address << endl;
}
```

Borrowing and reserving a book

The `borrowBook` method adds the book pointer to the loan set and removes it from the reservation set in case it was reserved:

```
void Customer::borrowBook(Book* bookPtr) {
  m_loanPtrSet.insert(bookPtr);
  m_reservationPtrSet.erase(bookPtr);
}
```

The `reserveBook` method simply adds the book pointer to the reservation list, and `returnBook` and `unreserveBook` remove the book pointer from the loan and reservation sets:

```
void Customer::reserveBook(Book* bookPtr) {
  m_reservationPtrSet.insert(bookPtr);
}

void Customer::returnBook(Book* bookPtr) {
  m_loanPtrSet.erase(bookPtr);
}
void Customer::unreserveBook(Book* bookPtr) {
  m_reservationPtrSet.erase(bookPtr);
```

}

Displaying the customer

The output stream operator works in the same way as in Chapter 3, *Building a Library Management System*. It writes the name and address of the customer, as well as the sets of borrowed and reserved books (if any):

```
ostream& operator<<(ostream& outStream, const Customer& customer){
  outStream << customer.m_name << ", "
    << customer.m_address << ".";
```

If the loan list of the customer is not empty, we iterate through it, and for each loan, we write the book:

```
  if (!customer.m_loanPtrSet.empty()) {
    outStream << endl << "  Borrowed books: ";

    bool first = true;
    for (const Book* bookPtr : customer.m_loanPtrSet) {
      outStream << (first ? "" : ", ") << bookPtr->author();
      first = false;
    }
  }
```

In the same way, if the reservation list of the customer is not empty, we iterate through it, and for each reservation, we write the book:

```
  if (!customer.m_reservationPtrSet.empty()) {
    outStream << endl << "  Reserved books: ";

    bool first = true;
    for (Book* bookPtr : customer.m_reservationPtrSet) {
      outStream << (first ? "" : ", ") << bookPtr->author();
      first = false;
    }
  }

  return outStream;
```

The Library class

The `Library` class is quite similar to its counterpart in Chapter 3, *Building a Library Management System*. However, we have added lookup `methods` to transform between pointers and list indexes when saving and loading the library information to a file:

Library.h:

```
class Library {
  public:
    Library();
```

The destructor deallocates all the dynamically allocated memory of this application:

```
    ~Library();

    private:
      static string s_binaryPath;
```

The `lookupBook` and `lookupCustomer` methods return pointers to `Book` and `Customer` objects. If the book or customer does not exist, `nullptr` is returned:

```
    Book* lookupBook(const string& author, const string& title);
    Customer* lookupCustomer(const string& name,
                             const string& address);

    void addBook();
    void deleteBook();
    void listBooks();
    void addCustomer();
    void deleteCustomer();
    void listCustomers();
    void borrowBook();
    void reserveBook();
    void returnBook();
```

The `lookupBookIndex` and `lookupCustomerIndex` methods take a pointer, search the book and customer lists after the object pointed at, and return its index in the lists:

```
    int lookupBookIndex(const Book* bookPtr);
    int lookupCustomerIndex(const Customer* customerPtr);
```

The `lookupBookPtr` and `lookupCustomerPtr` methods take an index and return a pointer to the object at the position in the book and customer lists:

```
Book* lookupBookPtr(int bookIndex);
Customer* lookupCustomerPtr(int customerIndex);
```

The `save` and `write` methods save and load the library information from a file. However, they are more complicated than their counterparts in Chapter 3, *Building a Library Management System*:

```
void save();
void load();
```

The `m_bookPtrList` and `m_customerPtrList` fields hold pointers to `Book` and `Customer` objects, rather than the objects themselves, as in Chapter 3, *Building a Library Management System*:

```
list<Book*> m_bookPtrList;
list<Customer*> m_customerPtrList;
};
```

Library.cpp:

```
#include <Set>
#include <Map>
#include <List>
#include <String>
#include <FStream>
#include <IOStream>
#include <CAssert>
using namespace std;

#include "Book.h"
#include "Customer.h"
#include "Library.h"

string Library::s_binaryPath("C:\Users\Stefan\Library.binary");
```

The constructor is identical to the constructor of Chapter 3, *Building a Library Management System*:

```
Library::Library() {
    load();

    bool quit = false;
    while (!quit) {
        cout << "1. Add Book" << endl
```

```
          << "2. Delete Book" << endl
          << "3. List Books" << endl
          << "4. Add Customer" << endl
          << "5. Delete Customer" << endl
          << "6. List Customers" << endl
          << "7. Borrow Book" << endl
          << "8. Reserve Book" << endl
          << "9. Return Book" << endl
          << "0. Quit" << endl
          << ": ";

    int choice;
    cin >> choice;
    cout << endl;

    switch (choice) {
      case 1:
      addBook();
      break;

      case 2:
      deleteBook();
      break;

      case 3:
      listBooks();
      break;

      case 4:
      addCustomer();
      break;

      case 5:
      deleteCustomer();
      break;

      case 6:
      listCustomers();
      break;

      case 7:
      borrowBook();
      break;

      case 8:
      reserveBook();
      break;
```

```
        case 9:
        returnBook();
        break;

        case 0:
        quit = true;
        break;
      }

    cout << endl;
  }

save();
}
```

Looking up books and customers

The `lookupBook` method of this chapter searches for the `Book` object with the author and title, in a way similar to `Chapter 3`, *Building a Library Management System*. However, if it finds a `Book` object that matches the author and title, it does not copy the information to a given object. Instead, it simply returns a pointer to the object. If it does not find the `Book` object, `nullptr` is returned:

```
Book* Library::lookupBook(const string& author,
                          const string& title) {
for (Book* bookPtr : m_bookPtrList) {
  if ((bookPtr->author() == author) &&
     (bookPtr->title() == title)) {
    return bookPtr;
  }
}

return nullptr;
}
```

In the same way, `lookupCustomer` tries to find a `Customer` object that matches the name and address. If it finds the object, its pointer is returned. If it does not find it, `nullptr` is returned:

```
Customer* Library::lookupCustomer(const string& name,
     const string& address) {
for (Customer* customerPtr : m_customerPtrList) {
  if ((customerPtr->name() == name) &&
     (customerPtr->address() == address)) {
    return customerPtr;
```

```
      }
   }
   return nullptr;
```

Adding a book

The `addBook` method prompts the user for the author and the title:

```
void Library::addBook() {
  string author;
  cout << "Author: ";
  cin >> author;

  string title;
  cout << "Title: ";
  cin >> title;
```

When checking if the book already exists, we call `lookupBook`. If the book exists, a pointer to the `Book` object is returned. If the book does not exist, `nullptr` is returned. Therefore, we test whether the return value does not equal `nullptr`. If it does not equal `nullptr`, the book already exists and an error message is displayed:

```
if (lookupBook(author, title) != nullptr) {
  cout << endl << "The book "" << title << "" by "
    << author << " already exists." << endl;
  return;
}
```

When adding the book, we dynamically create a new `Book` object with the `new` operator. We use the standard C++ `assert` macro to check that the book pointer is not null. If it is null, the execution will be aborted with an error message:

```
Book* bookPtr = new Book(author, title);
assert(bookPtr != nullptr);
m_bookPtrList.push_back(bookPtr);
cout << endl << "Added." << endl;
}
```

Deleting a book

The `deleteBook` method deletes a book from the library by prompting the user about the author and title of the book. If the book exists, we return, unreserve, and delete it:

```
void Library::deleteBook() {
  string author;
  cout << "Author: ";
  cin >> author;

  string title;
  cout << "Title: ";
  cin >> title;
```

We obtain a pointer to the Book object by calling lookupBook:

```
Book* bookPtr = lookupBook(author, title);
```

If the pointer is nullptr, the book does not exist and an error message is displayed:

```
if (bookPtr == nullptr) {
  cout << endl << "The book "" << title << "" by "
    << author << " does not exist." << endl;
  return;
}
```

We check whether the book has been borrowed by looking up the borrower:

```
Customer* borrowerPtr = bookPtr->borrowerPtr();
```

If the pointer returned by borrowerPtr is not nullptr, we return the book by calling returnBook of the borrower. In that way, the book is no longer registered as borrowed by the customer:

```
if (borrowerPtr != nullptr) {
  borrowerPtr->returnBook(bookPtr);
}
```

Moreover, we need to check whether the book has been reserved by any other customer. We do so by obtaining the reservation list of the book and, for every customer in the list, we unreserve the book:

```
list<Customer*> reservationPtrList =
  bookPtr->reservationPtrList();
```

Note that we do not check whether the book has actually been reserved by the customer, we simply unreserve the book. Also note that we do not need to put back any object to the list, since we work with pointers to objects and do not copy objects:

```
for (Customer* reserverPtr : reservationPtrList) {
  reserverPtr->unreserveBook(bookPtr);
}
```

When removing the book, we remove the book pointer from the book pointer list, and then deallocate the `Book` object. It may seem strange that we first display the message and then delete the book pointer. However, it has to be in that order. After we have deleted the object, we can do nothing with it. We cannot delete the object and then write it, it would cause memory errors:

```
m_bookPtrList.remove(bookPtr);
  n cout << endl << "Deleted:" << bookPtr << endl;
  delete bookPtr;
}
```

Listing the books

When listing the books, we first check whether the list is empty. If it is empty, we simply write `"No books."`:

```
void Library::listBooks() {
  if (m_bookPtrList.empty()) {
   cout << "No books." << endl;
   return;
  }
}
```

However, if the list is not empty, we iterate through the book pointer list and, for each book pointer, dereference the pointer and write the information:

```
for (const Book* bookPtr : m_bookPtrList) {
  cout << (*bookPtr) << endl;
  }
}
```

Adding a customer

The `addCustomer` method prompts the user for the name and address of the customer:

```
void Library::addCustomer() {
  string name;
   cout << "Name: ";
  cin >> name;

  string address;
  cout << "Address: ";
  cin >> address;
```

If a customer with the name and address already exists, an error message is displayed:

```
if (lookupCustomer(name, address) != nullptr) {
  cout << endl << "A customer with name " << name
    << " and address " << address << " already exists."
    << endl;
 return;
}
```

When adding the customer, we dynamically create a new `Customer` object that we add to the customer object pointer list:

```
Customer* customerPtr = new Customer(name, address);
  assert(customerPtr != nullptr);
  m_customerPtrList.push_back(customerPtr);
  cout << endl << "Added." << endl;
}
```

Deleting a customer

When deleting a customer, we look them up and display an error message if they do not exist:

```
void Library::deleteCustomer() {
  string name;
  cout << "Customer name: ";
  cin >> name;

  string address;
  cout << "Address: ";
  cin >> address;

  Customer* customerPtr = lookupCustomer(name, address);
```

If the customer with the given name and address does not exist, an error message is displayed. Consider the following code:

```
if (customerPtr == nullptr) {
  cout << endl << "Customer " << name
    << " does not exists." << endl;
  return;
}
```

If the customer has borrowed at least one book, they cannot be deleted, and an error message is displayed, which is shown as follows:

```
if (!customerPtr->loanPtrSet().empty()) {
  cout << "The customer " << customerPtr->name()
     << " has borrowed books and cannot be deleted." << endl;
  return;
}
```

However, if the customer has not borrowed any books, the customer is first removed from the reservation list of every book in the library, shown in the following code:

```
for (Book* bookPtr : m_bookPtrList) {
  bookPtr->removeReservation(customerPtr);
}
```

Then the customer is removed from the customer list, and the Customer object is deallocated by the delete operator. Again, note that we first must write the customer information, and then delete its object. The other way around would not have worked since we cannot inspect a deleted object. That would have caused memory errors:

```
m_customerPtrList.remove(customerPtr);
cout << endl << "Deleted." << (*customerPtr) << endl;
delete customerPtr;
}
```

Listing the customers

When listing the customer, we go through the customer list and, for each customer, dereference the Customer object pointer and write the information of the object:

```
void Library::listCustomers() {
  if (m_customerPtrList.empty()) {
    cout << "No customers." << endl;
    return;
  }
  for (const Customer* customerPtr: m_customerPtrList) {
    cout << (*customerPtr) << endl;
  }
}
```

Borrowing a book

When borrowing a book, we start by prompting the user for the author and title, which is shown in the following code snippet:

```
void Library::borrowBook() {
  string author;
  cout << "Author: ";
  cin >> author;

  string title;
  cout << "Title: ";
  cin >> title;
```

We look up the book and if the book does not exist, an error message is displayed, which is shown in the following code:

```
Book* bookPtr = lookupBook(author, title);

if (bookPtr == nullptr) {
  cout << endl << "There is no book "" << title
    << "" by " << author << "." << endl;
  return;
}
```

If the book has already been borrowed by another customer, it cannot be borrowed again:

```
if (bookPtr->borrowerPtr() != nullptr) {
  cout << endl << "The book "" << title << "" by " << author
    << " has already been borrowed." << endl;
  return;
}
```

We prompt the user for the name and address of the customer:

```
string name;
cout << "Customer name: ";
cin >> name;

string address;
cout << "Address: ";
cin >> address;

Customer* customerPtr = lookupCustomer(name, address);
```

If there is no customer with the given name and address, an error message is displayed:

```
if (customerPtr == nullptr) {
  cout << endl << "No customer with name " << name
     << " and address " << address << " exists." << endl;
  return;
}
```

Finally, we add the book to the customer's loan set and we mark the customer as the borrower of the book:

```
bookPtr->borrowerPtr() = customerPtr;
customerPtr->borrowBook(bookPtr);
cout << endl << "Borrowed." << endl;
}
```

Reserving a book

The reservation process is similar to the preceding borrowing process. We prompt the user for the author and title of the book, as well as the name and address of the customer, which is shown as follows:

```
void Library::reserveBook() {
  string author;
  cout << "Author: ";
  cin >> author;

  string title;
  cout << "Title: ";
  cin >> title;

Book* bookPtr = lookupBook(author, title);
```

If the book does not exist, an error message is displayed:

```
if (bookPtr == nullptr) {
  cout << endl << "There is no book "" << title
     << "" by " << author << "." << endl;
  return;
}
```

If the book has not been borrowed, it is not possible to reserve it. Instead, we encourage the user to borrow the book:

```
if (bookPtr->borrowerPtr() == nullptr) {
  cout << endl << "The book "" << title << "" by "
```

```
        << author << " has not been not borrowed. "
        << "Please borrow the book instead of reserving it."
        << endl;
    return;
}
```

We prompt the user for the name and address of the customer:

```
string name;
cout << "Customer name: ";
cin >> name;

string address;
cout << "Address: ";
cin >> address;

Customer* customerPtr = lookupCustomer(name, address);
```

If the customer does not exist, an error message is displayed:

```
if (customerPtr == nullptr) {
  cout << endl << "There is no customer with name " << name
     << " and address " << address << "." << endl;
  return;
}
```

If the customer has already borrowed the book, they cannot also reserve the book:

```
if (bookPtr->borrowerPtr() == customerPtr) {
  cout << endl << "The book has already been borrowed by "
     << name << "." << endl;
  return;
}
```

Finally, we add the customer to the reservation list of the book and we add the book to the reservation set of the customer. Note that there is a list of reservation customers for the book, while there is a set of reserved books for the customer. The reason for this is that when a book is returned, the first customer in the reservation list borrows the book. There are no such restrictions when it comes to a set of reservations for a customer:

```
int position = bookPtr->reserveBook(customerPtr);
customerPtr->reserveBook(bookPtr);
```

We notify the customer of its position on the reservation list:

```
cout << endl << position << "nd reserve." << endl;
}
```

Returning a book

When returning a book, we prompt the user for its author and title. However, we do not ask for the customer who has borrowed the book. That information is already stored in the Book object:

```
void Library::returnBook() {
  string author;
  cout << "Author: ";
  cin >> author;

  string title;
  cout << "Title: ";
  cin >> title;

  Book* bookPtr = lookupBook(author, title);
```

If the book with the given author and title does not exist, an error message is displayed:

```
if (bookPtr == nullptr) {
 cout << endl << "There is no book "" << title << "" by "
    << author << "." << endl;
 return;
}

Customer* customerPtr = bookPtr->borrowerPtr();
```

If the customer with the given name and address does not exist, an error message is displayed:

```
if (customerPtr == nullptr) {
 cout << endl << "The book "" << title << "" by "
    << author << " has not been borrowed." << endl;
 return;
}

bookPtr->returnBook();
customerPtr->returnBook(bookPtr);
cout << endl << "Returned." << endl;
```

When we have returned the book, we need to find out whether any customer has reserved it:

```
list<Customer*>& reservationPtrList =
  bookPtr->reservationPtrList();
```

If there is at least one customer in the reservation list of the book, we obtain that customer, remove them from the reservation list of the book, mark the customer as the borrower of the book, and add the book to the loan set of the customer:

```
if (!reservationPtrList.empty()) {
  Customer* newCustomerPtr = reservationPtrList.front();
  reservationPtrList.erase(reservationPtrList.begin());

  bookPtr->borrowBook(newCustomerPtr);
  newCustomerPtr->borrowBook(bookPtr);
  cout << endl << "Borrowed by "
     << newCustomerPtr->name() << endl;
  }
}
```

Looking up books and customers

When saving and loading the library information from a file, we need to transform between pointers to `Book` and `Customer` objects and indexes in the book and customer lists. The `lookupIndex` method takes a pointer to a `Book` object and returns its index in the book list:

```
int Library::lookupBookIndex(const Book* bookPtr) {
  int index = 0;

  for (Book* testPtr : m_bookPtrList) {
    if (bookPtr == testPtr) {
    return index;
  }

  ++index;
}
```

If we reach this point, the execution is aborted with an error message by the `assert` macro. However, we should not reach this point, since the `Book` pointer should be in the book pointer list:

```
assert(false);
  return -1;
}
```

The `lookupBookPtr` method performs the opposite task. It finds the `Book` object pointer at the position given by `bookIndex` in the book pointer list. The `assert` macro aborts the execution with an error message if the index is outside the scope of the list. However, that should not happen since all indexes shall be within the scope:

```
Book* Library::lookupBookPtr(int bookIndex) {
  assert((bookIndex >= 0) &&
    (bookIndex < ((int) m_bookPtrList.size())));

  auto iterator = m_bookPtrList.begin();
  for (int count = 0; count < bookIndex; ++count) {
    ++iterator;
  }

  return *iterator;
}
```

The `lookupCustomerIndex` method gives the index of the `Customer` pointer in the customer pointer list, in the same way as shown in the preceding `lookupBookIndex` method:

```
int Library::lookupCustomerIndex(const Customer* customerPtr) {
  int index = 0;

  for (Customer* testPtr : m_customerPtrList) {
    if (customerPtr == testPtr) {
    return index;
  }

  ++index;
  }

  assert(false);
  return -1;
}
```

The `lookupCustomerPtr` method looks up the index of the `Customer` pointer in the customer pointer list in the same way as shown in the preceding `lookupBookPtr` method:

```
Customer* Library::lookupCustomerPtr(int customerIndex) {
  assert((customerIndex >= 0) &&
    (customerIndex < ((int) m_customerPtrList.size())));

  auto iterator = m_customerPtrList.begin();
  for (int count = 0; count < customerIndex; ++count) {
    ++iterator;
```

```
    }
    return *iterator;
}
```

Marshmallowing

The `save` and `load` methods of the `Library` class of this chapter are a bit more complicated than their counterparts in Chapter 3, *Building a Library Management System*. The reason for this is that we cannot save pointers directly, since a pointer holds a memory address that can be changed between executions. Instead, we need to save their indexes to the file. The process of transforming pointers to indexes and indexes to pointers is called **marshmallowing**. When saving the library, we divide the saving process into several steps:

- Saving the book list: At this point, we save the author and title only.
- Saving the customer list: At this point, we save the name and address only.
- For each book: Save the borrower (if the book is borrowed) and the (possibly empty) reservation list. We save the customer list indexes, rather than the pointers to the customers.
- For each customer, we save the loan and reservation sets. We save the book list indexes, rather than the pointers to the books.

Saving the library information to a file

The `Save` method opens the file and, if it was successfully opened, reads the books and customers of the library:

```
void Library::save() {
    ofstream outStream(s_binaryPath);
```

Writing the book objects

We save the book objects. We only save the author and title of the books by calling `write` for each `Book` object. We do not save the potential borrower and reservation list at this point.

We start by writing the number of books in the list to the file:

```
if (outStream) {
    { int bookPtrListSize = m_bookPtrList.size();
        outStream.write((char*) &bookPtrListSize,
```

```
        sizeof bookPtrListSize);
```

Then we write the information of each book to the file by calling `write` on each `Book` object pointer:

```
for (const Book* bookPtr : m_bookPtrList) {
  bookPtr->write(outStream);
}
}
```

Writing the customer objects

We save the customer objects. Similar to the preceding book case, we only save the name and address of the customers by calling `write` for each `Customer` object. We do not save sets of borrowed and reserved books at this point.

In the same way, as in the preceding book case, we start by writing the number of customers on the list to the file:

```
{ int customerPtrListSize = m_customerPtrList.size();
  outStream.write((char*) &customerPtrListSize,
                  sizeof customerPtrListSize);
```

Then we write the information of each customer to the file by calling the `write` method on each `Customer` object pointer:

```
for (const Customer* customerPtr : m_customerPtrList) {
  customerPtr->write(outStream);
}
}
```

Writing the borrower index

For each `Book` object, if the book is borrowed we look up and save the index of the `Customer`, rather than the pointer to the object:

```
for (const Book* bookPtr : m_bookPtrList) {
  { const Customer* borrowerPtr = bookPtr->borrowerPtr();
```

For each book, we start by checking if it has been borrowed. If it has been borrowed, we write the value `true` to the file, to indicate that it is borrowed:

```
if (borrowerPtr != nullptr) {
  bool borrowed = true;
```

```
outStream.write((char*) &borrowed, sizeof borrowed);
```

Then we look up the index of the customer that has borrowed the book in the customer pointer list and write the index to the file:

```
    int loanIndex = lookupCustomerIndex(borrowerPtr);
    outStream.write((char*) &loanIndex, sizeof loanIndex);
}
```

If the book is not borrowed, we just write the value `false` to the file, to indicate that the book has not been borrowed:

```
    else {
      bool borrowed = false;
      outStream.write((char*) &borrowed, sizeof borrowed);
    }
  }
```

Writing the reservation indexes

As a book can be reserved for more than one customer, we iterate through the list of reservations and save the index of each customer in the reservation list:

```
  { const list<Customer*>& reservationPtrList =
      bookPtr->reservationPtrList();
```

For each book, we start by writing the number of reservations of the book to the file:

```
    int reserveSetSize = reservationPtrList.size();
    outStream.write((char*) &reserveSetSize,
                    sizeof reserveSetSize);
```

Then we iterate through the reservation list and, for each reservation, we look up and write the index of each customer that reserved the book:

```
    for (const Customer* customerPtr : reservationPtrList) {
      int customerIndex = lookupCustomerIndex(customerPtr);
      outStream.write((char*) &customerIndex,
                      sizeof customerIndex);
    }
  }
}
```

Writing the loan book indexes

For each customer, we save the indexes of the books they have borrowed. First, we save the size of the loan list and then the book indexes:

```
for (const Customer* customerPtr : m_customerPtrList) {
  { const set<Book*>& loanPtrSet =
      customerPtr->loanPtrSet();
```

For each customer, we start by writing the number of loans to the file:

```
int loanPtrSetSize = loanPtrSet.size();
outStream.write((char*) &loanPtrSetSize,
            sizeof loanPtrSetSize);
```

Then we iterate through the loan set and, for each loan, we look up and write the index of each book to the file:

```
for (const Book* customerPtr : loanPtrSet) {
  int customerIndex = lookupBookIndex(customerPtr);
  outStream.write((char*) &customerIndex,
              sizeof customerIndex);
}
}
```

Writing the reservation book indexes

In the same way, for each customer, we save the indexes of the books they have reserved. First, we save the size of the reservation list and then the indexes of the books they reserved:

```
{ const set<Book*>& reservedPtrSet =
    customerPtr->reservationPtrSet();
```

For each customer, we start by writing the number of reserved books to the file:

```
int reservationPtrSetSize = reservationPtrSet.size();
outStream.write((char*) &reservationPtrSetSize,
            sizeof reservationPtrSetSize);
```

Then we iterate through the reservation set and, for each reservation, we look up and write the index of each book to the file:

```
for (const Book* reservedPtr : reservationPtrSet) {
  int customerIndex = lookupBookIndex(reservedPtr);
  outStream.write((char*) &customerIndex,
```

```
                              sizeof customerIndex);
              }
            }
          }
        }
      }
```

Loading the library information from a file

When loading the file, we proceed in the same manner as when we saved the file:

```
void Library::load() {
  ifstream inStream(s_binaryPath);
```

Reading the book objects

We read the size of the book list, and then the books themselves. Remember that we have so far read the author and title of the books only:

```
if (inStream) {
  { int bookPtrListSize;
```

We start by reading the number of books:

```
    inStream.read((char*) &bookPtrListSize,
            sizeof bookPtrListSize);
```

Then we read the books themselves. For each book, we dynamically allocate a `Book` object, read its information by calling `read` on the pointer, and add the pointer to the book pointer list:

```
    for (int count = 0; count < bookPtrListSize; ++count) {
      Book *bookPtr = new Book();
      assert(bookPtr != nullptr);
      bookPtr->read(inStream);
      m_bookPtrList.push_back(bookPtr);
    }
  }
```

Reading the customer objects

In the same way, we read the size of the customer list and then the customers themselves. Up until this point, we read the name and address of the customers only:

```
{ int customerPtrListSize;
```

We start by reading the number of customers:

```
inStream.read((char*) &customerPtrListSize,
              sizeof customerPtrListSize);
```

Then we read the customers themselves. For each customer, we dynamically allocate a `Customer` object, read its information by calling `read` on the pointer, and add the pointer to the book pointer list:

```
for (int count = 0; count < customerPtrListSize; ++count) {
  Customer *customerPtr = new Customer();
  assert(customerPtr != nullptr);
  customerPtr->read(inStream);
  m_customerPtrList.push_back(customerPtr);
}
}
```

Reading the borrower index

For each book, we read the customers that have borrowed it (if any) and the list of customers that have reserved the book:

```
for (Book* bookPtr : m_bookPtrList) {
  { bool borrowed;
    inStream.read((char*) &borrowed, sizeof borrowed);
```

If `borrowed` is `true`, the book has been borrowed. In that case, we read the index of the customer. We then look up the pointer of the `Customer` object, which we add to the reservation list of the book:

```
if (borrowed) {
  int loanIndex;
  inStream.read((char*) &loanIndex, sizeof loanIndex);
  bookPtr->borrowerPtr() = lookupCustomerPtr(loanIndex);
}
```

If `borrowed` is `false`, the book has not been borrowed. In that case, we set the pointer to the customer that has borrowed the book to `nullptr`:

```
else {
  bookPtr->borrowerPtr() = nullptr;
}
}
```

Reading the reservation indexes

For each book, we also read the reservation list. First, we read the size of the list and then the customer indexes themselves:

```
{ list<Customer*>& reservationPtrList =
    bookPtr->reservationPtrList();
  int reservationPtrListSize;
```

We start by reading the number of reservations of the book:

```
inStream.read((char*) &reservationPtrListSize,
              sizeof reservationPtrListSize);
```

For each reservation, we read the index of the customer and call `lookupCustomerPtr` to obtain the pointer to the `Customer` object, which we add to the reservation pointer list of the book:

```
for (int count = 0; count < reservationPtrListSize;
     ++count) {
  int customerIndex;
  inStream.read((char*) &customerIndex,
               sizeof customerIndex);
  Customer* customerPtr =
    lookupCustomerPtr(customerIndex);
  reservationPtrList.push_back(customerPtr);
}
}
}
```

Reading the loan book indexes

For each customer, we read the set of borrowed books:

```
for (Customer* customerPtr : m_customerPtrList) {
  { set<Book*>& loanPtrSet = customerPtr->loanPtrSet();
    int loanPtrSetSize = loanPtrSet.size();
```

We start by reading the size of the loan list:

```
inStream.read((char*) &loanPtrSetSize,
            sizeof loanPtrSetSize);
```

For each loan, we read the index of the book and call `lookupBookPtr` to obtain the pointer to the `Book` object, which we add to the loan pointer list:

```
for (int count = 0; count < loanPtrSetSize; ++count) {
    int bookIndex;
    inStream.read((char*) &bookIndex, sizeof bookIndex);
    Book* bookPtr = lookupBookPtr(bookIndex);
    loanPtrSet.insert(bookPtr);
  }
}
```

Reading the reservation book indexes

In the same way, for each customer, we read the set of reserved books:

```
{ set<Book*>& reservationPtrSet =
    customerPtr->reservationPtrSet();
```

We start by reading the size of the reservation list:

```
int reservationPtrSetSize = reservationPtrSet.size();
inStream.read((char*) &reservationPtrSetSize,
            sizeof reservationPtrSetSize);
```

For each reservation, we read the index of the book and call `lookupBookPtr` to obtain the pointer to the `Book` object, which we add to the reservation pointer list:

```
for (int count = 0; count < reservationPtrSetSize;
    ++count) {
    int bookIndex;
    inStream.read((char*) &bookIndex, sizeof bookIndex);
    Book* bookPtr = lookupBookPtr(bookIndex);
    reservationPtrSet.insert(bookPtr);
  }
    }
      }
    }
  }
```

Deallocating memory

Since we have added dynamically allocated Book and Customer objects to the lists, we need to deallocate them at the end of the execution. The destructor iterates through the book and customer pointer lists and deallocates all the book and customer pointers:

```
Library::~Library() {
  for (const Book* bookPtr : m_bookPtrList) {
    delete bookPtr;
  }
  for (const Customer* customerPtr : m_customerPtrList) {
    delete customerPtr;
  }
}
```

The main function

Similar to Chapter 3, *Building a Library Management System*, the main function simply creates a Library object:

Main.cpp

```
#include <Set>
#include <Map>
#include <String>
#include <FStream>
#include <IOStream>
using namespace std;

#include "Book.h"
#include "Customer.h"
#include "Library.h"

void main() {
  Library();
}
```

Summary

In this chapter, we built a library management system similar to the system of Chapter 3, *Building a Library Management System*. However, we omitted all integer identity numbers and replaced them with pointers. This gives us the advantage that we can store loans and reservations more directly, but it also makes it harder for us to save and load them into a file.

In Chapter 5, *Qt Graphical Applications*, we will look at graphical applications.

5
Qt Graphical Applications

In Chapter 4, *Library Management System with Pointers*, we developed abstract datatypes and a library management system. However, those applications were text-based. In this chapter, we will look into three graphical applications that we will develop with the Qt graphical library:

- **Clock**: We will develop an analog clock with hour, minute, and second hands, with lines to mark hours, minutes, and seconds
- **The drawing program**: A program that draws lines, rectangles, and ellipses in different colors
- **The editor**: A program where the user can input and edit text

We will also learn about the Qt library:

- Windows and widgets
- Menus and toolbars
- Drawing figures and writing text in the window
- How to catch mouse and keyboard events

Creating the clock application

In this chapter and the next chapter, we will work with Qt, which is an object-oriented class library for graphical applications. We will also work with Qt Creator, instead of Visual Studio, which is an integrated development environment.

Setting up the environment

When creating a new graphical project in Qt Creator, we select **New File or Project** in the **File** menu, which makes the **New File or Project** dialog window become visible. We select **Qt Widgets Application**, and click the **Choose** button.

Then the **Introduction and Project Location** dialog becomes visible. We name the project `Clock`, place it in an appropriate location, and click the **Next** button. In the **KitSelection** dialog, we select the latest version of the Qt library, and click **Next**. In the **Class Information** dialog, we name the base class of the application `clock`. Normally, the window of a graphical application inherits a `window` class. In this case, however, we are dealing with a relatively simple application. Therefore, we inherit the Qt class `QWidget`, even though a widget often refers to a smaller graphical object that is often embedded in the window. In Qt Creator, it is possible to add forms. However, we do not use that feature in this chapter. Therefore, we uncheck the **Generate** form option.

 All class names in Qt start with the letter `Q`.

Finally, in the **Project Management** dialog, we simply accept the default values and click **Finish** to generate the project, with the files `Clock.h` and `Clock.cpp`.

The Clock class

The project is made up by the files `Clock.h`, `Clock.cpp`, and `Main.cpp`. The class definition looks a little bit different compared to the classes of the previous chapters. We enclose the class definition with *include guards*. That is, we must enclose the class definition with the preprocessor directive `ifndef`, `define`, and `endif`. The preprocessor performs text substitutions.

The `ifndef` and `endif` directives work as the `if` statement in C++. If the condition is not true, the code between the directives is omitted. In this case, the code is included only if the `CLOCK_H` macro has not previously been defined. If the code is included, the macro becomes defined at the next line with the `define` directive. In this way, the class definition is included in the project only once. Moreover, we also include the system header files `QWidget` and `QTimer` in the `Clock.h` header file rather than the `Clock.cpp` definition file.

Clock.h:

```
#ifndef CLOCK_H
#define CLOCK_H

#include <QWidget>
#include <QTimer>
```

Since `Clock` is a subclass of the Qt `QWidget` class, the `Q_OBJECT` macro must be included, which includes certain code from the Qt library. We need it to use the `SIGNAL` and `SLOT` macros shown here:

```
class Clock : public QWidget {
  Q_OBJECT
```

The constructor takes a pointer to its parent widget, for which the default is `nullptr`:

```
public:
  Clock(QWidget* parentWidgetPtr = nullptr);
```

The `paintEvent` method is called by the framework every time the window needs to be repainted. It takes a pointer to a `QPaintEvent` object as parameter, which can be used to determine in which way the repainting shall be performed:

```
void paintEvent(QPaintEvent *eventPtr);
```

`QTimer` is a Qt system class that handles a timer. We will use that to move the hands of the clock:

```
  private:
    QTimer m_timer;
};

#endif // CLOCK_H
```

The definition file is mainly made up of the `paintEvent` method, which handles the painting of the clock.

Clock.cpp:

```
#include <QtWidgets>
#include "Clock.h"
```

In the constructor, we call the base class `QWidget` with the `parentWidgetPtr` parameter (which may be `nullptr`):

```
Clock::Clock(QWidget* parentWidgetPtr /* = nullptr */)
 :QWidget(parentWidgetPtr) {
```

We set the title of the window to `Clock`. In Qt, we always use the `tr` function for literal text, which in turn calls the Qt method `translate` in the Qt `QCoreApplication` class that makes sure the text is translated into a form suitable to be displayed. We also resize the size of the window to 1000 x 500 pixels, which is appropriate for most screens:

```
setWindowTitle(tr("Clock"));
resize(1000, 500);
```

We need a way to connect the timer with the clock widget: when the timer has finished its countdown, the clock shall be updated. For that purpose, Qt provides us with the Signal and Slot system. When the timer reaches its countdown, it calls its method `timeout`. We use the `connect` method together with the `SIGNAL` and `SLOT` macros to connect the call to `timeout` with the call to the `update` method in the Qt `QWidget` class, which updates the drawing of the clock. The `SIGNAL` macro registers that the call to timeout shall raise a signal, the `SLOT` macro registers that the update method shall be called when the signal is raised, and the `connect` method connects the signal with the slot. We have set up a connection between the timer's timeout and the update of the clock:

```
m_timer.setParent(this);
connect(&m_timer, SIGNAL(timeout()), this, SLOT(update()));
m_timer.start(100);
}
```

The `paintEvent` method is called every time the window needs to be repainted. It may be due to some external cause, such as the user resizes the window. It may also be due to a call to the `update` method of the `QMainWindow` class, which in turn eventually calls `paintEvent`.

In this case, we do not need any information about the event, so we enclose the `eventPtr` parameter in comments. The `width` and `height` methods give the width and height of the paintable part of the window, in pixels. We call the `qMin` method to decide the minimum side of the window, and the `currentTime` method of the `QTime` class to find the current time for the clock:

```
void Clock::paintEvent(QPaintEvent* /* eventPtr */) {
    int side = qMin(width(), height());
    QTime time = QTime::currentTime();
```

The QPainter class can be viewed as a painting canvas. We start by initializing it to appropriate aliasing. We then call the translate and scale methods to transform the physical size in pixels to the logical size of 200 * 200 units:

```
QPainter painter(this);
painter.setRenderHint(QPainter::Antialiasing);
painter.setRenderHint(QPainter::TextAntialiasing);
painter.translate(width() / 2, height() / 2);
painter.scale(side / 200.0, side / 200.0);
```

We paint 60 lines for the minutes. Every fifth line shall be a little bit longer to mark the current hours. For each minute, we draw a line, and then we call the Qt rotate method, which rotates the drawing by 6 degrees. In this way, we rotate the drawing by 6 degrees 60 times, which sums up to 360 degrees, a whole lap:

```
for (int second = 0; second <= 60; ++second) {
  if ((second % 5) == 0) {
    painter.drawLine(QPoint(0, 81), QPoint(0, 98));
  }
  else {
    painter.drawLine(QPoint(0, 90), QPoint(0, 98));
  }
```

A complete leap is 360 degrees. For each line we rotate by 6 degrees, since 360 divided by 60 is 6 degrees. When we are finished with the rotations, the drawing is reset to its original settings:

```
    painter.rotate(6);
}
```

We obtain the current hour, minute, second, and millisecond from the QTime object:

```
double hours = time.hour(), minutes = time.minute(),
       seconds = time.second(), milliseconds = time.msec();
```

We set the pen color to black and the background color to gray:

```
painter.setPen(Qt::black);
painter.setBrush(Qt::gray);
```

We define the endpoints of the hour hand. The hour hand is a little bit thicker and shorter than the minute and second hands. We define three points that constitute the endpoint of the hour hand. The base of the hour hand is 16 units long and located 8 units from the origin. Therefore, we set the x coordinate of the base points to 8 and −8, and the y coordinate to 8. Finally, we define the length of the hour hand to 60 units. The value is negative in order to correspond with current rotation:

```
{ static const QPoint hourHand[3] =
    {QPoint(8, 8), QPoint(-8, 8), QPoint(0, -60)};
```

The `save` method saves the current settings of the `QPointer` object. The settings are later restored by the `restore` method:

```
painter.save();
```

We find out the exact angle of the current hour hand by calculating the hours, minutes, seconds, and milliseconds. We then rotate to set the hour hand. Each hour corresponds to 30 degrees, since we have 12 hours, and 360 degrees divided by 12 is 30 degrees:

```
double hour = hours + (minutes / 60.0) + (seconds / 3600.0) +
                (milliseconds / 3600000.0);
painter.rotate(30.0 * hour);
```

We call the `drawConvexPloygon` method with the three points of the hour hand:

```
painter.drawConvexPolygon(hourHand, 3);
painter.restore();
}
```

We draw the minute hand in the same way. It is a little bit thinner and longer than the hour hand. Another difference is that while we had 12 hours, we now have 60 minutes. This gives that each minute corresponds to 6 degrees, since 360 degrees divided by 60 is 6 degrees:

```
{ static const QPoint minuteHand[3] =
    {QPoint(6, 8), QPoint(-6, 8), QPoint(0, -70)};
painter.save();
```

When calculating the current minute angle, we use the minutes, seconds, and milliseconds:

```
double minute = minutes + (seconds / 60.0) +
                (milliseconds / 60000.0);
painter.rotate(6.0 * minute);
painter.drawConvexPolygon(minuteHand, 3);
painter.restore();
}
```

The drawing of the second hand is almost identical to the drawing of the previous minute hand. The only difference is that we only use seconds and milliseconds to calculate the second angle:

```
{ static const QPoint secondHand[3] =
    {QPoint(4, 8), QPoint(-4, 8), QPoint(0, -80)};

  painter.save();
  double second = seconds + (milliseconds / 1000);
  painter.rotate(6.0 * second);
  painter.drawConvexPolygon(secondHand, 3);
  painter.restore();
  }
}
```

The main function

In the `main` function, we initialize and start the Qt application. The `main` function can take the parameters `argc` and `argv`. It holds the command-line arguments of the applications; `argc` holds the number of arguments and the `argv` array holds the arguments themselves. The first entry of `argv` always holds the path to the execution file, and the last entry is always `nullptr`. The `QApplication` class takes `argc` and `argv` and initializes the Qt application. We create an object of our `Clock` class, and call `show` to make it visible. Finally, we call `exec` of the `QApplication` object.

Main.cpp:

```
#include <QApplication>
#include "Clock.h"

int main(int argc, char *argv[]) {
  QApplication application(argc, argv);
  Clock Clock;
  Clock.show();
  return application.exec();
}
```

To execute the application, we select the **Run** option on the project:

The execution will continue until the user closes the Clock window by pressing the close button in the top-right corner:

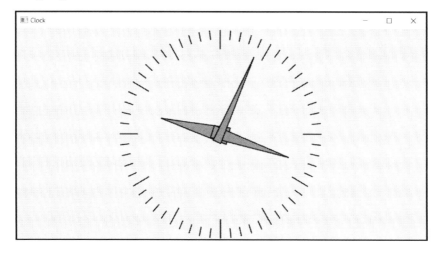

Setting up reusable classes for windows and widgets

In graphical applications, there are windows and widgets. A window is often a complete window with a frame holding title, menu bar, and buttons for closing and resizing the window. A widget is often a smaller graphical object, often embedded in a window. In the *Clock* project, we used only a `widget` class that inherits the `QWidget` class. However, in this section we will leave the *Clock* project and look into more advanced applications with both a window and a widget. The window holds the frame with the menu bar and toolbar, while the widget is located in the window and takes care of the graphical content.

In the following sections of this chapter, we will look into a drawing program and an editor. Those applications are typical document applications, where we open and save documents, as well as also cut, copy, paste, and delete elements of the document. In order to add menus and toolbars to the window, we need to inherit the two Qt classes, `QMainWindow` and `QWidget`. We need `QMainWindow` to add menus and toolbars to the window frame, and `QWidget` to draw images in the window's area.

In order to reuse the document code in the applications introduced in the remaining part of this chapter and in the next chapter, in this section, we define the classes `MainWindow` and `DocumentWidget`. Those classes will then be used by the drawing program and the editor later in the following sections of this chapter. `MainWindow` sets up a window with the `File` and `Edit` menus and toolbars, while `DocumentWidget` provides a framework that sets up skeleton code for the `New`, `Open`, `Save`, `SaveAs`, `Cut`, `Copy`, `Paste`, `Delete`, and `Exit` items. In this section, we will not create a new Qt project, we will just write the classes `MainWindow` and `DocumentWidget`, which are used as base classes in the drawing program and editor later in this chapter, and the `LISTENER` macro, which is used to set up menu and toolbar items.

Adding a listener

A listener is a method that is called when the user selects a menu item or a toolbar item. The `Listener` macro adds a listener to the class.

Listener.h:

```
#ifndef LISTENER_H
#define LISTENER_H

#include <QObject>
```

Due to Qt rules regarding menus and toolbars, the listener called by the Qt Framework in response to a user action must be a function rather than a method.

A method belongs to a class, while a function is free-standing.

The `DefineListener` macro defines both a friendly function and a method. The Qt Framework calls the function, which in turns calls the method:

```
#define DEFINE_LISTENER(BaseClass, Listener)
    friend bool Listener(QObject* baseObjectPtr) {
        return ((BaseClass*) baseObjectPtr)->Listener();
    }
    bool Listener()
```

The `Listener` macro is defined as a pointer to the method:

```
#define LISTENER(Listener) (&::Listener)
```

The listener method takes an `QObject` pointer as a parameter and returns a Boolean value:

```
typedef bool (*Listener)(QObject*);
#endif // LISTENER_H
```

The base window class

The `MainWindow` class sets up a document window with the `File` and `Edit` menus and toolbars. It also provides the `addAction` method, which is intended for subclasses to add application-specific menus and toolbars.

MainWindow.h:

```
#ifndef MAINWINDOW_H
#define MAINWINDOW_H

#include <QMainWindow>
#include <QActionGroup>
#include <QPair>
#include <QMap>

#include "Listener.h"
#include "DocumentWidget.h"
```

```
class MainWindow : public QMainWindow {
  Q_OBJECT

  public:
    MainWindow(QWidget* parentWidgetPtr = nullptr);
    ~MainWindow();

  protected:
    void addFileMenu();
    void addEditMenu();
```

The `addAction` method adds a menu item, with a potential accelerator key, toolbar icon, and listeners to mark the item with a checkbox or a radio button:

```
  protected:
    void addAction(QMenu* menuPtr, QString text,
                   const char* onSelectPtr,
                   QKeySequence acceleratorKey = 0,
                   QString iconName = QString(),
                   QToolBar* toolBarPtr = nullptr,
                   QString statusTip = QString(),
                   Listener enableListener = nullptr,
                   Listener checkListener = nullptr,
                   QActionGroup* groupPtr = nullptr);
```

We use the `DefineListener` macro to add a listener to decide whether a menu item shall be enabled. The listeners return `true` if the item shall be enabled. `DocumentWidget` is a sub class of the Qt class `QWidget`, which we will define in the next section. With the `DEFINE_LISTENER` macro, we add the `isSaveEnabled`, `isCutEnabled`, `isCopyEnabled`, `isPasteEnabled`, and `isDeleteEnabled` methods to the `MainWindow` class. They will be called when the user selects a menu item:

```
    DEFINE_LISTENER(DocumentWidget, isSaveEnabled);
    DEFINE_LISTENER(DocumentWidget, isCutEnabled);
    DEFINE_LISTENER(DocumentWidget, isCopyEnabled);
    DEFINE_LISTENER(DocumentWidget, isPasteEnabled);
    DEFINE_LISTENER(DocumentWidget, isDeleteEnabled);
```

The `onMenuShow` method is called before a menu becomes visible; it calls the listener of the items of the menu to decide whether they shall be disabled or annotated by a checkbox or a radio button. It is also called by the framework in order to disable toolbar icons:

```
  public slots:
    void onMenuShow();
```

The `m_enableMap` and `m_checkMap` fields hold maps of listeners for the menu items. The preceding `onMenuShow` method uses them to decide whether to disable the item, or annotate it with a checkbox or a radio button:

```
private:
  QMap<QAction*,QPair<QObject*,Listener>> m_enableMap,
                                          m_checkMap;
};

#endif // MAINWINDOW_H
```

MainWindow.cpp:

```
#include "MainWindow.h"
#include <QtWidgets>
```

The constructor calls the constructor of the Qt `QMainWindow` class, with the parent widget pointer as its parameter:

```
MainWindow::MainWindow(QWidget* parentWidgetPtr /*= nullptr*/)
 :QMainWindow(parentWidgetPtr) {
}
```

When a menu item is added, it is connected to an action. The destructor deallocates all actions of the menu bar:

```
MainWindow::~MainWindow() {
  for (QAction* actionPtr : menuBar()->actions()) {
    delete actionPtr;
  }
}
```

The `addFileMenu` method adds the standard `File` menu to the menu bar; `menubar` is a Qt method that returns a pointer to the menu bar of the window:

```
void MainWindow::addFileMenu() {
  QMenu* fileMenuPtr = menuBar()->addMenu(tr("&File"));
```

Similar to the `connect` method which connects the menu item with the `onMenuShow` method in the following code snippet. The Qt macros `SIGNAL` and `SLOT` ensure that `onMenuShow` is called before the menu becomes visible. The `onMenuShow` method sets the enable, checkbox, and radio bottom status for each item of the menu before the menu becomes visible. It also sets the enable status of toolbars images. The `aboutToShow` method is called before each menu becomes visible in order to enable or disable the items, and to possibly mark them with check boxes or radio buttons:

```
connect(fileMenuPtr, SIGNAL(aboutToShow()), this,
        SLOT(onMenuShow()));
```

The Qt `addToolBar` method adds a toolbar to the window's frame. When we call `addAction` here, the menu item will be added to the menu and, if present, to the toolbar:

```
QToolBar *fileToolBarPtr = addToolBar(tr("File"));
```

The `addAction` method adds the `New`, `Open`, `Save`, `SaveAs`, and `Exit` menu items. It takes the following parameters:

- A pointer to the menu the item shall belong to.
- The item text. The ampersand (`&`) before the text (`&New`) indicates that the next letter (`N`) will be underlined, and that the user can select that item by pressing *Alt-N*.
- Accelerator information. `QKeySequence` is a Qt enumeration holding accelerator key combinations. `QKeySequence::New` indicates that the user can select the item by pressing *Ctrl-N*. The text `Ctrl+N` will also be added to the item text.
- The name of an icon file (`new`). The icon of the file is displayed both to the left of the item text and on the toolbar. The icon file itself is added to the project in Qt Creator.
- A pointer to the toolbar, `nullptr` if the item is not connected to a toolbar.
- The text displayed when the user hovers with the mouse over the toolbar item. Ignored if the item is not connected to a toolbar.
- Listeners (default `nullptr`) that are called before the menu and toolbar become visible, and deciding whether the item is enabled or marked with a checkbox or a radio button:

```
addAction(fileMenuPtr, tr("&New"), SLOT(onNew()),
        QKeySequence::New, tr("new"), fileToolBarPtr,
        tr("Create a new file"));

addAction(fileMenuPtr, tr("&Open"), SLOT(onOpen()),
        QKeySequence::Open, tr("open"), fileToolBarPtr,
```

```
                    tr("Open an existing file"));
```

When there are no changes in the document since it was last saved, the document does not need to be saved and the `Save` item shall be disabled. Therefore, we add an extra parameter, indicating that the `isSaveEnabled` method shall be called to enable or disable the menu and toolbar item:

```
addAction(fileMenuPtr, tr("&Save"), SLOT(onSave()),
        QKeySequence::Save, tr("save"), fileToolBarPtr,
        tr("Save the document to disk"),
        LISTENER(isSaveEnabled));
```

The `SaveAs` menu item has no key sequence. Moreover, it does not have a toolbar entry. Therefore, the name of the icon file and the toolbar text are default `QString` objects and the toolbar pointer is `nullptr`:

```
addAction(fileMenuPtr, tr("Save &As"), SLOT(onSaveAs()),
        0, QString(), nullptr, QString(),
        LISTENER(isSaveEnabled));
```

The `addSeparator` method adds a horizontal line between two items:

```
fileMenuPtr->addSeparator();
addAction(fileMenuPtr, tr("E&xit"),
        SLOT(onExit()), QKeySequence::Quit);
}
```

The `addEditMenu` method adds the `Edit` menu to the window's menu bar in the same way as the preceding `File` menu:

```
void MainWindow::addEditMenu() {
  QMenu* editMenuPtr = menuBar()->addMenu(tr("&Edit"));
  QToolBar* editToolBarPtr = addToolBar(tr("Edit"));
  connect(editMenuPtr, SIGNAL(aboutToShow()),
          this, SLOT(onMenuShow()));

  addAction(editMenuPtr, tr("&Cut"), SLOT(onCut()),
          QKeySequence::Cut, tr("cut"), editToolBarPtr,
      tr("Cut the current selection's contents to the clipboard"),
          LISTENER(isCutEnabled));

  addAction(editMenuPtr, tr("&Copy"), SLOT(onCopy()),
          QKeySequence::Copy, tr("copy"), editToolBarPtr,
      tr("Copy the current selection's contents to the clipboard"),
          LISTENER(isCopyEnabled));

  addAction(editMenuPtr, tr("&Paste"), SLOT(onPaste()),
```

```
                QKeySequence::Paste, tr("paste"), editToolBarPtr,
        tr("Paste the current selection's contents to the clipboard"),
                LISTENER(isPasteEnabled)));

    editMenuPtr->addSeparator();
    addAction(editMenuPtr, tr("&Delete"), SLOT(onDelete()),
                QKeySequence::Delete, tr("delete"), editToolBarPtr,
                tr("Delete the current selection"),
                LISTENER(isDeleteEnabled)));
}
```

The addAction method adds a menu item to the menu bar and a toolbar icon to the toolbar. It also connects the item with the onSelectPtr method that is called when the user selects the item, and methods that enable the item and annotate it with a checkbox or radio button. An accelerator is added to the action, unless it is zero. The groupPtr parameter defines whether the item is part of a group. If checkListener is not nullptr, the item is annotated with a checkbox if groupPtr is nullptr, and with a radio button if it is not. In the case of radio buttons, only one radio button in the group will be marked at the same time:

```
    void MainWindow::addAction(QMenu* menuPtr, QString itemText,
                        const char* onSelectPtr,
                        QKeySequence acceleratorKey /* = 0 */,
                        QString iconName /*= QString()*/,
                        QToolBar* toolBarPtr /*= nullptr*/,
                        QString statusTip /*= QString()*/,
                        Listener enableListener /*= nullptr*/,
                        Listener checkListener /*= nullptr*/,
                        QActionGroup* groupPtr /*= nullptr*/) {
    QAction* actionPtr;
```

If iconName is not empty, we load the icon from the file in the project resource and then create a new QAction object with the icon:

```
    if (!iconName.isEmpty()) {
      const QIcon icon = QIcon::fromTheme("document-" + iconName,
                        QIcon(":/images/" + iconName + ".png"));
      actionPtr = new QAction(icon, itemText, this);
    }
```

If iconName is empty, we create a new QAction object without the icon:

```
    else {
      actionPtr = new QAction(itemText, this);
    }
```

We connect the menu item to the selection method. When the user selects the item, or clicks on the toolbar icon, `onSelectPtr` is called:

```
connect(actionPtr, SIGNAL(triggered()),
        centralWidget(), onSelectPtr);
```

If the accelerator key is not zero, we add it to the action pointer:

```
if (acceleratorKey != 0) {
  actionPtr->setShortcut(acceleratorKey);
}
```

Finally, we add the action pointer to the menu pointer in order for it to process the user's item selection:

```
menuPtr->addAction(actionPtr);
```

If `toolBarPtr` is not `nullptr`, we add the action to the toolbar of the window:

```
if (toolBarPtr != nullptr) {
  toolBarPtr->addAction(actionPtr);
}
```

If the status tip is not empty, we add it to the tooltip and status tip of the toolbar:

```
if (!statusTip.isEmpty()) {
    actionPtr->setToolTip(statusTip);
    actionPtr->setStatusTip(statusTip);
}
```

If the enable listener is not null, we add to `m_enableMap` a pair made up of a pointer to the central widget of the window and the listener. We also call the listener to initialize the enable status of the menu item and toolbar icon:

```
if (enableListener != nullptr) {
  QWidget* widgetPtr = centralWidget();
  m_enableMap[actionPtr] =
    QPair<QObject*,Listener>(widgetPtr, enableListener);
  actionPtr->setEnabled(enableListener(widgetPtr));
}
```

In the same way, if the check listener is not null, we add a pointer to the central widget of the window and the listener to `m_checkMap`. Both `m_enableMap` and `m_checkMap` are used by `onMenuShow`, as follows. We also call the listener to initialize the check status of the menu item (toolbar icons are not checked):

```
if (checkListener != nullptr) {
```

```
    actionPtr->setCheckable(true);
    QWidget* widgetPtr = centralWidget();
    m_checkMap[actionPtr] =
      QPair<QObject*,Listener>(widgetPtr, checkListener);
    actionPtr->setChecked(checkListener(widgetPtr));
  }
```

Finally, if the group pointer is not null, we add the action to it. In that way, the menu item will be annotated by a radio button rather than a checkbox. The framework does also keep track of the groups and makes sure only one of the radio buttons of each group is marked at the same time:

```
  if (groupPtr != nullptr) {
    groupPtr->addAction(actionPtr);
  }
}
```

The onMenuShow method is called before a menu or toolbar icon becomes visible. It makes sure each item is enabled or disabled, and that the items are annotated with checkboxes or radio buttons.

We start by iterating through the enable map. For each entry in the map, we look up the widget and the enable function. We call the function, which returns true or false, and use the result to enable or disable the item by calling setEnabled on the action object pointer:

```
void MainWindow::onMenuShow() {
  for (QMap<QAction*,QPair<QObject*,Listener>>::iterator i =
      m_enableMap.begin(); i != m_enableMap.end(); ++i) {
    QAction* actionPtr = i.key();
    QPair<QObject*,Listener> pair = i.value();
    QObject* baseObjectPtr = pair.first;
    Listener enableFunction = pair.second;
    actionPtr->setEnabled(enableFunction(baseObjectPtr));
  }
```

In the same way, we iterate through the check map. For each entry in the map, we look up the widget and the check function. We call the function and use the result to check the item by calling setCheckable and setChecked on the action object pointer. The Qt Framework makes sure the item is annotated by radio buttons if it belongs to a group, and a checkbox if it does not:

```
  for (QMap<QAction*,QPair<QObject*,Listener>>::iterator i =
      m_checkMap.begin(); i != m_checkMap.end(); ++i) {
    QAction* actionPtr = i.key();
    QPair<QObject*,Listener> pair = i.value();
    QObject* baseObjectPtr = pair.first;
```

```
        Listener checkFunction = pair.second;
        actionPtr->setCheckable(true);
        actionPtr->setChecked(checkFunction(baseObjectPtr));
    }
}
```

The base widget class

`DocumentWidget` is a skeleton framework for applications that handle documents. It handles the loading and saving of the document, and provides methods to be overridden by subclasses for the `Cut`, `Copy`, `Paste`, and `Delete` menu items.

While the preceding `MainWindow` class handles the window frame, with its menus and toolbars, the `DocumentWidget` class handles the drawing of the window's content. The idea is that the subclass of `MainWindow` creates an object of a subclass to `DocumentWidget` that it puts at the centrum of the window. See the constructors of `DrawingWindow` and `EditorWindow` in the following sections.

DocumentWidget.h:

```
#ifndef DOCUMENTWIDGET_H
#define DOCUMENTWIDGET_H

#include "Listener.h"
#include <QWidget>
#include <QtWidgets>
#include <FStream>
using namespace std;

class DocumentWidget : public QWidget {
  Q_OBJECT
```

The constructor takes the name of the application, to be displayed at the top banner of the window, the filename mask to be used when loading and storing documents with the standard file dialogs, and a pointer to a potential parent widget (normally the enclosing main window):

```
public:
    DocumentWidget(const QString& name, const QString& fileMask,
                   QWidget* parentWidgetPtr);
    ~DocumentWidget();
```

The `setFilePath` method sets the path of the current document. The path is displayed at the top banner of the window and is given as a default path in the standard load and save dialogs:

```
protected:
  void setFilePath(QString filePath);
```

When a document has been changed, the modified flag (sometimes called the dirty flag) is set. This causes an asterisk (*) to appear next to the file path at the top banner of the window, and the `Save` and `SaveAs` menu items to be enabled:

```
public:
  void setModifiedFlag(bool flag);
```

The `setMainWindowTitle` method is an auxiliary method that puts together the title of the window. It is made up by the file path and a potential asterisk (*) to indicate whether the modified flag is set:

```
private:
  void setMainWindowTitle();
```

The `closeEvent` method is overridden from `QWidget` and is called when the user closes the window. By setting fields of the `eventPtr` parameter, the closing can be prevented. For example, if the document has not been saved, the user can be asked if they want to save the document or cancel the closing of the window:

```
public:
  virtual void closeEvent(QCloseEvent* eventPtr);
```

The `isClearOk` method is an auxiliary method that displays a message box if the user tries to close the window or exit the application without saving the document:

```
private:
  bool isClearOk(QString title);
```

The following methods are called by the framework when the user selects a menu item or clicks a toolbar icon. In order for that to work, we mark the methods as slots, which is necessary for the `SLOT` macro in the `connect` call:

```
public slots:
  virtual void onNew();
  virtual void onOpen();
  virtual bool onSave();
  virtual bool onSaveAs();
  virtual void onExit();
```

When a document has not been changed, it is not necessary to save it. In that case, the `Save` and `SaveAs` menu items and toolbars images shall be disabled. The `isSaveEnabled` method is called by `onMenuShow` before the `File` menu becomes visible. It returns true only when the document has been changed and needs to be saved:

```
virtual bool isSaveEnabled();
```

The `tryWriteFile` method is an auxiliary method that tries to write the file. If it fails, a message box displays an error message:

```
private:
    bool tryWriteFile(QString filePath);
```

The following methods are virtual methods intended to be overridden by subclasses. They are called when the user selects the `New`, `Save`, `SaveAs`, and `Open` menu items:

```
protected:
    virtual void newDocument() = 0;
    virtual bool writeFile(const QString& filePath) = 0;
    virtual bool readFile(const QString& filePath) = 0;
```

The following methods are called before the edit menu becomes visible, and they decide whether the `Cut`, `Copy`, `Paste`, and `Delete` items shall be enabled:

```
public:
    virtual bool isCutEnabled();
    virtual bool isCopyEnabled();
    virtual bool isPasteEnabled();
    virtual bool isDeleteEnabled();
```

The following methods are called when the user selects the `Cut`, `Copy`, `Paste`, and `Delete` items or toolbar icons:

```
public slots:
    virtual void onCut();
    virtual void onCopy();
    virtual void onPaste();
    virtual void onDelete();
```

The `m_applicationName` field holds the name of the application, not the document. In the next sections, the names will be *Drawing* and *Editor*. The `m_fileMask` field holds the mask that is used when loading and saving the document with the standard dialogs. For instance, let us say that we have documents with the ending `.abc`. Then the mask could be `Abc files (.abc)`. The `m_filePath` field holds the path of the current document. When the document is new and not yet saved, the field holds the empty string.

Finally, `m_modifiedFlag` is true when the document has been modified and needs to be saved before the application quits:

```
    private:
      QString m_applicationName, m_fileMask, m_filePath;
      bool m_modifiedFlag = false;
};
```

Finally, there are some overloaded auxiliary operators. The addition and subtraction operators add and subtract a point with a size, and a rectangle with a size:

```
    QPoint& operator+=(QPoint& point, const QSize& size);
    QPoint& operator-=(QPoint& point, const QSize& size);

    QRect& operator+=(QRect& rect, int size);
    QRect& operator-=(QRect& rect, int size);
```

The `writePoint` and `readPoint` methods write and read a point from an input stream:

```
    void writePoint(ofstream& outStream, const QPoint& point);
    void readPoint(ifstream& inStream, QPoint& point);
```

The `writeColor` and `readColor` methods write and read a color from an input stream:

```
    void writeColor(ofstream& outStream, const QColor& color);
    void readColor(ifstream& inStream, QColor& color);
```

The `makeRect` method creates a rectangle with `point` as its center and `size` as its size:

```
    QRect makeRect(const QPoint& centerPoint, int halfSide);
    #endif // DOCUMENTWIDGET_H
```

DocumentWidget.cpp:

```
    #include <QtWidgets>
    #include <QMessageBox>

    #include "MainWindow.h"
    #include "DocumentWidget.h"
```

The constructor sets the name of the application, the file mask for the save and load standard dialogs, and a pointer to the enclosing parent widget (usually the enclosing main window):

```
    DocumentWidget::DocumentWidget(const QString& name,
                    const QString& fileMask, QWidget* parentWidgetPtr)
      :m_applicationName(name),
       m_fileMask(fileMask),
```

```
QWidget(parentWidgetPtr) {
  setMainWindowTitle();
}
```

The destructor does nothing, it is included for completeness only:

```
DocumentWidget::~DocumentWidget() {
  // Empty.
}
```

The `setFilePath` method calls `setMainWindowTitle` to update the text on the top banner of the window:

```
void DocumentWidget::setFilePath(QString filePath) {
  m_filePath = filePath;
  setMainWindowTitle();
}
```

The `setModifiedFlag` method also calls `setMainWindowTitle` to update the text on the top banner of the window. Moreover, it calls `onMenuShow` on the parent widget to update the icons of the toolbars:

```
void DocumentWidget::setModifiedFlag(bool modifiedFlag) {
  m_modifiedFlag = modifiedFlag;
  setMainWindowTitle();
  ((MainWindow*) parentWidget())->onMenuShow();
}
```

The title displayed at the top banner of the toolbar is the application name, the document file path (if not empty), and an asterisk if the document has been modified without being saved:

```
void DocumentWidget::setMainWindowTitle() {
  QString title= m_applicationName +
          (m_filePath.isEmpty() ? "" : (" [" + m_filePath + "]"))+
          (m_modifiedFlag ? " *" : "");
  this->parentWidget()->setWindowTitle(title);
}
```

The `isClearOk` method displays a message box if the document has been modified without being saved. The user can select one of the following buttons:

- **Yes**: The document is saved, and the application quits. However, if the saving fails, an error message is displayed and the application does not quit.
- **No**: The application quits without saving the document.

- **Cancel**: The closing of the application is cancelled. The document is not saved.

```
bool DocumentWidget::isClearOk(QString title) {
  if (m_modifiedFlag) {
    QMessageBox messageBox(QMessageBox::Warning,
                           title, QString());
    messageBox.setText(tr("The document has been modified."));
    messageBox.setInformativeText(
            tr("Do you want to save your changes?"));
    messageBox.setStandardButtons(QMessageBox::Yes |
                       QMessageBox::No | QMessageBox::Cancel);
    messageBox.setDefaultButton(QMessageBox::Yes);

    switch (messageBox.exec()) {
      case QMessageBox::Yes:
        return onSave();

      case QMessageBox::No:
        return true;

      case QMessageBox::Cancel:
        return false;
    }
  }

  return true;
}
```

If the document is cleared, `newDocument` is called, which is intended to be overridden by a subclass to perform application-specific initialization. Moreover, the modified flag and the file path are cleared. Finally, the Qt `update` method is called to force a repainting of the window's content:

```
void DocumentWidget::onNew() {
  if (isClearOk(tr("New File"))) {
    newDocument();
    setModifiedFlag(false);
    setFilePath(QString());
    update();
  }
}
```

If the document is cleared, `onOpen` uses the standard open dialog to obtain the file path of the document:

```
void DocumentWidget::onOpen() {
  if (isClearOk(tr("Open File"))) {
```

```
           QString file =
             QFileDialog::getOpenFileName(this, tr("Open File"),
                      tr("C:\Users\Stefan\Documents\"
                         "A A_Cpp_By_Example\Draw"),
                 m_fileMask + tr(";;Text files (*.txt)"));
```

If the file was successfully read, the modified flag is cleared, the file path is set, and `update` is called to force a repainting of the window:

```
       if (!file.isEmpty()) {
         if (readFile(file)) {
           setModifiedFlag(false);
           setFilePath(file);
           update();
         }
```

However, if the reading was not successful, a message box with an error message is displayed:

```
         else {
           QMessageBox messageBox;
           messageBox.setIcon(QMessageBox::Critical);
           messageBox.setText(tr("Read File"));
           messageBox.setInformativeText(tr("Could not read "") +
                                         m_filePath  + tr("""));
           messageBox.setStandardButtons(QMessageBox::Ok);
           messageBox.setDefaultButton(QMessageBox::Ok);
           messageBox.exec();
         }
       }
     }
   }
```

The `ifSaveEnabled` method simply returns the value of `m_modifiedFlag`. However, we need the method for the listener to work:

```
     bool DocumentWidget::isSaveEnabled() {
       return m_modifiedFlag;
     }
```

The `onSave` method is called when the user selects the `Save` or `SaveAs` menu item or toolbar icon. If the document has already been given a name, we simply try to write the file. However, if it has not yet been given a name we call `OnSaveAs`, which displays the standard Save dialog for the user:

```
     bool DocumentWidget::onSave() {
       if (!m_filePath.isEmpty()) {
```

```
      return tryWriteFile(m_filePath);
    }
    else {
      return onSaveAs();
    }
  }
```

The onSaveAs method is called when the user selects the SaveAs menu item (there is no
toolbar icon for this item). It opens the standard open dialog and tries to write the file. If the
writing was not successful, false is returned. The reason for this is that isClearOk closes
the window only if the writing was successful:

```
bool DocumentWidget::onSaveAs() {
  QString filePath =
        QFileDialog::getSaveFileName(this, tr("Save File"),
            tr("C:\Users\Stefan\Documents\"
              "A A_Cpp_By_Example\Draw"),
          m_fileMask + tr(";;Text files (*.txt)"));

  if (!filePath.isEmpty()) {
    return tryWriteFile(filePath);
  }
  else {
    return false;
  }
}
```

The tryWriteFile method tries to write the file by calling write, which is intended to be
overridden by a subclass. If it succeeded, the modified flag and the file path are set. If the
file was not successfully written, a message box with an error message is displayed:

```
bool DocumentWidget::tryWriteFile(QString filePath) {
  if (writeFile(filePath)) {
    setModifiedFlag(false);
    setFilePath(filePath);
    return true;
  }
  else {
    QMessageBox messageBox;
    messageBox.setIcon(QMessageBox::Critical);
    messageBox.setText(tr("Write File"));
    messageBox.setInformativeText(tr("Could not write "") +
                                  filePath  + tr("""));
    messageBox.setStandardButtons(QMessageBox::Ok);
    messageBox.setDefaultButton(QMessageBox::Ok);
    messageBox.exec();
    return false;
```

```
      }
   }
```

The `onExit` method is called when the user selects the `Exit` menu item. It checks whether it is clear to close the window, and exits the application if it is:

```
void DocumentWidget::onExit() {
  if (isClearOk(tr("Exit"))) {
    qApp->exit(0);
  }
}
```

The default behavior of `isCutEnabled` and `isDeleteEnabled` is to call `isCopyEnabled`, since they often are enabled on the same conditions:

```
bool DocumentWidget::isCutEnabled() {
  return isCopyEnabled();
}

bool DocumentWidget::isDeleteEnabled() {
  return isCopyEnabled();
}
```

The default behavior of `onCut` is to simply call `onCopy` and `onDelete`:

```
void DocumentWidget::onCut() {
  onCopy();
  onDelete();
}
```

The default behavior of the rest of the cut-and-copy methods is to return `false` and do nothing, which will leave the menu items disabled unless the subclass overrides the methods:

```
bool DocumentWidget::isCopyEnabled() {
  return false;
}

void DocumentWidget::onCopy() {
  // Empty.
}

bool DocumentWidget::isPasteEnabled() {
  return false;
}

void DocumentWidget::onPaste() {
```

```
    // Empty.
  }
  void DocumentWidget::onDelete() {
    // Empty.
  }
}
```

Finally, `closeEvent` is called when the user tries to close the window. If the window is ready to be cleared, `accept` is called on `eventPtr`, which causes the window to be closed, and `exit` is called on the global qApp object, which causes the application to quit:

```
void DocumentWidget::closeEvent(QCloseEvent* eventPtr) {
  if (isClearOk(tr("Close Window"))) {
    eventPtr->accept();
    qApp->exit(0);
  }
```

However, if the window is not ready to be cleared, `ignore` is called on `eventPtr`, which causes the window to remain open (and the application to continue):

```
  else {
    eventPtr->ignore();
  }
}
```

Moreover, there are also the set of auxiliary functions for handling points, sizes, rectangles, and color. The following operators add and subtract a point with a size, and return the resulting point:

```
QPoint& operator+=(QPoint& point, const QSize& size) {
  point.setX(point.x() + size.width());
  point.setY(point.y() + size.height());
  return point;
}

QPoint& operator-=(QPoint& point, const QSize& size) {
  point.setX(point.x() - size.width());
  point.setY(point.y() - size.height());
  return point;
}
```

The following operators add and subtract an integer from a rectangle, and return the resulting rectangle. The addition operator expands the size of the rectangle in every direction, while the subtraction operator shrinks the rectangle in every direction:

```
QRect& operator+=(QRect& rect, int size) {
  rect.setLeft(rect.left() - size);
  rect.setTop(rect.top() - size);
```

```
      rect.setWidth(rect.width() + size);
      rect.setHeight(rect.height() + size);
      return rect;
    }

    QRect& operator-=(QRect& rect, int size) {
      rect.setLeft(rect.left() + size);
      rect.setTop(rect.top() + size);
      rect.setWidth(rect.width() - size);
      rect.setHeight(rect.height() - size);
      return rect;
    }
```

The `writePoint` and `readPoint` functions write and read a point from a file. They write and read the *x* and *y* coordinates separately:

```
    void writePoint(ofstream& outStream, const QPoint& point) {
      int x = point.x(), y = point.y();
      outStream.write((char*) &x, sizeof x);
      outStream.write((char*) &y, sizeof y);
    }

    void readPoint(ifstream& inStream, QPoint& point) {
      int x, y;
      inStream.read((char*) &x, sizeof x);
      inStream.read((char*) &y, sizeof y);
      point = QPoint(x, y);
    }
```

The `writeColor` and `readColor` functions write and read a color from a file. A color is made up of the `red`, `green`, and `blue` components. Each component is an integer value between 0 and 255 inclusive. The methods write and read the components from a file stream:

```
    void writeColor(ofstream& outStream, const QColor& color) {
      int red = color.red(), green = color.green(),
      blue = color.blue();
      outStream.write((char*) &red, sizeof red);
      outStream.write((char*) &green, sizeof green);
      outStream.write((char*) &blue, sizeof blue);
    }

    void readColor(ifstream& inStream, QColor& color) {
      int red, green, blue;
      inStream.read((char*) &red, sizeof red);
      inStream.read((char*) &green, sizeof green);
      inStream.read((char*) &blue, sizeof blue);
```

When the components have been read, we create a QColor object that we assign the color parameter:

```
color = QColor(red, green, blue);
}
```

The makeRect function creates a rectangle centered around the point:

```
QRect makeRect(const QPoint& centerPoint, int halfSide) {
  return QRect(centerPoint.x() - halfSide,
               centerPoint.y() - halfSide,
               2 * halfSide, 2 * halfSide);
}
```

Building the drawing program

Let's now start a new project, where we take advantage of the main window and document widget classes of the previous section—*The drawing program*. We will start with a basic version in this chapter, and we will continue to build a more advanced version in the next chapter. With the drawing program of this chapter we can draw lines, rectangles, and ellipses in different colors. We can also save and load our drawings. Note that in this project the window and widget classes inherit from the MainWindow and DocumentWidget classes of the previous section.

The Figure base class

The figures of the application constitute a class hierarchy where the Figure is the base class. Its subclasses are Line, RectangleX, and EllipseX, which are described later on. We cannot use the names *Rectangle* and *Ellipse* for our classes, since that would clash with Qt methods with the same names. I have chosen to simply add an 'X' to the names.

The Figure class is abstract, which means that we cannot create an object of the class. We can only use it as a base class, which sub classes inherit.

Figure.h:

```
#ifndef FIGURE_H
#define FIGURE_H

enum FigureId {LineId, RectangleId, EllipseId};

#include <QtWidgets>
```

```
#include <FStream>
using namespace std;

class Figure {
  public:
    Figure();
```

The following methods are pure virtual, which means that they do not need to be defined. A class with at least one pure virtual method becomes abstract. The sub classes must define all the pure virtual methods of all its base classes, or become abstract themselves. In this way, it is guaranteed that all methods of all non-abstract classes are defined.

Each sub class defines `getId` and returns the identity enumeration of its class:

```
virtual FigureId getId() const = 0;
```

Each figure has a first and last point, and it is up to each sub class to define them:

```
virtual void initializePoints(QPoint point) = 0;
virtual void setLastPoint(QPoint point) = 0;
```

The `isClick` method returns `true` if the figure is hit by the point:

```
virtual bool isClick(QPoint mousePoint) = 0;
```

The `move` method moves the figures a certain distance:

```
virtual void move(QSize distance) = 0;
```

The `draw` method draws the figure on the painter area:

```
virtual void draw(QPainter &painter) const = 0;
```

The `write` and `read` methods write and read the figure from a file; `write` is constant since it does not change the figure:

```
virtual bool write(ofstream& outStream) const;
virtual bool read(ifstream& inStream);
```

The `color` method returns the color of the figure. It comes in two versions, where the first version is constant and returns a reference to a constant `QColor` object, while the second version is non-constant and returns a reference to a non-constant object:

```
const QColor& color() const {return m_color;}
QColor& color() {return m_color;}
```

The `filled` methods apply to two-dimensional figures (rectangles and ellipses) only. They return `true` if the figure is filled. Note that the second version returns a reference to the `m_filled` field, which allows the caller of the method to modify the value of `m_filled`:

```
virtual bool filled() const {return m_filled;}
virtual bool& filled() {return m_filled;}
```

When a figure is marked, it is drawn with small squares at its corners. The side of the squares are defined by the static field `Tolerance`:

```
static const int Tolerance;
```

The `writeColor` and `readColor` methods are auxiliary methods that read and write a color. They are static since they are called by methods outside the `Figure` class hierarchy:

```
static void writeColor(ofstream& outStream,

                       const QColor& color);
static void readColor(ifstream& inStream, QColor& color);
```

Each figure has a color, and it could be marked or filled:

```
  private:
    QColor m_color;
    bool m_marked = false, m_filled = false;
};

  #endif
```

The `Figure.cpp` file holds the definitions of the `Figure` class. It defines the `Tolerance` field as well as the `write` and `read` methods.

Figure.cpp:

```
#include "..\MainWindow\DocumentWidget.h"
#include "Figure.h"
```

`Tolerance` must be defined and initialized in global space since it is static. We define the size of the mark squares to be 6 pixels:

```
const int Figure::Tolerance(6);
```

The default constructor is called only when figures are read from a file:

```
Figure::Figure() {
  // Empty.
}
```

The `write` and `read` methods write and read the color of the figure, and whether the figure is filled:

```
bool Figure::write(ofstream& outStream) const {
  writeColor(outStream, m_color);
  outStream.write((char*) &m_filled, sizeof m_filled);
  return ((bool) outStream);
}

bool Figure::read(ifstream& inStream) {
  readColor(inStream, m_color);
  inStream.read((char*) &m_filled, sizeof m_filled);
  return ((bool) inStream);
}
```

The Line sub class

The `Line` class is a sub class of `Figure`. It becomes non-abstract by defining each pure virtual method of `Figure`. A line is drawn between two end-points, represented by the `m_firstPoint` to `m_lastPoint` fields in `Line`:

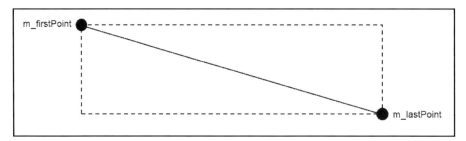

Line.h:

```
#ifndef LINE_H
#define LINE_H

#include <FStream>
using namespace std;

#include "Figure.h"

class Line : public Figure {
  public:
```

The default constructor is called only when reading `Line` objects from a file; `getId` simply returns the identity enumeration of the line:

```
Line();
FigureId getId() const {return LineId;}
```

A line has two endpoints. Both points are set when the line is created, the second point is then modified when the user moves it:

```
void initializePoints(QPoint point);
void setLastPoint(QPoint point);
```

The `isClick` method returns `true` if the mouse click is located on the line (with some tolerance):

```
bool isClick(QPoint mousePoint);
```

The `move` method moves the line (both its end-points) the given distance:

```
void move(QSize distance);
```

The `draw` method draws the line on the `QPainter` object:

```
void draw(QPainter& painter) const;
```

The `write` and `read` methods write and read the end-points of the line from a file stream:

```
bool write(ofstream& outStream) const;
bool read(ifstream& inStream);
```

The first and last points of the line are stored in the `Line` object:

```
private:
  QPoint m_firstPoint, m_lastPoint;
};

#endif
```

The `Line.cpp` file defines the methods of the `Line` class.

Line.cpp:

```
#include "..\MainWindow\DocumentWidget.h"
#include "Line.h"

Line::Line() {
  // Empty.
}
```

The `initializePoints` method is called when the user adds a new line to the drawing. It sets both its end-points:

```
void Line::initializePoints(QPoint point) {
  m_firstPoint = point;
  m_lastPoint = point;
}
```

The `setLastPoint` method is called when the user has added the line and modifies its shape. It sets the last point:

```
void Line::setLastPoint(QPoint point) {
  m_lastPoint = point;
}
```

The `isClick` method tests whether the user has clicked with the mouse on the line. We have two cases to consider. The first case is a special case that occurs when the line is completely vertical, when the x-coordinates of the end-points are equal. We use the Qt `QRect` class to create a rectangle surrounding the line, and test whether the point is enclosed in the rectangle:

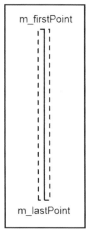

```
bool Line::isClick(QPoint mousePoint) {
  if (m_firstPoint.x() == m_lastPoint.x()) {
    QRect lineRect(m_firstPoint, m_lastPoint);
    lineRect.normalized();
    lineRect += Tolerance;
    return lineRect.contains(mousePoint);
  }
```

In a general case, where the line is not vertical, we start by creating an enclosing rectangle and test if the mouse point is in it. If it is, we set `leftPoint` to the leftmost point of `firstPoint` and `lastPoint`, and `rightPoint` to the rightmost point. We then calculate the width (`lineWidth`) and height (`lineHeight`) of the enclosing rectangle, as well as the distance between `rightPoint` and `mousePoint` in the *x* and *y* directions (`diffWidth` and `diffHeight`).

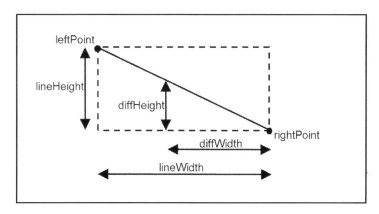

Due to uniformity, the following equation is true if the mouse pointer hits the line:

$$\frac{diffWidth}{diffHeight} = \frac{lineWidth}{lineHeight}$$

$$diffHeight - \frac{lineHeight}{lineWidth} diffWidth = 0$$

However, in order for the left-hand expression to become exactly zero, the user has to click exactly on the line. Therefore, let us allow for a small tolerance. Let's use the `Tolerance` field:

$$\left| diffHeight - \frac{lineHeight}{lineWidth} diffWidth \right| \le Tolerance$$

```
else {
  QPoint leftPoint = (m_firstPoint.x() < m_lastPoint.x())
                     ? m_firstPoint : m_lastPoint,
         rightPoint = (m_firstPoint.x() < m_lastPoint.x())
                      ? m_lastPoint : m_firstPoint;

  if ((leftPoint.x() <= mousePoint.x()) &&
      (mousePoint.x() <= rightPoint.x())) {
```

```
int lineWidth = rightPoint.x() - leftPoint.x(),
    lineHeight = rightPoint.y() - leftPoint.y();

int diffWidth = mousePoint.x() - leftPoint.x(),
    diffHeight = mousePoint.y() - leftPoint.y();
```

We must convert `lineHeight` to a double in order to perform non-integer division:

```
    return (fabs(diffHeight - (((double) lineHeight) /
            lineWidth) * diffWidth) <= Tolerance);
  }
```

If the mouse point is located outside the rectangle enclosing the line, we simply return `false`:

```
    return false;
  }
}
```

The `move` method simply moves both the endpoints of the line:

```
void Line::move(QSize distance) {
  m_firstPoint += distance;
  m_lastPoint += distance;
}
```

When drawing the line, we set the pen color and draw the line. The `color` method of the `Figure` class returns the color of the line:

```
void Line::draw(QPainter& painter) const {
  painter.setPen(color());
  painter.drawLine(m_firstPoint, m_lastPoint);
}
```

When writing the line, we first call `write` in `Figure` to write the color of the figure. We then write the endpoints of the line. Finally, we return the Boolean value of the output stream, which is `true` if the writing was successful:

```
bool Line::write(ofstream& outStream) const {
  Figure::write(outStream);
  writePoint(outStream, m_firstPoint);
  writePoint(outStream, m_lastPoint);
  return ((bool) outStream);
}
```

In the same way, when reading the line, we first call `read` in `Figure` to read the color of the line. We then read the endpoints of the line and return the Boolean value of the input stream:

```
bool Line::read(ifstream& inStream) {
  Figure::read(inStream);
  readPoint(inStream, m_firstPoint);
  readPoint(inStream, m_lastPoint);
  return ((bool) inStream);
}
```

The Rectangle sub class

`RectangleX` is a sub class of `Figure` that handles a rectangle. Similar to `Line`, it holds two points, which holds opposite corners of the rectangle:

Rectangle.h

```
#ifndef RECTANGLE_H
#define RECTANGLE_H

#include <FStream>
using namespace std;

#include "Figure.h"

class RectangleX : public Figure {
  public:
```

Similar to the preceding `Line` class, `RectangleX` has a default constructor that is used when reading the object from a file:

```
    RectangleX();
    virtual FigureId getId() const {return RectangleId;}

    RectangleX(const RectangleX& rectangle);

    virtual void initializePoints(QPoint point);
    virtual void setLastPoint(QPoint point);

    virtual bool isClick(QPoint mousePoint);
    virtual void move(QSize distance);
    virtual void draw(QPainter& painter) const;
    virtual bool write(ofstream& outStream) const;
    virtual bool read(ifstream& inStream);
```

```
    protected:
      QPoint m_topLeft, m_bottomRight;
};

#endif
```

Rectangle.cpp

```
#include "..\MainWindow\DocumentWidget.h"
#include "Rectangle.h"

RectangleX::RectangleX() {
  // Empty.
}
```

The `initializePoints` and `setLastPoint` methods work in a way similar to their counterparts in `Line`: `initializePoints` sets both the corner points, while `setLastPoint` sets the last corner point:

```
void RectangleX::initializePoints(QPoint point) {
  m_topLeft = point;
  m_bottomRight = point;
}

void RectangleX::setLastPoint(QPoint point) {
  m_bottomRight = point;
}
```

The `isClick` method is simpler than its counterpart in `Line`:

```
bool RectangleX::isClick(QPoint mousePoint) {
  QRect areaRect(m_topLeft, m_bottomRight);
```

If the rectangle is filled, we simply check whether the mouse click hit the rectangle by calling `contains` in `QRect`:

```
  if (filled()) {
    return areaRect.contains(mousePoint);
  }
```

If the rectangle is not filled, we need to check whether the mouse clicked on the border of the rectangle. To do so, we create two slightly smaller and larger rectangles. If the mouse click hit the larger rectangle, but not the smaller one, we consider the rectangle border to be hit:

```
  else {
    QRect largeAreaRect(areaRect), smallAreaRect(areaRect);
```

```
        largeAreaRect += Tolerance;
        smallAreaRect -= Tolerance;
        return largeAreaRect.contains(mousePoint) &&
               !smallAreaRect.contains(mousePoint);
    }

    return false;
}
```

When moving the rectangle, we simply move the first and last corners:

```
void RectangleX::move(QSize distance) {
  addSizeToPoint(m_topLeft, distance);
  addSizeToPoint(m_bottomRight, distance);
}
```

When drawing a rectangle, we first set the pen color by calling `color` in `Figure`:

```
void RectangleX::draw(QPainter& painter) const {
  painter.setPen(color());
```

If the rectangle is filled, we simply call `fillRect` on the `QPainter` object:

```
if (filled()) {
  painter.fillRect(QRect(m_topLeft, m_bottomRight), color());
}
```

If the rectangle is unfilled, we disable the brush to make the rectangle hollow, and we then call `drawRect` on the `QPainter` object to draw the border of the rectangle:

```
else {
  painter.setBrush(Qt::NoBrush);
  painter.drawRect(QRect(m_topLeft, m_bottomRight));
}
}
```

The `write` method first calls `write` in `Figure`, and it then writes the first and last corners of the rectangle:

```
bool RectangleX::write(ofstream& outStream) const {
  Figure::write(outStream);
  writePoint(outStream, m_topLeft);
  writePoint(outStream, m_bottomRight);
  return ((bool) outStream);
}
```

In the same way, read first calls read in Figure, and then reads the first and last corners of the rectangle:

```
bool RectangleX::read (ifstream& inStream) {
  Figure::read(inStream);
  readPoint(inStream, m_topLeft);
  readPoint(inStream, m_bottomRight);
  return ((bool) inStream);
}
```

The Ellipse sub class

EllipseX is a sub class of RectangleX that handles an ellipse. Part of the functionality of RectangleX is reused in EllipseX. More specifically, initializePoints, setLastPoint, move, write, and read are overridden from RectangleX.

Ellipse.h:

```
#ifndef ELLIPSE_H
#define ELLIPSE_H

#include "Rectangle.h"

class EllipseX : public RectangleX {
  public:
    EllipseX();
    FigureId getId() const {return EllipseId;}

    EllipseX(const EllipseX& ellipse);

    bool isClick(QPoint mousePoint);
    void draw(QPainter& painter) const;
};

#endif
```

Ellipse.cpp:

```
#include "..\MainWindow\DocumentWidget.h"
#include "Ellipse.h"

EllipseX::EllipseX() {
  // Empty.
}
```

The `isClick` method of `EllipseX` is similar to its counterpart in `RectangleX`. We use the Qt `QRegion` class to create elliptic objects that we compare to the mouse click:

```
bool EllipseX::isClick(QPoint mousePoint) {
  QRect normalRect(m_topLeft, m_bottomRight);
  normalRect.normalized();
```

If the ellipse is filled, we create an elliptic region and test whether the mouse click hit the region:

```
if (filled()) {
  QRegion normalEllipse(normalRect, QRegion::Ellipse);
  return normalEllipse.contains(mousePoint);
}
```

If the ellipse in unfilled, we create slightly smaller and larger elliptic regions. If the mouse click hit the smaller region, but not the smaller one, we consider the border of the ellipse to be hit:

```
else {
  QRect largeRect(normalRect), smallRect(normalRect);
  largeRect += Tolerance;
  smallRect -= Tolerance;

  QRegion largeEllipse(largeRect, QRegion::Ellipse),
          smallEllipse(smallRect, QRegion::Ellipse);

  return (largeEllipse.contains(mousePoint) &&
          !smallEllipse.contains(mousePoint));
  }
}
```

When drawing an ellipse, we first set the pen color by calling `color` in `Figure`:

```
void EllipseX::draw(QPainter& painter) const {
  painter.setPen(color());
```

If the ellipse is filled, we set the brush and draw the ellipse:

```
if (filled()) {
  painter.setBrush(color());
  painter.drawEllipse(QRect(m_topLeft, m_bottomRight));
  }
```

If the ellipse is unfilled, we set the brush to hollow and draw the ellipse border:

```
    else {
      painter.setBrush(Qt::NoBrush);
      painter.drawEllipse(QRect(m_topLeft, m_bottomRight));
    }
  }
```

Drawing the window

The DrawingWindow class is a sub class to the MainWindow class of the previous section.

DrawingWindow.h:

```
    #ifndef DRAWINGWINDOW_H
    #define DRAWINGWINDOW_H

    #include <QMainWindow>
    #include <QActionGroup>

    #include "..\MainWindow\MainWindow.h"
    #include "DrawingWidget.h"

    class DrawingWindow : public MainWindow {
      Q_OBJECT

      public:
        DrawingWindow(QWidget* parentWidgetPtr = nullptr);
        ~DrawingWindow();

      public:
        void closeEvent(QCloseEvent *eventPtr)
            { m_drawingWidgetPtr->closeEvent(eventPtr); }

      private:
        DrawingWidget* m_drawingWidgetPtr;
        QActionGroup* m_figureGroupPtr;
    };

    #endif // DRAWINGWINDOW_H
```

DrawingWindow.cpp:

```
    #include "..\MainWindow\DocumentWidget.h"
    #include "DrawingWindow.h"
```

The constructor sets the size of the window to $1000 * 500$ pixels:

```
DrawingWindow::DrawingWindow(QWidget* parentWidgetPtr
                            /* = nullptr */)
 :MainWindow(parentWidgetPtr) {
  resize(1000, 500);
```

The `m_drawingWidgetPtr` field is initialized to point at an object of the `DrawingWidget` class, which is then set to the center part of the window:

```
  m_drawingWidgetPtr = new DrawingWidget(this);
  setCentralWidget(m_drawingWidgetPtr);
```

The standard file menu is added to the window menu bar:

```
  addFileMenu();
```

We then add the application-specific format menu. It is connected to the `onMenuShow` method of the `DocumentWidget` class of the previous section:

```
  { QMenu* formatMenuPtr = menuBar()->addMenu(tr("F&ormat"));
    connect(formatMenuPtr, SIGNAL(aboutToShow()),
            this, SLOT(onMenuShow()));
```

The format menu holds the color and fill items:

```
    addAction(formatMenuPtr, tr("&Color"),
            SLOT(onColor()), QKeySequence(Qt::ALT + Qt::Key_C),
            QString(), nullptr, tr("Figure Color"));
```

The fill item will be enabled when the next figure of the drawing program is a two-dimensional figure (rectangle or ellipse):

```
    addAction(formatMenuPtr, tr("&Fill"),
            SLOT(onFill()), QKeySequence(Qt::CTRL + Qt::Key_F),
            QString(), nullptr, tr("Figure Fill"),
            LISTENER(isFillEnabled));
  }
```

For the figure menu, we create a new action group for the line, rectangle, and ellipse item. Only one of them shall be marked at the same time:

```
  { m_figureGroupPtr = new QActionGroup(this);

    QMenu* figureMenuPtr = menuBar()->addMenu(tr("F&igure"));
    connect(figureMenuPtr, SIGNAL(aboutToShow()),
            this, SLOT(onMenuShow()));
```

The currently selected item shall be marked with a radio button:

```
addAction(figureMenuPtr, tr("&Line"),
          SLOT(onLine()), QKeySequence(Qt::CTRL + Qt::Key_L),
          QString(), nullptr, tr("Line Figure"), nullptr,
          LISTENER(isLineChecked), m_figureGroupPtr);
addAction(figureMenuPtr, tr("&Rectangle"),
          SLOT(onRectangle()),
          QKeySequence(Qt::CTRL + Qt::Key_R),
          QString(), nullptr, tr("Rectangle Figure"), nullptr,
          LISTENER(isRectangleChecked), m_figureGroupPtr);
addAction(figureMenuPtr, tr("&Ellipse"),
          SLOT(onEllipse()),
          QKeySequence(Qt::CTRL + Qt::Key_E),
          QString(), nullptr, tr("Ellipse Figure"), nullptr,
          LISTENER(isEllipseChecked), m_figureGroupPtr);
  }
}
```

The destructor deallocates the figure group that was dynamically allocated in the constructor:

```
DrawingWindow::~DrawingWindow() {
  delete m_figureGroupPtr;
}
```

Drawing the widget

`DrawingWidget` is a sub class of `DocumentWidget` in the previous section. It handles mouse input, painting of the figures, as well as saving and loading of the drawing. It also provides methods for deciding when the menu items shall be marked and enabled.

DrawingWidget.h:

```
#ifndef DRAWINGWIDGET_H
#define DRAWINGWIDGET_H

#include "..\MainWindow\MainWindow.h"
#include "..\MainWindow\DocumentWidget.h"
#include "Figure.h"

class DrawingWidget : public DocumentWidget {
  Q_OBJECT

  public:
    DrawingWidget(QWidget* parentWidgetPtr);
```

```
~DrawingWidget();
```

The `mousePressEvent`, `mouseReleaseEvent`, and `mouseMoveEvent` are overridden methods that are called when the user presses or releases one of the mouse keys or moves the mouse:

```
public:
    void mousePressEvent(QMouseEvent *eventPtr);
    void mouseReleaseEvent(QMouseEvent *eventPtr);
    void mouseMoveEvent(QMouseEvent *eventPtr);
```

The `paintEvent` method is called when the window needs to be repainted. That can happen for several reasons. For instance, the user can modify the size of the window. The repainting can also be forced by a call to the `update` method, which causes `paintEvent` to be called eventually:

```
    void paintEvent(QPaintEvent *eventPtr);
```

The `newDocument` method is called when the user selects the new menu item, `writeFile` is called when the user selects the save or save as item, and `readFile` is called when the user selects the open item:

```
private:
    void newDocument() override;
    bool writeFile(const QString& filePath);
    bool readFile(const QString& filePath);
    Figure* createFigure(FigureId figureId);
```

The `onColor` and `onFill` methods are called when the user selects the color and fill menu items:

```
public slots:
    void onColor();
    void onFill();
```

The `isFillEnabled` method is called before the user selects the format menu. If it returns `true`, the fill item becomes enabled:

```
    DEFINE_LISTENER(DrawingWidget, isFillEnabled);
```

The `isLineChecked`, `isRectangleChecked`, and `isEllipseChecked` methods are also called before the figure menu becomes visible. The items become marked with a radio button if the methods return `true`:

```
DEFINE_LISTENER(DrawingWidget, isLineChecked);
DEFINE_LISTENER(DrawingWidget, isRectangleChecked);
DEFINE_LISTENER(DrawingWidget, isEllipseChecked);
```

The `onLine`, `onRectangle`, and `isEllipse` methods are called when the user selects the line, rectangle, and ellipse menu items:

```
void onLine();
void onRectangle();
void onEllipse();
```

When running, the application can hold the `Idle`, `Create`, or `Move` modes:

- `Idle`: When the application is waiting for input from the user.
- `Create`: When the user is adding a new figure to the drawing. Occurs when the user presses the left mouse button without hitting a figure. A new figure is added and its end-point is modified until the user releases the mouse button.
- `Move`: When the user is moving a figure. Occurs when the user presses the left mouse button and hitting a figure. The figure is moved until the user releases the mouse button.

```
private:
    enum ApplicationMode {Idle, Create, Move};
    ApplicationMode m_applicationMode = Idle;
    void setApplicationMode(ApplicationMode mode);
```

The `m_currColor` field holds the color of the next figure to be added by the user; `m_currFilled` decides whether the next figure (if it is a rectangle or an ellipse) shall be filled. The `m_addFigureId` method holds the identity integer of the next type of figure (line, rectangle, or ellipse) to be added by the user:

```
QColor m_currColor = Qt::black;
bool m_currFilled = false;
FigureId m_addFigureId = LineId;
```

When the user presses a mouse button and moves a figure, we need to store the previous mouse point in order to calculate the distance the figure has been moved since the last mouse events:

```
QPoint m_mousePoint;
```

Finally, `m_figurePtrList` holds pointers to the figures of the drawing. The top-most figure in the drawing is placed at the end of the list:

```
        QList<Figure*> m_figurePtrList;
    };

    #endif // DRAWINGWIDGET_H
```

DrawingWidget.cpp:

```
    #include "..\MainWindow\DocumentWidget.h"
    #include "DrawingWidget.h"

    #include "Line.h"
    #include "Rectangle.h"
    #include "Ellipse.h"
```

The constructor calls the constructor the base class `DocumentWidget` with the title `Drawing`. It also sets the save and load mask to `Drawing files (*.drw)`, which means that the default files selected by the standard save and load dialogs have the suffix `drw`:

```
    DrawingWidget::DrawingWidget(QWidget* parentWidgetPtr)
     :DocumentWidget(tr("Drawing"), tr("Drawing files (*.drw)"),
                    parentWidgetPtr) {
        // Empty.
    }
```

The destructor deallocates the figure pointers of the figure pointer list:

```
    DrawingWidget::~DrawingWidget() {
        for (Figure* figurePtr : m_figurePtrList) {
            delete figurePtr;
        }
    }
```

The `setApplicationMode` method sets the application mode and calls `onMenuShow` in the main window for the toolbar icons to be correctly enabled:

```
    void DrawingWidget::setApplicationMode(ApplicationMode mode) {
        m_applicationMode = mode;
        ((MainWindow*) parent())->onMenuShow();
    }
```

When the user selects the new menu item, `newDocument` is called. The figures of the figure pointer list are deallocated, and the list itself is cleared:

```
void DrawingWidget::newDocument() {
  for (Figure* figurePtr : m_figurePtrList) {
    delete figurePtr;
  }
  m_figurePtrList.clear();
```

The next figure to be added by the user is a black line, and the filled status is `false`:

```
  m_currColor = Qt::black;
  m_addFigureId = LineId;
  m_currFilled = false;
}
```

The `writeFile` method is called when the user selects the save or save as menu items:

```
bool DrawingWidget::writeFile(const QString& filePath) {
  ofstream outStream(filePath.toStdString());
```

We start by writing the current color and fill status. We then continue by writing the size of the figure pointer list, and the figures themselves:

```
  if (outStream) {
    writeColor(outStream, m_currColor);
    outStream.write((char*) &m_currFilled, sizeof m_currFilled);

    int size = m_figurePtrList.size();
    outStream.write((char*) &size, sizeof size);
```

For each figure, we first write its identity number, and we then write the figure itself:

```
    for (Figure* figurePtr : m_figurePtrList) {
      FigureId figureId = figurePtr->getId();
      outStream.write((char*) &figureId, sizeof figureId);
      figurePtr->write(outStream);
    }

    return ((bool) outStream);
  }
```

If the file was not possible to open, `false` is returned:

```
  return false;
}
```

The `readFile` method is called when the user selects the open menu item. In the same way as in `writeFile` previously, we read the color and fill status, the size of the figure pointer list, and then the figures themselves:

```
bool DrawingWidget::readFile(const QString& filePath) {
  ifstream inStream(filePath.toStdString());

  if (inStream) {
    readColor(inStream, m_currColor);
    inStream.read((char*) &m_currFilled, sizeof m_currFilled);

    int size;
    inStream.read((char*) &size, sizeof size);
```

When reading the figure, we first read its identity number, and call `createFigure` to create an object of the class corresponding to the figure's identity number. We then read the fields of the figure by calling `read` on its pointer. Note that we do not really know (or care) what kind of figure it is. We simply call read to the figure pointer, which in fact points to an object of `Line`, `RectangleX`, or `EllipseX`:

```
    for (int count = 0; count < size; ++count) {
      FigureId figureId = (FigureId) 0;
      inStream.read((char*) &figureId, sizeof figureId);
      Figure* figurePtr = createFigure(figureId);
      figurePtr->read(inStream);
      m_figurePtrList.push_back(figurePtr);
    }

    return ((bool) inStream);
  }

  return false;
}
```

The `createFigure` method dynamically creates an object of the `Line`, `RectangleX`, or `EllipseX` class, depending on the value of the `figureId` parameter:

```
Figure* DrawingWidget::createFigure(FigureId figureId) {
  Figure* figurePtr = nullptr;

  switch (figureId) {
    case LineId:
      figurePtr = new Line();
      break;

    case RectangleId:
```

```
            figurePtr = new RectangleX();
            break;

        case EllipseId:
            figurePtr = new EllipseX();
            break;
    }

    return figurePtr;
}
```

The `onColor` method is called when the user selects the color menu item. It sets the color of the next figure to be added by the user:

```
void DrawingWidget::onColor() {
    QColor newColor = QColorDialog::getColor(m_currColor, this);

    if (newColor.isValid() && (m_currColor != newColor)) {
        m_currColor = newColor;
        setModifiedFlag(true);
    }
}
```

The `isFillEnabled` method is called before the format menu becomes visible, and returns `true` if the next figure to be added by the user is a rectangle or an ellipse:

```
bool DrawingWidget::isFillEnabled() {
    return (m_addFigureId == RectangleId) ||
           (m_addFigureId == EllipseId);
}
```

The `onFill` method is called when the user selects fill menu item. It inverts the `m_currFilled` field. It also sets the modified flag since the document has been affected:

```
void DrawingWidget::onFill() {
    m_currFilled = !m_currFilled;
    setModifiedFlag(true);
}
```

The `isLineChecked`, `isRectangleChecked`, and `isEllipseChecked` methods are called before the figure menu becomes visible. If they return `true`, the items become checked with a radio button if the next figure to be added is the figure in question:

```
bool DrawingWidget::isLineChecked() {
    return (m_addFigureId == LineId);
}
```

```
bool DrawingWidget::isRectangleChecked() {
  return (m_addFigureId == RectangleId);
}

bool DrawingWidget::isEllipseChecked() {
  return (m_addFigureId == EllipseId);
}
```

The `onLine`, `onRectangle`, and `onEllipse` methods are called when the user selects the items in the figure menu. They set the next figure to be added by the user to the figure in question:

```
void DrawingWidget::onLine() {
  m_addFigureId = LineId;
}

void DrawingWidget::onRectangle() {
  m_addFigureId = RectangleId;
}

void DrawingWidget::onEllipse() {
  m_addFigureId = EllipseId;
}
```

The `mousePressEvent` method is called every time the user presses one of the mouse keys. First, we need to check if they have pressed the left mouse key:

```
void DrawingWidget::mousePressEvent(QMouseEvent* eventPtr) {
  if (eventPtr->buttons() == Qt::LeftButton) {
```

In the call to `mouseMoveEvent` in the following snippet, we need to keep track of the latest mouse point in order to calculate the distance between mouse movements. Therefore, we set `m_mousePoint` to the mouse point:

```
    m_mousePoint = eventPtr->pos();
```

We iterate through the figure pointer list and, for each figure, we check if the figure has been hit by the mouse click by calling `isClick`. We need to iterate backwards in a rather awkward manner in order to find the top-most figure first. We use the `reverse_iterator` class and the `rbegin` and `rend` methods in order to iterate backwards:

```
    for (QList<Figure*>::reverse_iterator iterator =
         m_figurePtrList.rbegin();
         iterator != m_figurePtrList.rend(); ++iterator) {
```

We use the dereference operator (`*`) to obtain the figure pointer in the list:

```
Figure* figurePtr = *iterator;
```

If the figure has been hit by the mouse click, we set the application mode to move. We also place the figure at the end of the list, so that it appears to be top-most in the drawing, by calling `removeOne` and `push_back` on the list. Finally, we break the loop since we have found the figure we are looking for:

```
if (figurePtr->isClick(m_mousePoint)) {
  setApplicationMode(Move);
  m_figurePtrList.removeOne(figurePtr);
  m_figurePtrList.push_back(figurePtr);
  break;
}
}
```

If the application mode is still idle (has not moved), we have not found a figure hit by the mouse click. In that case, we set the application mode to create and call `createFigure` to find a figure to copy. We then set the color and filled status as well as the points of the figure. Finally, we add the figure pointer to the figure pointer list by calling `push_back` (which is added at the end of the list in order for it to appear at the top of the drawing) and set the modified flag to `true`, since the drawing has been modified:

```
if (m_applicationMode == Idle) {
  setApplicationMode(Create);
  Figure* newFigurePtr = createFigure(m_addFigureId);
  newFigurePtr->color() = m_currColor;
  newFigurePtr->filled() = m_currFilled;
  newFigurePtr->initializePoints(m_mousePoint);
  m_figurePtrList.push_back(newFigurePtr);
  setModifiedFlag(true);
}
}
}
```

The `mouseMoveEvent` is called every time the user moves the mouse. First, we need to check that the user presses the left mouse key when they move the mouse:

```
void DrawingWidget::mouseMoveEvent(QMouseEvent* eventPtr) {
  if (eventPtr->buttons() == Qt::LeftButton) {
    QPoint newMousePoint = eventPtr->pos();
```

We then check the application mode. If we are in the process of adding a new figure to the drawing, we modify its last point:

```
switch (m_applicationMode) {
  case Create:
    m_figurePtrList.back()->setLastPoint(m_mousePoint);
    break;
```

If we are in the process of moving a figure, we calculate the distance since the last mouse event and move the figure placed at the end of the figure pointer list. Remember that the figure hit by the mouse click was placed at the end of the figure pointer list in the preceding mousePressEvent:

```
  case Move: {
      QSize distance(newMousePoint.x() - m_mousePoint.x(),
                     newMousePoint.y() - m_mousePoint.y());
      m_figurePtrList.back()->move(distance);
      setModifiedFlag(true);
    }
    break;
}
```

Finally, we update the current mouse point for the next call to mouseMoveEvent. We also call the update method to force a repainting of the window:

```
    m_mousePoint = newMousePoint;
    update();
  }
}
```

The mouseReleaseEvent method is called when the user releases one of the mouse buttons. We set the application mode to idle:

```
void DrawingWidget::mouseReleaseEvent(QMouseEvent* eventPtr) {
  if (eventPtr->buttons() == Qt::LeftButton) {
    setApplicationMode(Idle);
  }
}
```

The paintEvent method is called every time the window needs to be repainted. It may happen for several reasons. For instance, the user may have changed the size of the window. It may also be a result of a call to update in the Qt QWidget class, which forces a repainting of the window and an eventual call to paintEvent.

We start by creating a `QPainter` object, which can be regarded as canvas to paint on, and set suitable rendering. We then iterate through the figure pointer list, and draw each figure. In this way, the last figure in the list is drawn at the top of the drawing:

```
void DrawingWidget::paintEvent(QPaintEvent* /* eventPtr */) {
  QPainter painter(this);
  painter.setRenderHint(QPainter::Antialiasing);
  painter.setRenderHint(QPainter::TextAntialiasing);

  for (Figure* figurePtr : m_figurePtrList) {
    figurePtr->draw(painter);
  }
}
```

The main function

Finally, we start the application in the `main` function by creating an application object, showing the main window and executing the application.

Main.cpp:

```
#include "DrawingWindow.h"
#include <QApplication>

int main(int argc, char *argv[]) {
  QApplication application(argc, argv);
  DrawingWindow drawingWindow;
  drawingWindow.show();
  return application.exec();
}
```

The following output is received:

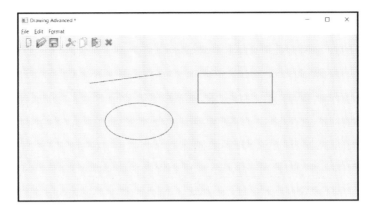

Building an editor

The next application is an editor, where the user can input and edit text. The current input position is indicated by a caret. It is possible to move the caret with the arrow keys and by clicking with the mouse.

The Caret class

The Caret class handles the caret; that is, the blinking vertical line marking the position of the next character to be input.

Caret.h:

```
#ifndef CARET_H
#define CARET_H

#include <QObject>
#include <QWidget>
#include <QTimer>

class Caret : public QObject {
  Q_OBJECT

  public:
    Caret(QWidget* parentWidgetPtr = nullptr);
```

The `show` and `hide` methods show and hide the caret. In this application, the caret is never hidden. However, in the advanced version in the next chapter, the caret will be hidden on some occasions:

```
void show();
void hide();
```

The `set` method sets the current size and position of the caret, and `paint` paints it on the `QPainter` object:

```
void set(QRect rect);
void paint(QPainter& painter);
```

The `onTimer` method is called every time the caret blinks:

```
public slots:
  void onTimer(void);

private:
  QWidget* m_parentWidgetPtr;
```

The `m_visible` field is true when the caret is visible:

```
bool m_visible, m_blink;
```

The `m_rect` field handles the timer that makes the caret blink:

```
QRect m_rect;
```

The `m_timer` field handles the timer that makes the caret blink:

```
QTimer m_timer;
};

#endif // CARET_H
```

The `Caret.cpp` file holds the definitions of the methods of the `Caret` class.

Caret.cpp:

```
#include "Caret.h"
#include <QPainter>
```

The constructor connects the timer signal to onTimer, with the result that onTimer is called for every timeout. The timer is then initialized to 500 milliseconds. That is, onTimer will be called every 500 milliseconds, and the caret becomes shown and hidden every 500 milliseconds:

```
Caret::Caret(QWidget* parentWidgetPtr)
  :m_parentWidgetPtr(parentWidgetPtr) {
  m_timer.setParent(this);
  connect(&m_timer, SIGNAL(timeout()), this, SLOT(onTimer()));
  m_timer.start(500);
}
```

The show and hide methods set the m_visible field and force a repainting of the caret area by calling update on the parent window:

```
void Caret::show() {
  m_visible = true;
  m_parentWidgetPtr->update(m_rect);
}

void Caret::hide() {
  m_visible = false;
  m_parentWidgetPtr->update(m_rect);
}
```

The set method sets the size and position of the caret. However, the width of the caret is always set to one, which makes it appear as a thin vertical line:

```
void Caret::set(QRect rect) {
  m_rect = rect;
  m_rect.setWidth(1);
  m_parentWidgetPtr->update(m_rect);
}
```

The onTimer method is called every 500 milliseconds. It inverts m_blink and forces a repaint of the caret. This gives the result that the caret blinks at an interval of one second:

```
void Caret::onTimer(void) {
  m_blink = !m_blink;
  m_parentWidgetPtr->update(m_rect);
}
```

The `paint` method is called every time the caret needs to be repainted. The caret is drawn if both `m_visible` and `m_blink` are true, which they are if the caret is set to be visible and the caret is blinking; that is, that the caret is visible in the blinking interval. The area of the caret is cleared before the call to paint, so that if no drawing occurs, the caret is cleared:

```
void Caret::paint(QPainter& painter) {
  if (m_visible && m_blink) {
    painter.save();
    painter.setPen(Qt::NoPen);
    painter.setBrush(Qt::black);
    painter.drawRect(m_rect);
    painter.restore();
  }
}
```

Drawing the editor window

`EditorWindow` is a sub class of `MainWindow` in the previous section. It handles the closing of the window. Moreover, it also handles the key press event.

EditorWindow.h:

```
#ifndef EDITORWINDOW_H
#define EDITORWINDOW_H

#include <QMainWindow>
#include <QActionGroup>
#include <QPair>
#include <QMap>

#include "..\MainWindow\MainWindow.h"
#include "EditorWidget.h"

class EditorWindow : public MainWindow {
  Q_OBJECT

  public:
    EditorWindow(QWidget* parentWidgetPtr = nullptr);
    ~EditorWindow();
```

The `keyPressEvent` method is called every time the user presses a key, and `closeEvent` is called when the user tries closing the window:

```
    protected:
      void keyPressEvent(QKeyEvent* eventPtr);
```

```
      void closeEvent(QCloseEvent* eventPtr);

   private:
      EditorWidget* m_editorWidgetPtr;
};

#endif // EDITORWINDOW_H
```

The `EditorWindow` class is in fact rather small. It only defines the constructor and the destructor, as well as the `keyPressEvent` and `closePressEvent` methods.

EditorWindow.cpp:

```
#include "EditorWindow.h"
#include <QtWidgets>
```

The constructor sets the size of the window to 1000 * 500 pixels and adds the standard file menu to the menu bar:

```
EditorWindow::EditorWindow(QWidget* parentWidgetPtr /*= nullptr*/)
 :MainWindow(parentWidgetPtr) {
  resize(1000, 500);
  m_editorWidgetPtr = new EditorWidget(this);
  setCentralWidget(m_editorWidgetPtr);
  addFileMenu();
}

EditorWindow::~EditorWindow() {
  // Empty.
}
```

The `keyPressEvent` and `closeEvent` methods just pass the message to their counterpart methods in the editor widget, which is located at the center of the window:

```
void EditorWindow::keyPressEvent(QKeyEvent* eventPtr) {
  m_editorWidgetPtr->keyPressEvent(eventPtr);
}

void EditorWindow::closeEvent(QCloseEvent* eventPtr) {
  m_editorWidgetPtr->closeEvent(eventPtr);
}
```

Drawing the editor widget

The `EditorWidget` class is a sub class of `DocumentWidget` of the previous section. It catches the key, mouse, resizing, and closing events. It also overrides the methods for saving and loading documents.

EditorWidget.h:

```
#ifndef EDITORWIDGET_H
#define EDITORWIDGET_H

#include <QWidget>
#include <QMap>
#include <QMenu>
#include <QToolBar>
#include <QPair>
#include "Caret.h"

#include "..\MainWindow\DocumentWidget.h"

class EditorWidget : public DocumentWidget {
  Q_OBJECT

  public:
    EditorWidget(QWidget* parentWidgetPtr);
```

The `keyPressEvent` is called when the user presses a key, and `mousePressEvent` is called when the user clicks with the mouse:

```
    void keyPressEvent(QKeyEvent* eventPtr);
    void mousePressEvent(QMouseEvent* eventPtr);
```

The `mouseToIndex` method is an auxiliary method that calculates the index of the character the user clicks at with the mouse:

```
  private:
    int mouseToIndex(QPoint point);
```

The `paintEvent` method is called when the window needs to be repainted, and `resizeEvent` is called when the user resizes the window. We catch the resize event in this application because we want to recalculate the number of characters that fits on each line:

```
  public:
    void paintEvent(QPaintEvent* eventPtr);
    void resizeEvent(QResizeEvent* eventPtr);
```

Similar to the drawing program in the previous section, `newDocument` is called when the user selects the New menu item, `writeFile` is called when the user selects the save or save as items, and `readFile` is called when the user selects the open item:

```
private:
    void newDocument(void);
    bool writeFile(const QString& filePath);
    bool readFile(const QString& filePath);
```

The `setCaret` method is called to set the caret as a response to user input or a mouse click:

```
private:
    void setCaret();
```

When the user moves the caret up or down, we need to find the index of character over or under the caret. The easiest way to do that is to simulate a mouse click:

```
    void simulateMouseClick(int x, int y);
```

The `calculate` method is an auxiliary method that calculates the number of lines, and the position of each character on each line:

```
private:
    void calculate();
```

The `m_editIndex` field holds the index of the position for the user to input text. That position is also where the caret is visible:

```
    int m_editIndex = 0;
```

The `m_caret` field holds the caret of the application:

```
    Caret m_caret;
```

The text of the editor is stored in `m_editorText`:

```
    QString m_editorText;
```

The text of the editor may be distributed over several lines; `m_lineList` keeps track of the first and last index of each line:

```
    QList<QPair<int,int>> m_lineList;
```

The preceding `calculate` method calculates the rectangle of each character in the editor text, and places them in `m_rectList`:

```
    QList<QRect> m_rectList;
```

In the application of this chapter, all characters hold the same font, which is stored in `TextFont`:

```
static const QFont TextFont;
```

`FontWidth` and `FontHeight` hold the width and height of a character in `TextFont`:

```
int FontWidth, FontHeight;
};

#endif // EDITORWIDGET_H
```

The `EditorWidget` class is rather large. It defines the functionality of the editor.

EditorWidget.cpp:

```
#include "EditorWidget.h"
#include <QtWidgets>
using namespace std;
```

We initialize the text font to 12-point `Courier New`:

```
const QFont EditorWidget::TextFont("Courier New", 12);
```

The constructor sets the title to `Editor` and the file suffix for the standard Load and Save dialogs to `edi`. The height and average width, in pixels, of a character in the text font are set with the Qt `QMetrics` class. The rectangle of each character is calculated, and the caret is set to the first character in the text:

```
EditorWidget::EditorWidget(QWidget* parentWidgetPtr)
 :DocumentWidget(tr("Editor"), tr("Editor files (*.edi)"),
                 parentWidgetPtr),
  m_caret(this),
  m_editorText(tr("Hello World")) {
  QFontMetrics metrics(TextFont);
  FontHeight = metrics.height();
  FontWidth = metrics.averageCharWidth();
  calculate();
  setCaret();
  m_caret.show();
}
```

The `newDocument` method is called when the user selects the new menu item. It clears the text, sets the caret, and recalculates the character rectangles:

```
void EditorWidget::newDocument(void) {
  m_editIndex = 0;
```

```
    m_editorText.clear();
    calculate();
    setCaret();
  }
```

The `writeFile` method is called when the user selects the save or save as menu items. It simply writes the current text of the editor:

```
bool EditorWidget::writeFile(const QString& filePath) {
  QFile file(filePath);
  if (file.open(QIODevice::WriteOnly | QIODevice::Text)) {
    QTextStream outStream(&file);
    outStream << m_editorText;
```

We use the `Ok` field of the input stream to decide if the writing was successful:

```
    return ((bool) outStream.Ok);
  }
```

If it was not possible to open the file for writing, `false` is returned:

```
  return false;
}
```

The `readFile` method is called when the user selects the load menu item. It reads all the text of the editor by calling `readAll` on the input stream:

```
bool EditorWidget::readFile(const QString& filePath) {
  QFile file(filePath);

  if (file.open(QIODevice::ReadOnly | QIODevice::Text)) {
    QTextStream inStream(&file);
    m_editorText = inStream.readAll();
```

When the text has been read, the character rectangles are calculated, and the caret is set:

```
    calculate();
    setCaret();
```

We use the `Ok` field of the input stream to decide if the reading was successful:

```
    return ((bool) inStream.Ok);
  }
```

If it was not possible to open the file for reading, `false` is returned:

```
  return false;
}
```

The `mousePressEvent` is called when the user presses one of the mouse buttons. If the user presses the left button, we call `mouseToIndex` to calculate the index of the character clicked at, and set the caret to that index:

```
void EditorWidget::mousePressEvent(QMouseEvent* eventPtr) {
  if (eventPtr->buttons() == Qt::LeftButton) {
    m_editIndex = mouseToIndex(eventPtr->pos());
    setCaret();
  }
}
```

The `keyPressEvent` is called when the user presses a key. First, we check if it is an arrow key, the delete, backspace, or return key. If it is not, we insert the character at the position indicated by the caret:

```
void EditorWidget::keyPressEvent(QKeyEvent* eventPtr) {
  switch (eventPtr->key()) {
```

If the key is the left-arrow key, and if the edit caret is not already located at the beginning of the text, we decrease the edit index:

```
case Qt::Key_Left:
  if (m_editIndex > 0) {
    --m_editIndex;
  }
  break;
```

If the key is the right-arrow key, and if the edit caret is not already located at the end of the text, we increase the edit index:

```
case Qt::Key_Right:
  if (m_editIndex < m_editorText.size()) {
    ++m_editIndex;
  }
  break;
```

If the key is the up-arrow key, and if the edit caret is not already located at the top of the editor, we call `similateMouseClick` to simulate that the user clicks with the mouse at a point slightly over the current index. In that way, the new edit index will at the line over the current line:

```
case Qt::Key_Up: {
    QRect charRect = m_rectList[m_editIndex];

    if (charRect.top() > 0) {
      int x = charRect.left() + (charRect.width() / 2),
```

```
            y = charRect.top() - 1;
         simulateMouseClick(x, y);
      }
   }
   break;
```

If the key is the down-arrow key, we call `similateMouseClick` to simulate that the user clicks with the mouse at a point slightly under the current index. In that way, we the edit carat will be located at the character directly beneath the current character. Note that if the index is already at the bottom line, nothing happens:

```
case Qt::Key_Down: {
   QRect charRect = m_rectList[m_editIndex];
   int x = charRect.left() + (charRect.width() / 2),
       y = charRect.bottom() + 1;
   simulateMouseClick(x, y);
}
break;
```

If the user presses the delete key, and the edit index is not already beyond the end of the text, the current character is removed:

```
case Qt::Key_Delete:
   if (m_editIndex < m_editorText.size()) {
     m_editorText.remove(m_editIndex, 1);
     setModifiedFlag(true);
   }
   break;
```

If the user presses the backspace key, and the edit index is not already at the beginning of the text, the character before the current character is removed:

```
case Qt::Key_Backspace:
   if (m_editIndex > 0) {
     m_editorText.remove(--m_editIndex, 1);
     setModifiedFlag(true);
   }
   break;
```

If the user presses the return key, the newline character (n) is inserted:

```
case Qt::Key_Return:
   m_editorText.insert(m_editIndex++, 'n');
   setModifiedFlag(true);
   break;
```

If the user presses a readable character, it is given by the `text` method, and we insert its first character at the edit index:

```
default: {
    QString text = eventPtr->text();

    if (!text.isEmpty()) {
      m_editorText.insert(m_editIndex++, text[0]);
      setModifiedFlag(true);
    }
  }
  break;
}
```

When the text has been modified, we need to calculate the character rectangles, set the caret, and force a repaint by calling `update`:

```
calculate();
setCaret();
update();
}
```

The `similateMouseClick` method simulates a mouse click by calling `mousePressEvent` and `mousePressRelease` with the given point:

```
void EditorWidget::simulateMouseClick(int x, int y) {
  QMouseEvent pressEvent(QEvent::MouseButtonPress, QPointF(x, y),
               Qt::LeftButton, Qt::NoButton, Qt::NoModifier);
  mousePressEvent(&pressEvent);
  QMouseEvent releaseEvent(QEvent::MouseButtonRelease,
                QPointF(x, y), Qt::LeftButton,
                Qt::NoButton, Qt::NoModifier);
  mousePressEvent(&releaseEvent);
}
```

The `setCaret` method creates a rectangle holding the size and position of the caret, and then hides, sets, and shows the caret:

```
void EditorWidget::setCaret() {
  QRect charRect = m_rectList[m_editIndex];
  QRect caretRect(charRect.left(), charRect.top(),
            1, charRect.height());
  m_caret.hide();
  m_caret.set(caretRect);
  m_caret.show();
}
```

The `mouseToIndex` method calculates the edit index of the given mouse point:

```
int EditorWidget::mouseToIndex(QPoint mousePoint) {
    int x = mousePoint.x(), y = mousePoint.y();
```

First, we set the y coordinate to the text, in case it is below the text:

```
if (y > (FontHeight * m_lineList.size())) {
    y = ((FontHeight * m_lineList.size()) - 1);
}
```

We calculate the line of the mouse point:

```
int lineIndex = y / FontHeight;
QPair<int,int> lineInfo = m_lineList[lineIndex];
int firstIndex = lineInfo.first, lastIndex = lineInfo.second;
```

We find the index on that line:

```
if (x > ((lastIndex - firstIndex + 1) * FontWidth)) {
    return (lineIndex == (m_lineList.size() - 1))
            ? (lineInfo.second + 1) : lineInfo.second;
}
else {
    return firstIndex + (x / FontWidth);
}
return 0;
}
```

The `resizeEvent` method is called when the user changes the size of the window. The character rectangles are recalculated since the lines may be shorter or longer:

```
void EditorWidget::resizeEvent(QResizeEvent* eventPtr) {
    calculate();
    DocumentWidget::resizeEvent(eventPtr);
}
```

The `calculate` method is called every time there has been a change in the text or when the window size has been changed. It iterates through the text and calculates the rectangle for each character:

```
void EditorWidget::calculate() {
    m_lineList.clear();
    m_rectList.clear();
    int windowWidth = width();
```

First, we need to divide the text into lines. Each line continues until it does not fit in the window, until we reach a new line, or until the text ends:

```
{ int firstIndex = 0, lineWidth = 0;
  for (int charIndex = 0; charIndex < m_editorText.size();
       ++charIndex) {
    QChar c = m_editorText[charIndex];

    if (c == 'n') {
      m_lineList.push_back
                 (QPair<int,int>(firstIndex, charIndex));
      firstIndex = charIndex + 1;
      lineWidth = 0;
    }
    else {
      if ((lineWidth + FontWidth) > windowWidth) {
        if (firstIndex == charIndex) {
          m_lineList.push_back
                     (QPair<int,int>(firstIndex, charIndex));
          firstIndex = charIndex + 1;
        }
        else {
          m_lineList.push_back(QPair<int,int>(firstIndex,
                                              charIndex - 1));
          firstIndex = charIndex;
        }

        lineWidth = 0;
      }
      else {
        lineWidth += FontWidth;
      }
    }
  }

  m_lineList.push_back(QPair<int,int>(firstIndex,
                                      m_editorText.size() - 1));
}
```

We then iterate through the lines and, for each line, calculate the rectangle of each character:

```
{ int top = 0;
  for (int lineIndex = 0; lineIndex < m_lineList.size();
       ++lineIndex) {
    QPair<int,int> lineInfo = m_lineList[lineIndex];
    int firstIndex = lineInfo.first,
        lastIndex = lineInfo.second, left = 0;
```

```
          for (int charIndex = firstIndex;
                   charIndex <= lastIndex; ++charIndex){
            QRect charRect(left, top, FontWidth, FontHeight);
            m_rectList.push_back(charRect);
            left += FontWidth;
          }

          if (lastIndex == (m_editorText.size() - 1)) {
            QRect lastRect(left, top, 1, FontHeight);
            m_rectList.push_back(lastRect);
          }

          top += FontHeight;
        }
      }
    }
```

The `paintEvent` method is called when the window needs to be repainted:

```
    void EditorWidget::paintEvent(QPaintEvent* /*eventPtr*/) {
      QPainter painter(this);
      painter.setRenderHint(QPainter::Antialiasing);
      painter.setRenderHint(QPainter::TextAntialiasing);
      painter.setFont(TextFont);
      painter.setPen(Qt::black);
      painter.setBrush(Qt::white);
```

We iterate through the text of the editor and, for each character except the new line, we write in its appropriate position:

```
      for (int index = 0; index < m_editorText.length(); ++index) {
        QChar c = m_editorText[index];

        if (c != 'n') {
          QRect rect = m_rectList[index];
          painter.drawText(rect, c);
        }
      }

      m_caret.paint(painter);
    }
```

The main function

Finally, the `main` function works in a way similar to the previous applications of this chapter—we create an application, create an editor window, and execute the application.

Main.cpp:

```
#include "EditorWindow.h"
#include <QApplication>

int main(int argc, char *argv[]) {
  QApplication application(argc, argv);
  EditorWindow editorWindow;
  editorWindow.show();
  return application.exec();
}
```

The following output is obtained:

Summary

In this chapter, we have developed three graphical applications with the Qt library—an analog clock, a drawing program, and an editor. The clock shows the current hour, minute, and second. In the drawing program we can draw lines, rectangles, and ellipses, and in the editor, we can input and edit text.

In the next chapter, we will continue to work with the applications, and develop more advanced versions.

6

Enhancing the Qt Graphical Applications

In Chapter 5, *Qt Graphical Applications*, we developed graphical Qt applications involving an analog clock, a drawing program, and an editor. In this chapter, we will continue to work on the three graphical applications of Chapter 5, *Qt Graphical Applications*. However, we will make the following improvements:

- **Clock**: We will add digits to the clock dial
- **The drawing program**: We will add the ability to move and modify figures, to cut and paste them, and to mark one or several figures
- **The editor**: We will add the ability to change font and alignment as well as to mark a text block

In this chapter, we will continue to work with the Qt libraries:

- Windows and widgets
- Menus and toolbars
- Mouse and keyboard events

Improving the clock

In this chapter, we will replace the version of clock dial markings with digits.

The Clock class

The `Clock` class definition is similar to the one in Chapter 5, *Qt Graphical Applications*. The timer updates the window 10 times each second. The constructor initializes the clock and `paintEvent` is called every time the window needs to be repainted.

Clock.h:

```
#ifndef CLOCK_H
#define CLOCK_H

#include <QWidget>
#include <QTimer>

class Clock : public QWidget {
  Q_OBJECT

  public:
    Clock(QWidget *parentWidget = nullptr);
    void paintEvent(QPaintEvent *eventPtr);

  private:
  QTimer m_timer;
};

#endif // CLOCK_H
```

Clock.cpp:

```
#include <QtWidgets>
#include "Clock.h"
```

Similar to Chapter 5, *Qt Graphical Applications*, the constructor sets the header of the window to `Clock Advanced`, the window size to *1000 x 500* pixels, initializes the timer to send a timeout message every `100` milliseconds, and connect the `timeout` message to the `update` method, which forces the window to be repainted for each timeout:

```
Clock::Clock(QWidget *parentWidget /*= nullptr*/)
:QWidget(parentWidget) {
  setWindowTitle(tr("Clock Advanced"));
  resize(1000, 500);

  m_timer.setParent(this);
  connect(&m_timer, SIGNAL(timeout()), this, SLOT(update()));
  m_timer.start(100);
}
```

The `paintEvent` method is called every time the window needs to be repainted. We will start by calculating the side of the clock and obtaining the current time:

```
void Clock::paintEvent(QPaintEvent* /*event*/) {
  int side = qMin(width(), height());
  QTime time = QTime::currentTime();
```

We then create and initialize a `QPainter` object. We call `translate` and `scale` to match the physical size (pixels) to the logical size of *200 x 200* units:

```
QPainter painter(this);
painter.setRenderHint(QPainter::Antialiasing);
painter.setRenderHint(QPainter::TextAntialiasing);
painter.translate(width() / 2, height() / 2);
painter.scale(side / 200.0, side / 200.0);
```

As we write digits to the clock in this version of the chapter, we add the font `Times New Roman`, 12 points, to the painter:

```
painter.setFont(QFont(tr("Times New Roman"), 12));
```

We write the digits of the clock, 1 to 12, as shown in the following code:

```
for (int hour = 1; hour <= 12; ++hour) {
  QString text;
  text.setNum(hour);
```

A whole leap is 360° and the angle between two consecutive digits is 30°, since 360 divided by 12 is 30:

```
double angle = (30.0 * hour) - 90;
double radius = 90.0;
```

The x and y coordinates of the digits are calculated by the sine and cosine functions. However, first, we need to transform the degrees to radians since sine and cosine accept radians only. This is shown in the following code:

```
double x = radius * qCos(qDegreesToRadians(angle)),
       y = radius * qSin(qDegreesToRadians(angle));
```

The `drawText` methods write the digit, as follows:

```
QRect rect(x - 100, y - 100, 200, 200);
painter.drawText(rect, Qt::AlignHCenter |
                       Qt::AlignVCenter, text);
}
```

When the digits have been written, we draw the hour, minute, and second hands in the same way as in Chapter 5, *Qt Graphical Applications*:

```cpp
double hours = time.hour(), minutes = time.minute(),
    seconds = time.second(), milliseconds = time.msec();

painter.setPen(Qt::black);
painter.setBrush(Qt::gray);

{ static const QPoint hourHand[3] =
    {QPoint(8, 8), QPoint(-8, 8), QPoint(0, -60)};

    painter.save();
    double hour = hours + (minutes / 60.0) + (seconds / 3600.0) +
                (milliseconds / 3600000.0);
    painter.rotate(30.0 * hour);
    painter.drawConvexPolygon(hourHand, 3);
    painter.restore();
}

{ static const QPoint minuteHand[3] =
    {QPoint(6, 8), QPoint(-6, 8), QPoint(0, -70)};

    painter.save();
    double minute = minutes + (seconds / 60.0) +
                (milliseconds / 60000.0);
    painter.rotate(6.0 * minute);
    painter.drawConvexPolygon(minuteHand, 3);
    painter.restore();
}

{ static const QPoint secondHand[3] =
    {QPoint(4, 8), QPoint(-4, 8), QPoint(0, -80)};

    painter.save();
    double second = seconds + (milliseconds / 1000);
    painter.rotate(6.0 * second);
    painter.drawConvexPolygon(secondHand, 3);
    painter.restore();
}
}
```

The main function

The `main` function is similar to the one in `Chapter 5`, *Qt Graphical Applications*. It creates an application object, initializes the clock, and executes the application.

Main.cpp:

```
#include <QApplication>
#include "Clock.h"

int main(int argc, char *argv[]) {
  QApplication application(argc, argv);
  Clock Clock;
  Clock.show();
  return application.exec();
}
```

Output:

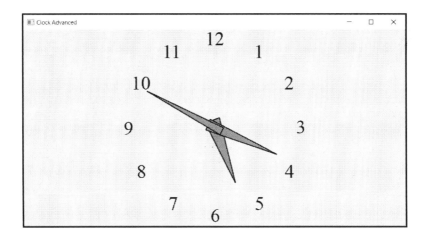

Improving the drawing program

The drawing program of this chapter is a more advanced version of the drawing program of `Chapter 5`, *Qt Graphical Applications*. In this version, it is possible to modify a figure, to enclose one or more figures and then change their colors, and to cut and paste figures.

The Figure class

The `Figure` class is rather similar to the one in Chapter 5, *Qt Graphical Applications*. However, `isInside`, `doubleClick`, `modify`, and `marked` have been added.

Figure.h:

```
#ifndef FIGURE_H
#define FIGURE_H

enum FigureId {LineId, RectangleId, EllipseId};

#include <QtWidgets>
#include <FStream>
using namespace std;

class Figure {
  public:
    Figure();
```

In this version, the pure virtual `clone` method has been added. That is due to the cut and paste. When pasting a figure we want to create a copy of it, without actually knowing which class the object belongs to. We could not do that with the copy constructor only. This is actually the main point of this section: how to use pure virtual methods and how to take advantage of dynamic binding. We need `clone`, which calls the copy constructor of its class to return a pointer to the new object:

```
virtual Figure* clone() const = 0;

virtual FigureId getId() const = 0;
virtual void initializePoints(QPoint point) = 0;
```

In this version of the drawing program, `onClick` sets fields to indicate whether the figure shall be modified or moved. If the user grabs one of the marked points of the figure (which varies between different kinds of figures), the figure shall be modified. Otherwise, it shall be moved. The `modify` method is called when the user grabs one of the corners of the figure. In that case, the figure shall be modified rather than moved:

```
virtual bool isClick(QPoint mousePoint) = 0;
virtual void modify(QSize distance) = 0;
```

The `isInside` method returns `true` if the figure is completely enclosed in the area. It is called when the user encloses figures with the mouse:

```
virtual bool isInside(QRect area) = 0;
```

The `doubleClick` method is called when the user double-clicks at the figure, each figure performs some suitable action:

```
virtual void doubleClick(QPoint mousePoint) = 0;

virtual void move(QSize distance) = 0;
virtual void draw(QPainter &painter) const = 0;

virtual bool write(ofstream& outStream) const;
virtual bool read(ifstream& inStream);
```

The `marked` methods return and set the `m_marked` field. When a figure is marked, it is annotated with small squares:

```
bool marked() const {return m_marked;}
bool& marked() {return m_marked;}

const QColor& color() const {return m_color;}
QColor& color() {return m_color;}

virtual bool filled() const {return m_filled;}
virtual bool& filled() {return m_filled;}

static const int Tolerance;

private:
QColor m_color;
bool m_marked = false, m_filled = false;
};

#endif
```

Figure.cpp:

```
#include "..\MainWindow\DocumentWidget.h"
#include "Figure.h"

const int Figure::Tolerance(6);

Figure::Figure() {
   // Empty.
}
```

The `write` and `read` methods write and read the color of the figure and whether it is filled. However, they do not write or read the marked status. A figure is always unmarked when written or read:

```
bool Figure::write(ofstream& outStream) const {
  writeColor(outStream, m_color);
  outStream.write((char*) &m_filled, sizeof m_filled);
  return ((bool) outStream);
}

bool Figure::read(ifstream& inStream) {
  readColor(inStream, m_color);
  inStream.read((char*) &m_filled, sizeof m_filled);
  return ((bool) inStream);
}
```

The Line class

The `Line` class is a subclass of `Figure`.

Line.h:

```
#ifndef LINE_H
#define LINE_H
#include <FStream>
using namespace std;

#include "Figure.h"

class Line : public Figure {
  public:
  Line();
  FigureId getId() const {return LineId;}
  In addition to the
  Line(const Line& line);
  Figure* clone() const;

  void initializePoints(QPoint point);
```

As mentioned in the preceding `Figure` section, `isClick` decided whether the line shall be modified or moved. If the user grabs one of its endpoints, only that endpoint shall be moved. If the user grabs the line between the endpoints, the line shall be moved. That is, both the endpoints of the line shall be moved:

```
bool isClick(QPoint mousePoint);
```

The `isInside` method checks whether the line is completely enclosed by the area:

```
bool isInside(QRect area);
```

The `doubleClick` method does nothing in the `Line` class. However, we still need to define it, since it is pure virtual in `Figure`. If we had not defined it, `Line` would have been abstract:

```
void doubleClick(QPoint /* mousePoint */) {/* Empty. */}
```

The `modify` method modifies the line in accordance with the settings of the preceding `isClick`. If the user grabs one of the endpoints, that endpoint is moved. Otherwise, the whole line (both the endpoints) is moved:

```
void modify(QSize distance);
void move(QSize distance);
```

The `area` method returns a slightly larger area if the line is marked, in order to include the marking squares:

```
QRect area() const;
void draw(QPainter& painter) const;

bool write(ofstream& outStream) const;
bool read(ifstream& inStream);
```

The `m_lineMode` field keeps track of the movement or modification of the line. When the line is created, `m_lineMode` is set to `LastPoint`. When the user grabs the first or last endpoint of the line, `m_lineMode` is set to `FirstPoint` or `LastPoint`. When the user grabs the line between the endpoints, `m_lineMode` is set to `MoveLine`:

```
private:
    enum {FirstPoint, LastPoint, MoveLine} m_lineMode;
    QPoint m_firstPoint, m_lastPoint;
```

The `isPointInLine` method decides whether the user has clicked on the line, with some tolerance:

```
static bool isPointInLine(QPoint m_firstPoint,
                          QPoint m_lastPoint, QPoint point);
};

#endif
```

Line.cpp:

```
#include "..\MainWindow\DocumentWidget.h"
#include "Line.h"
```

When a line becomes created, the line mode is set to the last point. That means that the last point of the line will be changed when the user moves the mouse:

```
Line::Line()
:m_lineMode(LastPoint) {
  // Empty.
}
```

The `clone` method is called when a line is being pasted. The copy constructor of `Figure` is called to set the color of the figure. Note that we call the `Figure` constructor with a `Line` object as a parameter, even though it takes a reference to a `Figure` object as a parameter. We are allowed to do this since `Line` is a subclass of `Figure` and the `Line` object will be transformed into a `Figure` object during the call. Moreover, the first and last endpoints are copied. Note that we do need to copy the value `m_lineMode` since its value is set when the user creates, modifies, or moves the line only:

```
Line::Line(const Line& line)
 :Figure(line),
   m_firstPoint(line.m_firstPoint),
   m_lastPoint(line.m_lastPoint) {
  // Empty.
 }
```

The `clone` method uses the copy constructor to create a new object, which is then returned:

```
Figure* Line::clone() const {
  Line* linePtr = new Line(*this);
  return linePtr;
}
```

The `initializePoints` method is called shortly after the line is being created. The reason for this call is that we do not create a `Line` object directly. Instead, we create the line indirectly by calling `clone`. We then need to initialize the end-points by calling `initializePoints`:

```
void Line::initializePoints(QPoint point) {
  m_firstPoint = point;
  m_lastPoint = point;
}
```

The `isClick` method is called when the user clicks with the mouse. First, we check whether they have clicked at the first endpoint. We use the `Tolerance` field to create a small square, with the first endpoint in its center. If the user clicks on the square, `m_lineMode` is set to `FirstPoint` and `true` is returned:

```
bool Line::isClick(QPoint mousePoint) {
  QRect firstSquare(makeRect(m_firstPoint, Tolerance));

  if (firstSquare.contains(mousePoint)) {
    m_lineMode = FirstPoint;
    return true;
  }
```

In the same way, we create a small square with the last endpoint in its center. If the user clicks at the square, `m_lineMode` is set to `LastPoint` and `true` is returned:

```
QRect lastSquare(makeRect(m_lastPoint, Tolerance));

if (lastSquare.contains(mousePoint)) {
  m_lineMode = LastPoint;
  return true;
}
```

If the user does not click on either of the endpoints, we check if they click on the line itself. If they do, `m_lineMode` is set to `ModeLine` and `true` is returned:

```
if (isPointInLine(m_firstPoint, m_lastPoint, mousePoint)) {
  m_lineMode = MoveLine;
  return true;
}
```

Finally, if the user does not click on one of the endpoints or the line itself, they missed the line altogether and `false` is returned:

```
  return false;
}
```

The `isInside` method returns `true` if the line is completely enclosed by the area. It is quite easy, we just check whether the two end-points are located inside the area:

```
bool Line::isInside(QRect area) {
  return area.contains(m_firstPoint) &&
    area.contains(m_lastPoint);
}
```

The isPointInLine method is identical to isClick in the version of Chapter 5, *Qt Graphical Applications*:

```
bool Line::isPointInLine(QPoint m_firstPoint, QPoint m_lastPoint,
                         QPoint point) {
    if (m_firstPoint.x() == m_lastPoint.x()) {
        QRect lineRect(m_firstPoint, m_lastPoint);
        lineRect.normalized();
        lineRect += Tolerance;
        return lineRect.contains(point);
    }
    else {
        QPoint leftPoint = (m_firstPoint.x() < m_lastPoint.x())
                           ? m_firstPoint : m_lastPoint,
               rightPoint = (m_firstPoint.x() < m_lastPoint.x())
                           ? m_lastPoint : m_firstPoint;

        if ((leftPoint.x() <= point.x()) &&
            (point.x() <= rightPoint.x())) {
            int lineWidth = rightPoint.x() - leftPoint.x(),
                lineHeight = rightPoint.y() - leftPoint.y();

            int diffWidth = point.x() - leftPoint.x(),
                diffHeight = point.y() - leftPoint.y();

            double delta = fabs(diffHeight -
                    (diffWidth * ((double) lineHeight) / lineWidth));
            return (delta <= Tolerance);
        }

        return false;
    }
}
```

The modify method moves the first or last endpoint, or both of them, depending on the settings of m_lineMode in the preceding isClick method:

```
void Line::modify(QSize distance) {
    switch (m_lineMode) {
        case FirstPoint:
            m_firstPoint += distance;
            break;

        case LastPoint:
            m_lastPoint += distance;
            break;
```

```
        case MoveLine:
        move(distance);
        break;
    }
}
```

The `move` method simply moves both the end-points of the line:

```
void Line::move(QSize distance) {
  m_firstPoint += distance;
  m_lastPoint += distance;
}
```

The `draw` method draws the line. The difference between this version and the version of Chapter 5, *Qt Graphical Applications*, is that it also draws the squares at the end-points of the line if it is marked:

```
void Line::draw(QPainter& painter) const {
  painter.setPen(color());
  painter.drawLine(m_firstPoint, m_lastPoint);

  if (marked()) {
    painter.fillRect(makeRect(m_firstPoint, Tolerance),
                Qt::black);
    painter.fillRect(makeRect(m_lastPoint, Tolerance),
                Qt::black);
  }
}
```

The `area` method returns the area covering the line. If the line is marked, the area is slightly expanded in order to cover the squares marking the endpoints:

```
QRect Line::area() const {
  QRect lineArea(m_firstPoint, m_lastPoint);
  lineArea.normalized();

  if (marked()) {
    lineArea += Tolerance;
  }

  return lineArea;
}
```

Similar to the version of Chapter 5, *Qt Graphical Applications*, write and read call their counterparts in Figure and then write and read the two endpoints of the line:

```
bool Line::write(ofstream& outStream) const {
  Figure::write(outStream);
  writePoint(outStream, m_firstPoint);
  writePoint(outStream, m_lastPoint);
  return ((bool) outStream);
}

bool Line::read(ifstream& inStream) {
  Figure::read(inStream);
  readPoint(inStream, m_firstPoint);
  readPoint(inStream, m_lastPoint);
  return ((bool) inStream);
}
```

The Rectangle class

RectangleX is a subclass of Figure. It is an expanded version of the version of Chapter 5, *Qt Graphical Applications*. The isClick method has been modified, doubleClick and modify have been added.

Rectangle.h:

```
#ifndef RECTANGLE_H
#define RECTANGLE_H

#include <FStream>
using namespace std;

#include "Figure.h"

class RectangleX : public Figure {
  public:
  RectangleX();
  virtual FigureId getId() const {return RectangleId;}

  RectangleX(const RectangleX& rectangle);
  Figure* clone() const;

  virtual void initializePoints(QPoint point);

  virtual bool isClick(QPoint mousePoint);
  virtual void modify(QSize distance);
```

```
virtual bool isInside(QRect area);
virtual void doubleClick(QPoint mousePoint);

virtual void move(QSize distance);
virtual QRect area() const;
virtual void draw(QPainter& painter) const;

virtual bool write(ofstream& outStream) const;
virtual bool read(ifstream& inStream);

private:
  enum {TopLeftPoint, TopRightPoint, BottomRightPoint,
      BottomLeftPoint, MoveRectangle} m_rectangleMode;

protected:
  QPoint m_topLeft, m_bottomRight;
};

#endif
```

Rectangle.cpp:

```
#include <CAssert>
#include "..\MainWindow\DocumentWidget.h"
#include "Rectangle.h"
```

When a rectangle is added by the user, its mode is `BottomRightPoint`. That means that the bottom-right corner of the rectangle will be moved when the user moves the mouse:

```
RectangleX::RectangleX()
:m_rectangleMode(BottomRightPoint) {
  // Empty.
}
```

The copy constructor copies the rectangle. More specifically, first it calls the copy constructor of the `Figure` class, then it copies the top-left and bottom-right corner. Note that it does not copy the `m_rectangleMode` field, since it is used when the user moves the mouse only:

```
RectangleX::RectangleX(const RectangleX& rectangle)
:Figure(rectangle),
  m_topLeft(rectangle.m_topLeft),
  m_bottomRight(rectangle.m_bottomRight) {
  // Empty.
}
```

The `clone` method creates and returns a pointer to a new object by calling the copy constructor:

```
Figure* RectangleX::clone() const {
  RectangleX* rectanglePtr = new RectangleX(*this);
  return rectanglePtr;
}

void RectangleX::initializePoints(QPoint point) {
  m_topLeft = point;
  m_bottomRight = point;
}
```

The `isClick` method is called when the user clicks with the mouse. Similar to the preceding bool `Line`, we start by checking whether they have clicked at any of the corners. If they have not, we check whether they have clicked on the rectangle border or inside the rectangle, depending on whether it is filled.

We start by defining a small square covering the top-left corner. If the user clicks on it, we set the `m_rectangleMode` field to `TopLeftPoint` and return `true`:

```
bool RectangleX::isClick(QPoint mousePoint) {
  QRect topLeftRect(makeRect(m_topLeft, Tolerance));

  if (topLeftRect.contains(mousePoint)) {
    m_rectangleMode = TopLeftPoint;
    return true;
  }
```

We continue by defining a square covering the top-right corner. If the user clicks on it, we set `m_rectangleMode` to `TopRightPoint` and return `true`:

```
QPoint topRightPoint(m_bottomRight.x(), m_topLeft.y());
QRect topRectRight(makeRect(topRightPoint, Tolerance));

if (topRectRight.contains(mousePoint)) {
  m_rectangleMode = TopRightPoint;
  return true;
}
```

If the user clicks at the square covering the bottom-right corner, we set `m_rectangleMode` to `BottomRightPoint` and return `true`:

```
QRect m_bottomRightRect(makeRect(m_bottomRight, Tolerance));
if (m_bottomRightRect.contains(mousePoint)) {
  m_rectangleMode = BottomRightPoint;
```

```
    return true;
  }
```

If the user clicks at the square covering the bottom-left corner, we set m_rectangleMode to BottomLeftPoint **and return** true:

```
QPoint bottomLeftPoint(m_topLeft.x(), m_bottomRight.y());
QRect bottomLeftRect(makeRect(bottomLeftPoint, Tolerance));

if (bottomLeftRect.contains(mousePoint)) {
  m_rectangleMode = BottomLeftPoint;
  return true;
}
```

If the user does not click at any of the corners of the rectangle, we check the rectangle itself. If it is filled, we check whether the mouse pointer is located inside the rectangle itself. If it is, we set m_rectangleMode to MoveRectangle **and return** true:

```
QRect areaRect(m_topLeft, m_bottomRight);

if (filled()) {
  if (areaRect.contains(mousePoint)) {
    m_rectangleMode = MoveRectangle;
    return true;
  }
}
```

If the rectangle is not filled, we define slightly larger and smaller rectangles. If the mouse click is located inside the larger rectangle, but not in the smaller one, we set m_rectangleMode to MoveRectangle **and return** true:

```
else {
  QRect largeAreaRect(areaRect), smallAreaRect(areaRect);

  largeAreaRect += Tolerance;
  smallAreaRect -= Tolerance;

  if (largeAreaRect.contains(mousePoint) &&
      !smallAreaRect.contains(mousePoint)) {
    m_rectangleMode = MoveRectangle;
    return true;
  }
}
```

Finally, if the user does not click at one of the corners or the rectangle itself, they missed the rectangle and we return false:

```
        return false;
    }
```

The `isInside` method is quite simple. We simply check if the top-left and bottom-right corners are located inside the rectangle:

```
bool RectangleX::isInside(QRect area) {
    return area.contains(m_topLeft) &&
        area.contains(m_bottomRight);
}
```

The `doubleClick` method is called when the user double-clicks with the mouse. If the call to `onClick` returns `true`, `doubleClick` is called. In the rectangle case, the filled status is changed—a filled rectangle becomes unfilled and an unfilled rectangle becomes filled:

```
void RectangleX::doubleClick(QPoint mousePoint) {
    if (isClick(mousePoint)) {
```

The first call to `filled` is a call to the version that returns a reference to the `m_filled` field, which allows us to change the returned value:

```
        filled() = !filled();
    }
}
```

The `modify` method modifies the rectangle in accordance with the `m_rectangleMode` field, which was set by the preceding `isClick`. If it is set to one of the four corners, we modify that corner. If not, we move the whole rectangle:

```
void RectangleX::modify(QSize distance) {
    switch (m_rectangleMode) {
        case TopLeftPoint:
        m_topLeft += distance;
        break;

        case TopRightPoint:
        m_topLeft.setY(m_topLeft.y() + distance.height());
        m_bottomRight.setX(m_bottomRight.x() + distance.width());
        break;

        case BottomRightPoint:
        m_bottomRight += distance;
        break;

        case BottomLeftPoint:
        m_topLeft.setX(m_topLeft.x() + distance.width());
        m_bottomRight.setY(m_bottomRight.y() + distance.height());
```

```
       break;

       case MoveRectangle:
       move(distance);
       break;
       }
    }
```

The `move` method is quite simple. It just changes the top-left and bottom-right corners:

```
void RectangleX::move(QSize distance) {
  m_topLeft += distance;
  m_bottomRight += distance;
}
```

The `area` method returns the area covering the rectangle. If it is marked, we slightly expand the area in order for it to cover the marking squares:

```
QRect RectangleX::area() const {
  QRect areaRect(m_topLeft, m_bottomRight);
  areaRect.normalized();

  if (marked()) {
    areaRect += Tolerance;
  }

  return areaRect;
}
```

The `draw` method draws the rectangle; with a full brush it is filled and with a hollow brush if it is unfilled:

```
void RectangleX::draw(QPainter& painter) const {
  painter.setPen(color());

  if (filled()) {
    painter.fillRect(QRect(m_topLeft, m_bottomRight), color());
  }
  else {
    painter.setBrush(Qt::NoBrush);
    painter.drawRect(QRect(m_topLeft, m_bottomRight));
  }
```

If the rectangle is marked, the four squares covering the corners of the rectangle are also drawn:

```
if (marked()) {
    painter.fillRect(makeRect(m_topLeft, Tolerance), Qt::black);
```

```
      QPoint topRight(m_bottomRight.x(), m_topLeft.y());
      painter.fillRect(makeRect(topRight, Tolerance), Qt::black);
      painter.fillRect(makeRect(m_bottomRight, Tolerance),
                   Qt::black);
      QPoint bottomLeft(m_topLeft.x(), m_bottomRight.y());
      painter.fillRect(makeRect(bottomLeft, Tolerance), Qt::black);
   }
}
```

The `write` and `read` methods first call their counterparts in `Figure` in order to write and read the color of the rectangle. Then it writes and reads the top-left and bottom-right corners:

```
bool RectangleX::write(ofstream& outStream) const {
 Figure::write(outStream);
 writePoint(outStream, m_topLeft);
 writePoint(outStream, m_bottomRight);
 return ((bool) outStream);
}
bool RectangleX::read (ifstream& inStream) {
  Figure::read(inStream);
  readPoint(inStream, m_topLeft);
  readPoint(inStream, m_bottomRight);
  return ((bool) inStream);
}
```

The Ellipse class

`EllipseX` is a direct sub class of `RectangleX` and an indirect subclass of `Figure` that draws a filled or unfilled ellipse:

EllipseX.h:

```
#ifndef ELLIPSE_H
#define ELLIPSE_H

#include "Rectangle.h"

class EllipseX : public RectangleX {
  public:
  EllipseX();
  FigureId getId() const {return EllipseId;}

  EllipseX(const EllipseX& ellipse);
  Figure* clone() const;
```

Similar to the preceding rectangle case, isClick checks whether the user grabs the ellipse in one of its four corners, or if the ellipse itself shall be moved:

```
bool isClick(QPoint mousePoint);
```

The modify method modifies the ellipse in accordance with the settings of following m_ellipseMode in preceding isClick:

```
void modify(QSize distance);
void draw(QPainter& painter) const;
```

While the preceding rectangle could be grabbed by its four corners, the ellipse can be grabbed by its left, top, right, and bottom points. Therefore, we need to add the CreateEllipse enumeration value, which modifies the bottom-right corner of the area covering the ellipse:

```
private:
  enum {CreateEllipse, LeftPoint, TopPoint, RightPoint,
      BottomPoint, MoveEllipse} m_ellipseMode;
  };

  #endif
```

EllipseX.cpp:

```
#include <CAssert>
#include "..\MainWindow\DocumentWidget.h"
#include "Ellipse.h"
```

In contrast to the preceding line and rectangle cases, we set the m_ellipseMode field to CreateEllipse, which is valid when the ellipse is being created only:

```
EllipseX::EllipseX()
 :m_ellipseMode(CreateEllipse) {
 // Empty.
 }
```

The copy constructor does not need to set the m_topLeft and m_bottomRight fields, since it is taken care of by the copy constructor of RectangleX, which is being called by the copy constructor of EllipseX:

```
EllipseX::EllipseX(const EllipseX& ellipse)
 :RectangleX(ellipse) {
 // Empty.
 }
```

```
Figure* EllipseX::clone() const {
  EllipseX* ellipsePtr = new EllipseX(*this);
  return ellipsePtr;
}
```

Similar to the preceding rectangle case, `isClick` checks whether the user grabs the ellipse by one of its four points. However, in the ellipse case, we do not check the corners of the rectangle. Instead, we check the left, top, right, and bottom position of the ellipse. We create a small square for each of those positions and check whether the user clicks on them. If they do, we set the `m_ellipseMode` field to an appropriate value and return `true`:

```
bool EllipseX::isClick(QPoint mousePoint) {
  QPoint leftPoint(m_topLeft.x(),
              (m_topLeft.y() + m_bottomRight.y()) / 2);
  QRect leftRect(makeRect(leftPoint, Tolerance));

  if (leftRect.contains(mousePoint)) {
    m_ellipseMode = LeftPoint;
    return true;
  }

  QPoint topPoint((m_topLeft.x() + m_bottomRight.x()) / 2,
           m_topLeft.y());
  QRect topRect(makeRect(topPoint, Tolerance));
  if (topRect.contains(mousePoint)) {
    m_ellipseMode = TopPoint;
    return true;
  }

  QPoint rightPoint(m_bottomRight.x(),
            (m_topLeft.y() + m_bottomRight.y()) / 2);
  QRect rightRect(makeRect(rightPoint, Tolerance));

  if (rightRect.contains(mousePoint)) {
    m_ellipseMode = RightPoint;
    return true;
  }

  QPoint bottomPoint((m_topLeft.x() + m_bottomRight.x()) / 2,
             m_bottomRight.y());
  QRect bottomRect(makeRect(bottomPoint, Tolerance));

  if (bottomRect.contains(mousePoint)) {
    m_ellipseMode = BottomPoint;
    return true;
  }
```

If the user does not click on any of the four positions, we check whether they click on the ellipse itself. If it is filled, we use the Qt QRegion class to create an elliptic region and we check whether the mouse point is located inside the region:

```
QRect normalRect(m_topLeft, m_bottomRight);
normalRect.normalized();

if (filled()) {
  QRegion normalEllipse(normalRect, QRegion::Ellipse);

  if (normalEllipse.contains(mousePoint)) {
    m_ellipseMode = MoveEllipse;
    return true;
  }
}
```

If the ellipse is unfilled, we create slightly larger and smaller elliptic regions and then check whether the mouse point is located inside the larger region, and also inside the smaller one:

```
else {
  QRect largeRect(normalRect), smallRect(normalRect);
  largeRect += Tolerance;
  smallRect -= Tolerance;

  QRegion largeEllipse(largeRect, QRegion::Ellipse),
      smallEllipse(smallRect, QRegion::Ellipse);

  if (largeEllipse.contains(mousePoint) &&
      !smallEllipse.contains(mousePoint)) {
    m_ellipseMode = MoveEllipse;
    return true;
  }
}
```

Finally, if the user does not click at any of the grabbing positions or the ellipse itself, we return `false`:

```
  return false;
}
```

The `modify` method modifies the ellipse in accordance with the settings of `m_ellipseMode` in `onClick`:

```
void EllipseX::modify(QSize distance) {
  switch (m_ellipseMode) {
    case CreateEllipse:
    m_bottomRight += distance;
```

```
      break;

    case LeftPoint:
    m_topLeft.setX(m_topLeft.x() + distance.width());
    break;

    case RightPoint:
    m_bottomRight.setX(m_bottomRight.x() + distance.width());
    break;

    case TopPoint:
    m_topLeft.setY(m_topLeft.y() + distance.height());
    break;

    case BottomPoint:
    m_bottomRight.setY(m_bottomRight.y() + distance.height());
    break;

    case MoveEllipse:
    move(distance);
    break;
  }
}
```

The `draw` method draws the ellipse with a solid brush if it is filled, and with a hollow brush if it is unfilled:

```
void EllipseX::draw(QPainter& painter) const {
  painter.setPen(color());
  if (filled()) {
    painter.setBrush(color());
    painter.drawEllipse(QRect(m_topLeft, m_bottomRight));
  }
  else {
    painter.setBrush(Qt::NoBrush);
    painter.drawEllipse(QRect(m_topLeft, m_bottomRight));
  }
```

If the ellipse is marked, the four squares covering the top, left, right, and bottom points of the ellipse are also drawn:

```
if (marked()) {
 QPoint leftPoint(m_topLeft.x(),
                  (m_topLeft.y() + m_bottomRight.y())/2);
 painter.fillRect(makeRect(leftPoint, Tolerance), Qt::black);

 QPoint topPoint((m_topLeft.x() + m_bottomRight.x()) / 2,
```

```
                        m_topLeft.y());
     painter.fillRect(makeRect(topPoint, Tolerance), Qt::black);

     QPoint rightPoint(m_bottomRight.x(),
                      (m_topLeft.y() + m_bottomRight.y()) / 2);
     painter.fillRect(makeRect(rightPoint, Tolerance), Qt::black);

     QPoint bottomPoint((m_topLeft.x() + m_bottomRight.x()) / 2,
                      m_bottomRight.y());
     painter.fillRect(makeRect(bottomPoint, Tolerance), Qt::black);
   }
}
```

The DrawingWindow class

The `DrawingWindow` class is similar to the version of the previous chapter. It overrides the `closeEvent` method.

DrawingWindow.h:

```
#ifndef DRAWINGWINDOW_H
#define DRAWINGWINDOW_H

#include <QMainWindow>
#include <QActionGroup>

#include "..\MainWindow\MainWindow.h"
#include "DrawingWidget.h"

class DrawingWindow : public MainWindow {
  Q_OBJECT

  public:
  DrawingWindow(QWidget *parentWidget = nullptr);
  ~DrawingWindow();

  public:
  void closeEvent(QCloseEvent *eventPtr)
      { m_drawingWidgetPtr->closeEvent(eventPtr); }

  private:
    DrawingWidget* m_drawingWidgetPtr;
    QActionGroup* m_figureGroupPtr;
};

#endif // DRAWINGWINDOW_H
```

DrawingWindow.cpp:

```
#include "..\MainWindow\DocumentWidget.h"
#include "DrawingWindow.h"
```

The constructor initializes the window size to *1000 x 500* pixels, puts the drawing widget in the middle of the window, adds the standard **File** and **Edit** menus, and adds the application-specific **Format** and Figure menus:

```
DrawingWindow::DrawingWindow(QWidget *parentWidget /*= nullptr*/)
 :MainWindow(parentWidget) {
  resize(1000, 500);

  m_drawingWidgetPtr = new DrawingWidget(this);
  setCentralWidget(m_drawingWidgetPtr);
  addFileMenu();
  addEditMenu();
```

The **Format** menu holds the `Color`, `Fill`, and `Modify` items as well as the Figure submenu:

```
{ QMenu* formatMenuPtr = menuBar()->addMenu(tr("F&ormat"));
  connect(formatMenuPtr, SIGNAL(aboutToShow()),
        this, SLOT(onMenuShow()));

  addAction(formatMenuPtr, tr("&Color"),
        SLOT(onColor()), QKeySequence(Qt::ALT + Qt::Key_C),
        QString(), nullptr, tr("Figure Color"));

  addAction(formatMenuPtr, tr("&Fill"),
        SLOT(onFill()), QKeySequence(Qt::CTRL + Qt::Key_F),
        QString(), nullptr, tr("Figure Fill"),
        LISTENER(isFillEnabled));
```

The user selects the **Modify** item when they want to mark or modify existing figures instead of adding new figures:

```
  m_figureGroupPtr = new QActionGroup(this);
  addAction(formatMenuPtr, tr("&Modify"),
        SLOT(onModify()),
        QKeySequence(Qt::CTRL + Qt::Key_M),
        QString(), nullptr, tr("Modify Figure"), nullptr,
        LISTENER(isModifyChecked), m_figureGroupPtr);
```

The Figure menu is a submenu holding the Line, Rectangle, and Ellipse items. It becomes a submenu when we add it to the **Format** menu:

```
{ QMenu* figureMenuPtr =
        formatMenuPtr->addMenu(tr("&Figure"));
  connect(figureMenuPtr, SIGNAL(aboutToShow()),
        this, SLOT(onMenuShow()));

  addAction(figureMenuPtr, tr("&Line"),
        SLOT(onLine()),
        QKeySequence(Qt::CTRL + Qt::Key_L),
        QString(), nullptr, tr("Line Figure"), nullptr,
        LISTENER(isLineChecked), m_figureGroupPtr);

  addAction(figureMenuPtr, tr("&Rectangle"),
        SLOT(onRectangle()),
        QKeySequence(Qt::CTRL + Qt::Key_R),
        QString(), nullptr, tr("Rectangle Figure"),
        nullptr, LISTENER(isRectangleChecked),
        m_figureGroupPtr);

  addAction(figureMenuPtr, tr("&Ellipse"),
        SLOT(onEllipse()),
        QKeySequence(Qt::CTRL + Qt::Key_E),
        QString(), nullptr, tr("Ellipse Figure"), nullptr,
        LISTENER(isEllipseChecked), m_figureGroupPtr);
  }
 }
}

DrawingWindow::~DrawingWindow() {
  delete m_figureGroupPtr;
}
```

The DrawingWidget class

The DrawingWidget class is the main class of the application. It catches the mouse and paint events. It also catches the menu item selections of the **File**, **Edit**, and Figure menus.

DrawingWidget.h:

```
#ifndef DRAWINGWIDGET_H
#define DRAWINGWIDGET_H

#include "..\MainWindow\MainWindow.h"
```

```
#include "..\MainWindow\DocumentWidget.h"
#include "Figure.h"

class DrawingWidget : public DocumentWidget {
  Q_OBJECT

  public:
  DrawingWidget(QWidget* parentWidget);
  ~DrawingWidget();
  public:
  void mousePressEvent(QMouseEvent *eventPtr);
  void mouseMoveEvent(QMouseEvent *eventPtr);
  void mouseReleaseEvent(QMouseEvent *eventPtr);
  void mouseDoubleClickEvent(QMouseEvent *eventPtr);
  void paintEvent(QPaintEvent *eventPtr);

  private:
  void newDocument(void);
  bool writeFile(const QString& filePath);
  bool readFile(const QString& filePath);
  Figure* createFigure(FigureId figureId);
```

Unlike the version of Chapter 5, *Qt Graphical Applications,* this version overrides the cut and copy event methods:

```
public slots:
  bool isCopyEnabled();
  void onCopy(void);
  bool isPasteEnabled();
  void onPaste(void);
  void onDelete(void);
  void onColor(void);

  DEFINE_LISTENER(DrawingWidget, isFillEnabled);
  void onFill(void);
  DEFINE_LISTENER(DrawingWidget, isModifyChecked);
  void onModify(void);

  DEFINE_LISTENER(DrawingWidget, isLineChecked);
  void onLine(void);

  DEFINE_LISTENER(DrawingWidget, isRectangleChecked);
  void onRectangle(void);

  DEFINE_LISTENER(DrawingWidget, isEllipseChecked);
  void onEllipse(void);
```

The m_applicationMode field holds the values Idle, ModifySingle, or ModifyRectangle. The Idle mode is active when the user is not pressing the mouse. The ModifySingle mode becomes active when the user grabs a figure and modifies or moves it (depending on which part of the figure the user grabs). Finally, the ModifyRectangle mode becomes active when the user clicks at the window without hitting a figure. In that case, a rectangle is shown, and every figure enclosed by the rectangle becomes marked when the user releases the mouse button. The user can delete or cut and paste the marked figure, or change their color or the filled status. When the user releases the mouse button, the Application mode again becomes Idle:

```
private:
    enum ApplicationMode {Idle, ModifySingle, ModifyRectangle};
    ApplicationMode m_applicationMode = Idle;
    void setApplicationMode(ApplicationMode mode);
```

The m_actionMode field holds the values Modify or Add. In Modify mode, when the user clicks with the mouse, m_applicationMode is set to ModifySingle or ModifyRectangle, depending on whether they hit a figure. In Add mode, a new figure is added, regardless of whether the user hits a figure. The kind of figure to be added is set by m_addFigureId, which holds the values LineId, RectangleId, or EllipseId:

```
enum ActionMode {Modify, Add};
ActionMode m_actionMode = Add;
FigureId m_addFigureId = LineId;
```

The color of the next figure to be added to the drawing is initialized to black, and the filled status is initialized to false (unfilled). In both cases, it can later be changed by the user:

```
QColor m_nextColor = Qt::black;
bool m_nextFilled = false;
```

We need to save the latest mouse point in order to calculate distances between mouse movements:

```
QPoint m_mousePoint;
```

Pointers to the figures of the drawing are stored in m_figurePtrList. The top-most figure is stored at the end of the list. When the user cuts or copies one or several figures, the figures are copied and the pointers to the copies are stored in m_copyPtrList:

```
QList<Figure*> m_figurePtrList, m_copyPtrList;
```

When `m_actionMode` holds `Modify` and the user presses the mouse button without hitting a figure, a rectangle becomes visible in the window. That rectangle is stored in `m_insideRectangle`:

```
    QRect m_insideRectangle;
};

#endif // DRAWINGWIDGET_H
```

DrawingWidget.cpp:

```
#include <CAssert>
#include "..\MainWindow\DocumentWidget.h"

#include "DrawingWidget.h"
#include "Line.h"
#include "Rectangle.h"
#include "Ellipse.h"
```

The constructor calls the constructor of the base class `DocumentWidget` to set the header of the window to `Drawing Advanced`, and to set the file suffix of the drawing files to `drw`:

```
DrawingWidget::DrawingWidget(QWidget* parentWidget)
:DocumentWidget(tr("Drawing Advanced"),
        tr("Drawing files (*.drw)"),
        parentWidget) {
  // Empty.
}
```

The destructor does nothing, it has been included for the sake of completeness only:

```
DrawingWidget::~DrawingWidget() {
  // Empty.
}
```

The `setApplicationMode` method sets the application mode and calls `onMenuShow` in the main window for the toolbar icons to be correctly enabled:

```
void DrawingWidget::setApplicationMode(ApplicationMode mode) {
  m_applicationMode = mode;
  ((MainWindow*) parent())->onMenuShow();
}
```

The `newDocument` method is called when the user selects the `New` menu item. We start by deallocating every figure in the figure and copy pointer lists, and they clear the list themselves:

```
void DrawingWidget::newDocument(void) {
  for (Figure* figurePtr : m_figurePtrList) {
    delete figurePtr;
  }

  for (Figure* copyPtr : m_copyPtrList) {
    delete copyPtr;
  }

  m_figurePtrList.clear();
  m_copyPtrList.clear();
```

The current color and filled status are set to black and false (unfilled). The action mode is set to `Add` and the add figure identity is set to `LineId`, which means that when the user presses the mouse button a black line is added to the drawing:

```
  m_nextColor = Qt::black;
  m_nextFilled = false;
  m_actionMode = Add;
  m_addFigureId = LineId;
}
```

The `writeFile` method is called when the user selects the `Save` or `Save As` menu items:

```
bool DrawingWidget::writeFile(const QString& filePath) {
  ofstream outStream(filePath.toStdString());
```

If the file was successfully opened, we start by writing the next color and filled status:

```
  if (outStream) {
    writeColor(outStream, m_nextColor);
    outStream.write((char*) &m_nextFilled, sizeof m_nextFilled);
```

We then write the number of figures in the drawing, and then we write the figures themselves:

```
    int size = m_figurePtrList.size();
    outStream.write((char*) &size, sizeof size);
```

For each figure, first we write its identity value, we then write the figure itself by calling `write` on its pointer. Note that we do not know which class the figure pointer points at. We do not need to know that, since `write` is a pure virtual method in the base class `Figure`:

```
for (Figure* figurePtr : m_figurePtrList) {
  FigureId figureId = figurePtr->getId();
  outStream.write((char*) &figureId, sizeof figureId);
  figurePtr->write(outStream);
}
```

We return the output stream converted to `bool`, which is true if the writing was successful:

```
  return ((bool) outStream);
}
```

If the file was not successfully opened, we return `false`:

```
  return false;
}
```

The `readFile` method is called when the user selects the **Open** menu item. We read the parts of the file in the same order as we wrote them in the preceding `writeFile`:

```
bool DrawingWidget::readFile(const QString& filePath) {
  ifstream inStream(filePath.toStdString());
```

If the file was successfully opened, we start by reading the next color and filled status:

```
  if (inStream) {
    readColor(inStream, m_nextColor);
    inStream.read((char*) &m_nextFilled, sizeof m_nextFilled);
```

We then write the number of figures in the drawing, and then we write the figures themselves:

```
    int size;
    inStream.read((char*) &size, sizeof size);
```

For each figure, first we read its identity value, we then create a figure of the class indicated by the identity value by calling `createFigure`. Finally, we read the figure itself by calling `write` on its pointer:

```
    for (int count = 0; count < size; ++count) {
      FigureId figureId = (FigureId) 0;
      inStream.read((char*) &figureId, sizeof figureId);
      Figure* figurePtr = createFigure(figureId);
      figurePtr->read(inStream);
```

```
                m_figurePtrList.push_back(figurePtr);
        }
```

We return the input stream converted to `bool`, which is true if the reading was successful:

```
            return ((bool) inStream);
        }
```

If the file was not successfully opened, we return `false`:

```
        return false;
    }
```

The `createFigure` method dynamically creates an object of the `Line`, `RectangleX`, or `EllipseX` class, depending on the value of the `figureId` parameter:

```
            Figure* DrawingWidget::createFigure(FigureId figureId) {
              Figure* figurePtr = nullptr;

              switch (figureId) {
                case LineId:
                  figurePtr = new Line();
                  break;

                case RectangleId:
                  figurePtr = new RectangleX();
                  break;

                case EllipseId:
                  figurePtr = new EllipseX();
                  break;
              }

              return figurePtr;
            }
```

The `isCopyEnable` method is called before the **Edit** menu becomes visible in order to enable the Copy item. It is also called by the framework in order to enable the Copy toolbar icon. It returns `true` if at least one figure is marked, and by then it is ready to be copied. If it returns `true`, the Copy item and toolbar icon become enabled:

```
            bool DrawingWidget::isCopyEnabled() {
              for (Figure* figurePtr : m_figurePtrList) {
                if (figurePtr->marked()) {
                  return true;
                }
              }
```

```
        return false;
    }
```

The `onCopy` method is called when the user selects the **Copy** menu item. To start with, it deallocates every figure in the copy pointer list and clears the list itself:

```
void DrawingWidget::onCopy(void) {
    for (Figure* copyPtr : m_copyPtrList) {
        delete copyPtr;
    }
    m_copyPtrList.clear();
```

Then, we iterate through the figure pointer list and add the pointer to a copy of each marked figure to the copy pointer list. We call `clone` on each figure pointer to provide us with the copy:

```
    for (Figure* figurePtr : m_figurePtrList) {
        if (figurePtr->marked()) {
            m_copyPtrList.push_back(figurePtr->clone());
        }
    }
}
```

The `isPasteEnabled` method is called before the **Edit** menu becomes visible to enable the Paste item. It is also called by the framework to enable the paste toolbar icon. If the copy pointer list is not empty, it returns `true`, and thereby enables the Paste item and image. That is, it returns `true` if there are figures ready to be pasted:

```
bool DrawingWidget::isPasteEnabled() {
    return !m_copyPtrList.isEmpty();
}
```

The `onPaste` method is called when the user selects the **Paste** item in the **Edit** menu, or when they select the paste image in the edit toolbar. We iterate through the copy pointer list and add a copy (which we obtain by calling `clone`) of the figure to the figure pointer list, after we have moved it 10 pixels downwards and to the right:

```
void DrawingWidget::onPaste(void) {
    for (Figure* copyPtr : m_copyPtrList) {
        Figure* pastePtr = copyPtr->clone();
        pastePtr->move(QSize(10, 10));
        m_figurePtrList.push_back(pastePtr);
    }
```

Finally, when the figures have been added to the list, we force an eventual call to the
`paintEvent` by calling `update`:

```
        update();
    }
```

The `onDelete` method is called every time the user selects the **Delete** menu item or toolbar
icon. We iterate through the figure pointer list and remove every marked figure:

```
void DrawingWidget::onDelete(void) {
    for (Figure* figurePtr : m_figurePtrList) {
      if (figurePtr->marked()) {
      m_figurePtrList.removeOne(figurePtr);
      delete figurePtr;
      }
    }
```

Also, in this case, we force an eventual call to `paintEvent` by calling the `update` method,
after the figures have been deleted:

```
        update();
    }
```

The `onColor` method is called every time the user selects the `Color` item in the **Format**
menu. We start by obtaining the new color by calling the static method `getColor` in the Qt
`QColorDialog` class:

```
void DrawingWidget::onColor(void) {
    QColor newColor = QColorDialog::getColor(m_nextColor, this);
```

If the color is valid, which it is if the user has closed the dialog by pressing the **Ok** button
rather than the **Cancel** button, and if they have chosen a new color, we set the next color to
the new color and set the modified flag. We also iterate through the figure pointer list and,
for each marked figure, set the color of the figure:

```
    if (newColor.isValid() && (m_nextColor != newColor)) {
      m_nextColor = newColor;
      setModifiedFlag(true);

      for (Figure* figurePtr : m_figurePtrList) {
        if (figurePtr->marked()) {
          figurePtr->color() = m_nextColor;
```

If at least one figure is marked, we force an eventual call to `paintEvent` by calling update:

```
            update();
        }
    }
  }
}
```

The `isFillEnabled` method is called before the `Fill` item in the **Format** menu becomes visible:

```
bool DrawingWidget::isFillEnabled(void) {
  switch (m_actionMode) {
```

In `Modify` mode, we iterate through the figure pointer list. If at least one rectangle or ellipse is marked, we return `true` and the item becomes enabled:

```
case Modify:
  for (Figure* figurePtr : m_figurePtrList) {
    if (figurePtr->marked() &&
        ((figurePtr->getId() == RectangleId) ||
         (figurePtr->getId() == EllipseId))) {
      return true;
    }
  }
```

If no rectangle or ellipse is marked, we return `false` and the item becomes disabled:

```
    return false;
```

In the `Add` mode, we return `true` if the next figure to be added by the user is a rectangle or an ellipse:

```
case Add:
  return (m_addFigureId == RectangleId) ||
         (m_addFigureId == EllipseId);
}
```

We are not supposed to reach this point. The `assert` macro call is for debugging purposes only. However, we still must return a value at the end of the method:

```
  assert(false);
  return true;
}
```

The `onFill` method is called when the user selects the `Fill` item in the **Format** menu:

```
void DrawingWidget::onFill(void) {
  switch (m_actionMode) {
```

In the `Modify` mode, we iterate through the figure pointer list and invert the filled status of all marked figures. If at least one figure changes, we force an eventual call to `paintEvent` by calling `update`:

```
case Modify:
  for (Figure* figurePtr : m_figurePtrList) {
    if (figurePtr->marked()) {
      figurePtr->filled() = !figurePtr->filled();
      update();
    }
  }
```

We also invert the filled status of the next figure to be added:

```
m_nextFilled = !m_nextFilled;
break;
```

In the `Add` mode, we invert the filled status of the next figure to be added by the user:

```
case Add:
  m_nextFilled = !m_nextFilled;
  break;
  }
}
```

The `isModifyChecked` method is called before the `Modify` item in the **Format** menu becomes visible. In `Modify` mode, it returns `true` and enables the item:

```
bool DrawingWidget::isModifyChecked(void) {
  return (m_actionMode == Modify);
}
```

The `onModify` method is called when the user selects the `Modify` item in the **Format** menu. It sets the action mode to `Modify`:

```
void DrawingWidget::onModify(void) {
  m_actionMode = Modify;
}
```

The isLineChecked method is called before the Line item in the Add submenu becomes visible. It returns true, and the item becomes checked (with a radio button, since the item belongs to a group) in case of add action mode, and the next figure to be added is a line:

```
bool DrawingWidget::isLineChecked(void) {
    return (m_actionMode == Add) && (m_addFigureId == LineId);
}
```

The onLine method is called when the user selects the Line item in the Add submenu. It set the action mode to Add and the next figure to be added by the user to a line:

```
void DrawingWidget::onLine(void) {
    m_actionMode = Add;
    m_addFigureId = LineId;
}
```

The isRectangleChecked method is called before the Rectangle item in the Add submenu becomes visible. It returns true in case of Add action mode and if the next figure to be added is a rectangle:

```
bool DrawingWidget::isRectangleChecked(void) {
    return (m_actionMode == Add) && (m_addFigureId == RectangleId);
}
```

The onRectangle method is called when the user selects the Rectangle item. It sets the action mode to Add and the next figure to be added by the user to a rectangle:

```
void DrawingWidget::onRectangle(void) {
    m_actionMode = Add;
    m_addFigureId = RectangleId;
}
```

The isEllipseChecked method is called before the Ellipse item in the Add submenu becomes visible. It returns true in case of Add action mode and if the next figure to be added is an ellipse:

```
bool DrawingWidget::isEllipseEnabled(void) {
    return !isEllipseChecked();
}
```

The onEllipse method is called when the user selects the Ellipse item. It sets the action mode to Add and the next figure to be added by the user to an ellipse:

```
void DrawingWidget::onEllipse(void) {
    m_actionMode = Add;
    m_addFigureId = EllipseId;
```

```
    }
```

The `mousePressEvent` method is called when the user presses one of the mouse buttons. We store the mouse point in `m_mousePoint`, to be used in `mouseMoveEvent` as follows:

```
void DrawingWidget::mousePressEvent(QMouseEvent* eventPtr) {
    if (eventPtr->buttons() == Qt::LeftButton) {
    m_mousePoint = eventPtr->pos();
```

In case of `Modify` mode, we first iterate through the figure pointer list and unmark every figure:

```
switch (m_actionMode) {
  case Modify: {
      for (Figure* figurePtr : m_figurePtrList) {
       figurePtr->marked() = false;
      }
```

We then iterate through the list again, to find if the user has hit a figure. Since the top-most figure is placed at the end of the list, we need to iterate through the list backward. We do so by using the `reverse_iterator` type of the Qt `QList` class:

```
m_clickedFigurePtr = nullptr;
for (QList<Figure*>::reverse_iterator iterator =
    m_figurePtrList.rbegin();
iterator != m_figurePtrList.rend(); ++iterator) {
    Figure* figurePtr = *iterator;
```

If we found out (by calling `isClick` on the figure) that a figure has been hit by the user's mouse click, we set the application mode to `ModifySingle` and mark the figure. We also remove it from the list and add it to the end of the list, to make it appear top-most in the drawing. Finally, we break the loop since we have found a figure:

```
if (figurePtr->isClick(m_mousePoint)) {
  setApplicationMode(ModifySingle);
  m_clickedFigurePtr = figurePtr;
  figurePtr->marked() = true;
  m_figurePtrList.removeOne(figurePtr);
  m_figurePtrList.push_back(figurePtr);
  break;
}
}
```

If we have not found a figure, we set the application mode to ModifyRectangle and initialize the top-most and bottom-right corners of the enclosing rectangle to the mouse point:

```
      if (m_clickedFigurePtr == nullptr) {
        setApplicationMode(ModifyRectangle);
        m_insideRectangle = QRect(m_mousePoint, m_mousePoint);
      }
    }
    break;
```

In case of Add action mode, we create a new figure by calling createFigure with the identity of the next figure to be added by the user as a parameter. We then set the color, filled status of the new figure, and initialize its endpoints:

```
    case Add: {
        Figure* newFigurePtr = createFigure(m_addFigureId);
        newFigurePtr->color() = m_nextColor;
        newFigurePtr->filled() = m_nextFilled;
        newFigurePtr->initializePoints(m_mousePoint);
```

When the new figure has been created and initialized, we add it at the end of the figure pointer list and set the application mode to ModifySingle, since the mouseMoveEvent method will continue to modify the last figure in the list, just as if the user had hit a figure in the Modify mode. We also set the modified flag since we have added a figure to the drawing:

```
      m_figurePtrList.push_back(newFigurePtr);
      setApplicationMode(ModifySingle);
      setModifiedFlag(true);
      }
      break;
    }
```

Finally, we force an eventual call to paintEvent by calling update:

```
        update();
      }
    }
```

The mouseMoveEvent method is called when the user moves the mouse. If they also press the left mouse button, we save the mouse point to future calls to mouseMoveEvent and calculate the distance since the last call to mousePressEvent or mouseMoveEvent:

```
    void DrawingWidget::mouseMoveEvent(QMouseEvent* eventPtr) {
        if (eventPtr->buttons() == Qt::LeftButton) {
```

```
QPoint newMousePoint = eventPtr->pos();
QSize distance(newMousePoint.x() - m_mousePoint.x(),
               newMousePoint.y() - m_mousePoint.y());
m_mousePoint = newMousePoint;
```

In the `Modify` mode, we modify the current figure (the figure placed at the end of the figure pointer list) by calling `modify`. Remember that the figure can be either modified or moved, depending on the settings in the call to `isClick` in `onMousePress` previously. We also set the modified flag since the figure has been altered:

```
switch (m_applicationMode) {
  case ModifySingle:
    m_figurePtrList.back()->modify(distance);
    setModifiedFlag(true);
    break;
```

In case of the enclosing rectangle, we just update its bottom-right corner. Note that we do not set the modified flag since no figure has yet been altered:

```
case ModifyRectangle:
  m_insideRectangle.setBottomRight(m_mousePoint);
  break;
}
```

Finally, we force an eventual call to `paintEvent` by calling `update`:

```
    update();
  }
}
```

The `mouseReleaseEvent` method is called when the user releases a mouse button. If it is the left mouse button, we check the application mode. The only mode we actually are interested in is the enclosing rectangle mode:

```
void DrawingWidget::mouseReleaseEvent(QMouseEvent* eventPtr) {
  if (eventPtr->buttons() == Qt::LeftButton) {
    switch (m_applicationMode) {
      case ModifyRectangle: {
        QList<Figure*> insidePtrList;
```

We iterate through the figure pointer list and call `isInside` on each figure. Each figure that is completely enclosed by the rectangle becomes marked, removed from the list, and added to `insidePtrList` to be later added at the end of the figure pointer list:

```
for (Figure* figurePtr : m_figurePtrList) {
  if (figurePtr->isInside(m_insideRectangle)) {
    figurePtr->marked() = true;
```

```
        m_figurePtrList.removeOne(figurePtr);
        insidePtrList.push_back(figurePtr);
      }
    }
```

Each figure which is completely enclosed by the rectangle is removed from the figure pointer list:

```
    for (Figure* figurePtr : insidePtrList) {
      m_figurePtrList.removeOne(figurePtr);
    }
```

Finally, all enclosed figures are added at the end of the list in order to appear top-most in the drawing:

```
    m_figurePtrList.append(insidePtrList);
    }
    break;
  }
```

When the user has released the mouse button, the application mode is set to idle, and we force an eventual call to `paintEvent` by calling `update`:

```
    setApplicationMode(Idle);
    update();
   }
  }
```

The `mouseDoubleClick` method is called when the user double-clicks one of the buttons. However, `mouseClickEvent` is always called before `mouseDoubleClickEvent`. If the preceding call to `mouseClickEvent` has made `m_clickedFigurePtr` point at the clicked figure, we call `doubleClick` on that figure. This may cause some change in the figure, depending on which kind of figure it is:

```
    void DrawingWidget::mouseDoubleClickEvent(QMouseEvent
      *eventPtr) {
    if ((eventPtr->buttons() == Qt::LeftButton) &&
        (m_clickedFigurePtr != nullptr)) {
      m_clickedFigurePtr->doubleClick(eventPtr->pos());
      update();
    }
  }
```

Finally, `paintEvent` is called when the content of the window needs to be repainted. Before the call, the framework clears the window:

```
void DrawingWidget::paintEvent(QPaintEvent* /*
   eventPtr */) {
QPainter painter(this);
painter.setRenderHint(QPainter::Antialiasing);
painter.setRenderHint(QPainter::TextAntialiasing);
```

We iterate through the figure pointer list and draw every figure. The last figure in the list is placed at the end of the list, to appear at the top of the drawing:

```
for (Figure* figurePtr : m_figurePtrList) {
   figurePtr->draw(painter);
}
```

In case of enclosing rectangle mode, we draw a hollow rectangle with a light-gray border:

```
if (m_applicationMode == ModifyRectangle) {
   painter.setPen(Qt::lightGray);
   painter.setBrush(Qt::NoBrush);
   painter.drawRect(m_insideRectangle);
}
}
```

The main function

The `main` function is similar to the `main` function of the previous applications—it creates an application, shows the drawing window, and starts the execution of the application.

Main.cpp:

```
#include "DrawingWindow.h"
#include <QApplication>

int main(int argc, char *argv[]) {
  QApplication application(argc, argv);
  DrawingWindow drawingWindow;
  drawingWindow.show();
  return application.exec();
}
```

The output is shown in the following screenshot:

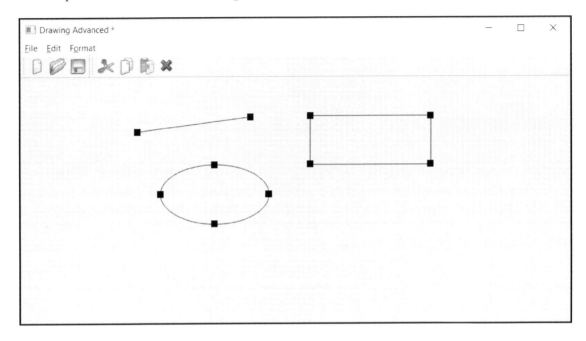

Improving the editor

The editor of this chapter is a more advanced version of the editor of Chapter 5, *Qt Graphical Applications*. In this version, it is possible to change the font and alignment of the text, to mark text, and to cut and paste text.

The EditorWindow class

The EditorWindow class of this chapter is similar to the class of Chapter 5, *Qt Graphical Applications*. It catches the key pressing event and the window closing event.

EditorWindow.h:

```
#ifndef EDITORWINDOW_H
#define EDITORWINDOW_H

#include <QMainWindow>
#include <QActionGroup>
```

```
#include <QPair>
#include <QMap>

#include "..\MainWindow\MainWindow.h"
#include "EditorWidget.h"

class EditorWindow : public MainWindow {
  Q_OBJECT

  public:
  EditorWindow(QWidget *parentWidgetPtr = nullptr);
  ~EditorWindow();

  protected:
  void keyPressEvent(QKeyEvent* eventPtr);
  void closeEvent(QCloseEvent* eventPtr);

  private:
  EditorWidget* m_editorWidgetPtr;
  QActionGroup* m_alignmentGroupPtr;
};

#endif // EDITORWINDOW_H
```

EditorWindow.cpp:

```
#include "EditorWindow.h"
#include <QtWidgets>
```

The constructor initializes the editor window. It sets the size of the window to *1000 x 500* pixels. It also dynamically creates an editor widget and adds the standard **File** and **Edit** menus:

```
EditorWindow::EditorWindow(QWidget *parentWidgetPtr /*= nullptr*/)
 :MainWindow(parentWidgetPtr) {
  resize(1000, 500);

  m_editorWidgetPtr = new EditorWidget(this);
  setCentralWidget(m_editorWidgetPtr);
  addFileMenu();
  addEditMenu();
```

The Figure menu is different, compared to Chapter 5, *Qt Graphical Applications*. We add the item Font and the submenu Alignment, to which, in turn, we add the three items: left, center, and right:

```
{ QMenu* formatMenuPtr = menuBar()->addMenu(tr("F&ormat"));
```

```
connect(formatMenuPtr, SIGNAL(aboutToShow()), this,
    SLOT(onMenuShow()));
addAction(formatMenuPtr, tr("&Font"), SLOT(onFont()),
    0, QString(), nullptr, QString(),
    LISTENER(isFontEnabled));

{ QMenu* alignmentMenuPtr =
    formatMenuPtr->addMenu(tr("&Alignment"));
 connect(alignmentMenuPtr, SIGNAL(aboutToShow()),
    this, SLOT(onMenuShow()));
```

We also add a toolbar for the `Alignment` menu:

```
QToolBar* alignmentToolBarPtr = addToolBar(tr("Alignment"));
m_alignmentGroupPtr = new QActionGroup(this);

addAction(alignmentMenuPtr, tr("&Left"), SLOT(onLeft()),
    QKeySequence(Qt::ALT + Qt::Key_L), tr("left"),
    alignmentToolBarPtr, tr("Left-aligned text"),
    nullptr, LISTENER(isLeftChecked));
addAction(alignmentMenuPtr, tr("&Center"),
    SLOT(onCenter()),
    QKeySequence(Qt::ALT + Qt::Key_C),
    tr("center"), alignmentToolBarPtr,
    tr("Center-aligned text"), nullptr,
    LISTENER(isCenterChecked));
addAction(alignmentMenuPtr, tr("&Right"),
    SLOT(onRight()),
    QKeySequence(Qt::ALT + Qt::Key_R),
    tr("right"), alignmentToolBarPtr,
    tr("Right-aligned text"), nullptr,
    LISTENER(isRightChecked));
    }
  }

 m_editorWidgetPtr->setModifiedFlag(false);
}

EditorWindow::~EditorWindow() {
 delete m_alignmentGroupPtr;
}
```

The key pressing event and the window closing event are passed on to the editor widget:

```
void EditorWindow::keyPressEvent(QKeyEvent* eventPtr) {
  m_editorWidgetPtr->keyPressEvent(eventPtr);
}
```

```
void EditorWindow::closeEvent(QCloseEvent* eventPtr) {
  m_editorWidgetPtr->closeEvent(eventPtr);
}
```

The EditorWidget class

The `EditorWidget` class is similar to the version of Chapter 5, *Qt Graphical Applications*. However, methods and listeners to handle the font and alignment have been added.

EditorWidget.h:

```
#ifndef EDITORWIDGET_H
#define EDITORWIDGET_H

#include <QWidget>
#include <QMap>
#include <QMenu>
#include <QToolBar>
#include <QPair>
#include "Caret.h"

#include "..\MainWindow\Listener.h"
#include "..\MainWindow\DocumentWidget.h"

class EditorWidget : public DocumentWidget {
  Q_OBJECT

  public:
  EditorWidget(QWidget* parentWidgetPtr);
  void keyPressEvent(QKeyEvent* eventPtr);

  private:
  void keyEditPressEvent(QKeyEvent* eventPtr);
  void keyMarkPressEvent(QKeyEvent* eventPtr);
```

The `mousePresseEvent`, `mouseMoveEvent`, and `mouseReleaseEvent` are called when the user presses a mouse button, moves the mouse, and releases the mouse button:

```
  public:
    void mousePressEvent(QMouseEvent* eventPtr);
    void mouseMoveEvent(QMouseEvent* eventPtr);
    void mouseReleaseEvent(QMouseEvent* eventPtr);

  private:
    int mouseToIndex(QPoint point);
```

```
public:
    void paintEvent(QPaintEvent* eventPtr);
    void resizeEvent(QResizeEvent* eventPtr);
```

The `newDocument` method is called when the user selects the **New** menu item, `writeFile` is called when they select **Save** or **Save As**, and `readFile` is called when they select the **Open** menu item:

```
private:
    void newDocument(void);
    bool writeFile(const QString& filePath);
    bool readFile(const QString& filePath);

public slots:
    bool isCopyEnabled();
    void onCopy(void);
    bool isPasteEnabled();
    void onPaste(void);
    void onDelete(void);

    DEFINE_LISTENER(EditorWidget, isFontEnabled);
    void onFont(void);
```

The `isLeftChecked`, `isCenterChecked`, and `isRightChecked` methods are called before the `Alignment` submenu becomes visible. They then annotate a radio button to the selected alignment:

```
    DEFINE_LISTENER(EditorWidget, isLeftChecked);
    DEFINE_LISTENER(EditorWidget, isCenterChecked);
    DEFINE_LISTENER(EditorWidget, isRightChecked);
```

The `onLeft`, `onCenter`, and `onRight` methods are called when the user selects one of the items of the Alignment submenu:

```
    void onLeft(void);
    void onCenter(void);
    void onRight(void);

private:
    void setCaret();
    void simulateMouseClick(int x, int y);
```

In this version of the editor, we have two modes—edit and mark. The edit mark is active when the user inputs text or moves the caret with the arrow key, while the mark mode is active when the user has marked a block of the code with the mouse. The caret is visible in edit mode, but not in mark mode:

```
private:
   enum Mode {Edit, Mark} m_mode;
```

The text can be aligned in the left, center, and right direction:

```
enum Alignment {Left, Center, Right} m_alignment;
```

In edit mode, m_editIndex holds the index to place the next character to be input by the user, which also is the position of the caret. In mark mode, m_firstIndex and m_lastIndex hold the indexes of the first and last marked character:

```
int m_editIndex, m_firstIndex, m_lastIndex;
```

The m_caret object holds the caret of the editor. The caret is visible in edit mode, but not in mark mode:

```
Caret m_caret;
```

The m_editorText field holds the text of the editor, and m_copyText holds the text which is cut or pasted by the user:

```
QString m_editorText, m_copyText;
```

The text of the editor is divided into lines; the index of the first and last character of each line is stored in m_lineList:

```
QList<QPair<int,int>> m_lineList;
```

The current font of the text is stored in m_textFont. The height in pixels of a character of the current font is stored in m_fontHeight:

```
QFont m_textFont;
int m_fontHeight;
```

The mousePressEvent and mouseMoveEvent methods store the last mouse point in order to calculate the distance between mouse events:

```
Qt::MouseButton m_button;
```

Similar to the method of Chapter 5, *Qt Graphical Applications*, calculate is an auxiliary method that calculates the enclosing rectangle of each character of the text. However, the version of this chapter is more complicated since it has to take into consideration whether the text is left, center, or right-aligned:

```
void calculate();
```

The enclosing rectangles are stored in m_rectList, and then used by the caret and paintEvent:

```
QList<QRect> m_rectList;
};
```

```
#endif // EDITORWIDGET_H
```

EditorWidget.cpp:

```
#include "EditorWidget.h"
#include <QtWidgets>
#include <CAssert>
using namespace std;
```

The constructor sets the window header to Editor Advanced and the file suffix to edi:

```
EditorWidget::EditorWidget(QWidget* parentWidgetPtr)
  :DocumentWidget(tr("Editor Advanced"),
     tr("Editor files (*.edi)"), parentWidgetPtr),
```

The text font is initialized to 12 point Times New Roman. The application mode is set to edit, the index of the next character to be input by the user is set to zero, and the text is left-aligned from the beginning:

```
m_textFont(tr("Times New Roman"), 12),
  m_mode(Edit),
  m_editIndex(0),
  m_alignment(Left),
  m_caret(this) {
```

The rectangles enclosing the characters are calculated by calculate, the caret is initialized and shown since the application holds edit mode from the beginning:

```
calculate();
setCaret();
m_caret.show();
}
```

The `newDocument` method is called when the user selects the **New** menu item. We start by setting the application mode to edit and the edit index to zero. The text font is set to 12 point Times New Roman. The text of the editor is cleared, the rectangles enclosing the characters are calculated by `calculate`, and the caret is set:

```
void EditorWidget::newDocument(void) {
    m_mode = Edit;
    m_editIndex = 0;
    m_textFont = QFont(tr("Times New Roman"), 12);
    m_editorText.clear();
    calculate();
    setCaret();
}
```

The `writeFile` method is called when the user selects the **Save** or **Save As** menu items. The file format is quite simple: we write the font on the first line, and then the text of the editor on the following lines:

```
bool EditorWidget::writeFile(const QString& filePath) {
    QFile file(filePath);
    if (file.open(QIODevice::WriteOnly | QIODevice::Text)) {
        QTextStream outStream(&file);
        outStream << m_textFont.toString() << endl << m_editorText;
```

We use the `Ok` field of the input stream to decide if the writing was successful:

```
        return ((bool) outStream.Ok);
    }
```

If we could not open the file for writing, we return `false`:

```
    return false;
}
```

The `readFile` method is called when the user selects the **Open** menu items. Similar to `writeFile` previously, we read the first line and initialize the text font with the text. We then read the editor text:

```
bool EditorWidget::readFile(const QString& filePath) {
    QFile file(filePath);

    if (file.open(QIODevice::ReadOnly | QIODevice::Text)) {
        QTextStream inStream(&file);
        m_textFont.fromString(inStream.readLine());
        m_editorText = inStream.readAll();
```

When the text is read, we call `calculate` to calculate the rectangles enclosing the characters of the text. We then set the caret and return `true`, since the reading was successful:

```
calculate();
setCaret();
```

We use the `Ok` field of the input stream to decide if the reading was successful:

```
    return ((bool) inStream.Ok);
}
```

If we could not open the file for reading, we `return false`:

```
    return false;
}
```

The `isCopyEnabled` method is called before the **Edit** menu becomes visible. It is also called by the framework to decide whether the copy toolbar icon shall be enabled. It returns true (and the item becomes enabled) if the application holds mark mode, which means that the user has marked a part of the text, which can be copied:

```
bool EditorWidget::isCopyEnabled() {
    return (m_mode == Mark);
}
```

The `onCopy` method is called when the user selects the **Copy** item. We copy the marked text into `m_EditorText`:

```
void EditorWidget::onCopy(void) {
    int minIndex = qMin(m_firstIndex, m_lastIndex),
    maxIndex = qMax(m_firstIndex, m_lastIndex);

    m_copyText =
        m_editorText.mid(minIndex, maxIndex - minIndex + 1);
}
```

The `isPasteEnabled` method is also called before the **Edit** menu becomes visible. It returns `true` (and the item becomes visible) if the copy text is not empty. That is, if there is a block of text that has been copied and is ready to be pasted:

```
bool EditorWidget::isPasteEnabled() {
    return !m_copyText.isEmpty();
}
```

The `onPaste` method is called when the user selects the Paste menu item. In mark mode, we call `onDelete`, which causes the marked text to be deleted:

```
void EditorWidget::onPaste(void) {
  if (m_mode == Mark) {
    onDelete();
  }
```

We then insert the copied text into the editor text. We also update `m_editIndex`, since the edit index after the text has been copied shall be the position after the inserted text:

```
m_editorText.insert(m_editIndex, m_copyText);
m_editIndex += m_copyText.size();
```

Finally, we calculate the rectangles enclosing the characters of the text, set the caret to the new index, set the modified flag since the text has been altered, and call `update` to force an eventual call to `paintEvent` in order to display the new text:

```
calculate();
setCaret();
setModifiedFlag(true);
update();
}
```

The `onDelete` method is called when the user selects the **Delete** menu item or the **Delete** toolbar icon. The effect is similar to the event when the user presses the *Delete* key. Therefore, we prepare a keypress event with the *Delete* key, which we use as a parameter in the call to `keyPressEvent`.

Note that there is no `isDeleteEnabled` method because the user can always use the **Delete** item. In edit mode, the next character is deleted. In mark mode, the marked text is deleted:

```
void EditorWidget::onDelete(void) {
  QKeyEvent event(QEvent::KeyPress, Qt::Key_Delete,
            Qt::NoModifier);
  keyPressEvent(&event);
}
```

`isCopyEnabled` is called before the **Format** menu becomes visible. It returns `true` in edit mode, since it would be illogical to change the font on all characters when a subset of them is marked:

```
bool EditorWidget::isFontEnabled() {
  return (m_mode == Edit);
}
```

The onFont method is called when the user selects the Font menu item. We let the user select the new font with the Qt QFontDialog class:

```
void EditorWidget::onFont(void) {
  bool pressedOkButton;
  QFont newFont =
    QFontDialog::getFont(&pressedOkButton, m_textFont, this);
```

If the user closes the dialog by pressing the **Ok** button, we set the font of the editor (m_textFont) field and the modified flag:

```
if (pressedOkButton) {
  m_textFont = newFont;
  setModifiedFlag(true);
```

We calculate the newly enclosed rectangles by calling calculate, set the caret, and force an eventual call to paintEvent by calling update:

```
    calculate();
    m_caret.set(m_rectList[m_editIndex]);
    update();
  }
}
```

The isLeftChecked, isCenterChecked, and isRightChecked methods are called before the alignment submenu becomes visible. They return true to the current alignment:

```
bool EditorWidget::isLeftChecked(void) {
  return (m_alignment == Left);
}

bool EditorWidget::isCenterChecked(void) {
  return (m_alignment == Center);
}

bool EditorWidget::isRightChecked(void) {
  return (m_alignment == Right);
}
```

The onLeft, onCenter, and onRight methods are called when the user selects the Left, Center, and Right menu item. They set the alignment and the modified flag.

They also calculate the new enclosing rectangles, set the caret, and force an eventual call to `paintEvent` by calling `update`:

```
void EditorWidget::onLeft(void) {
  m_alignment = Left;
  setModifiedFlag(true);
  calculate();
  setCaret();
  update();
}

void EditorWidget::onCenter(void) {
  m_alignment = Center;
  setModifiedFlag(true);
  calculate();
  setCaret();
  update();
}

void EditorWidget::onRight(void) {
  m_alignment = Right;
  setModifiedFlag(true);
  calculate();
  setCaret();
  update();
}
```

The `mousePressEvent` method is called when the user presses one of the mouse buttons. We call `mouseToIndex` to find the character index the user clicked on. For the time being, both the first and last mark index is set to the mouse index. The last index may later be changed by a call to `mouseMoveEvent` in the following snippet. Finally, the mode is set to mark, and the caret is hidden:

```
void EditorWidget::mousePressEvent(QMouseEvent* eventPtr) {
  if (eventPtr->buttons() == Qt::LeftButton) {
    m_firstIndex = m_lastIndex = mouseToIndex(eventPtr->pos());
    m_mode = Mark;
    m_caret.hide();
  }
}
```

The `mouseMoveEvent` method is called when the user moves the mouse. We set the last mark index to the mouse index and force an eventual call to `paintEvent` by calling `update`:

```
void EditorWidget::mouseMoveEvent(QMouseEvent* eventPtr) {
  if (eventPtr->buttons() == Qt::LeftButton) {
    m_lastIndex = mouseToIndex(eventPtr->pos());
    update();
  }
}
```

The `mouseReleaseEvent` method is called when the user releases the mouse button. If the user has moved the mouse to the original start position of the mouse movement, there is nothing to mark and we set the application in edit mode. In that case, we set the edit index to the first mark index, and set and show the caret (since it shall be visible in edit mode). Finally, we force an eventual call to `paintEvent` by calling `update`:

```
void EditorWidget::mouseReleaseEvent(QMouseEvent* eventPtr) {
  if (eventPtr->buttons() == Qt::LeftButton) {
    if (m_firstIndex == m_lastIndex) {
      m_mode = Edit;
      m_editIndex = m_firstIndex;
      setCaret();
      m_caret.show();
      update();
    }
  }
}
```

`keyPressEvent` is called when the user presses a key on the keyboard. Depending on the application mode (edit or mark), we call `keyEditPressEvent` or the following `keyMarkPressEvent` to further process the key event:

```
void EditorWidget::keyPressEvent(QKeyEvent* eventPtr) {
  switch (m_mode) {
    case Edit:
    keyEditPressEvent(eventPtr);
    break;

    case Mark:
    keyMarkPressEvent(eventPtr);
    break;
  }
}
```

`keyEditPressEvent` handles the key press in edit mode. First, we check if the key is an arrow key, page up or down, *Delete*, *Backspace*, or return key:

```
void EditorWidget::keyEditPressEvent(QKeyEvent* eventPtr) {
    switch (eventPtr->key()) {
```

In the case of the left-arrow key, we move the edit index one step backward, unless it is already at the beginning of the text:

```
case Qt::Key_Left:
  if (m_editIndex > 0) {
    --m_editIndex;
  }
  break;
```

In the case of the right-arrow key, we mode the edit index one step forward, unless it is already at the end of the text:

```
case Qt::Key_Right:
  if (m_editIndex < m_editorText.size()) {
    ++m_editIndex;
  }
  break;
```

In the case of the up-arrow key, we calculate the appropriate x and y position for the character on the previous line, unless it is already on top of the text. We then call `simulateMouseClick`, which has the same effect as if the user has clicked on the character above the line:

```
case Qt::Key_Up: {
  QRect charRect = m_rectList[m_editIndex];

  if (charRect.top() > 0) {
    int x = charRect.left() + (charRect.width() / 2),
        y = charRect.top() - 1;
    simulateMouseClick(x, y);
  }
}
break;
```

In the same way, in the case of the down-arrow key, we move the edit index one line downwards unless it is already at the bottom of the text.

We calculate the appropriate x and y position for the character on the line below and call simulateMouseClick, which has the same effect as if the user has clicked at the point:

```
case Qt::Key_Down: {
  QRect charRect = m_rectList[m_editIndex];
  int x = charRect.left() + (charRect.width() / 2),
      y = charRect.bottom() + 1;
  simulateMouseClick(x, y);
}
break;
```

In the case of the *Delete* key, we remove the current key, unless we are at the end of the text. That is, if we are one step beyond the last character:

```
case Qt::Key_Delete:
  if (m_editIndex < m_editorText.size()) {
    m_editorText.remove(m_editIndex, 1);
    setModifiedFlag(true);
  }
  break;
```

In the case of the backspace key, we move the edit index one step backward, unless it already is at the beginning of the text, and call onDelete. In this way, we remove the previous character and move the edit index one step backward:

```
case Qt::Key_Backspace:
if (m_editIndex > 0) {
  --m_editIndex;
  onDelete();
}
break;
```

In the case of the return key, we simply insert the new line character to the text:

```
case Qt::Key_Return:
  m_editorText.insert(m_editIndex++, 'n');
  setModifiedFlag(true);
  break;
```

If the key is not a special key, we check whether it is a regular character by calling text on the key event pointer. If the text is not empty, add its first character to the text:

```
default: {
  QString text = eventPtr->text();

  if (!text.isEmpty()) {
    m_editorText.insert(m_editIndex++, text[0]);
```

```
              setModifiedFlag(true);
            }
          }
          break;
        }
```

Finally, we calculate the enclosing rectangles, set the caret, and force an eventual call to paintEvent by calling update:

```
            calculate();
            setCaret();
            update();
          }
```

keyMarkPressEvent is called when the user presses a key in mark mode:

```
          void EditorWidget::keyMarkPressEvent(QKeyEvent* eventPtr) {
            switch (eventPtr->key()) {
```

In case of the left-arrow key, we set the application to edit mode and the edit index to the minimum of the first and last marked index. However, if the minimum index is located at the beginning of the text, we do nothing:

```
          case Qt::Key_Left: {
              int minIndex = qMin(m_firstIndex, m_lastIndex);

              if (minIndex > 0) {
                m_mode = Edit;
                m_caret.show();
                m_editIndex = minIndex;
              }
            }
            break;
```

On the other hand, in the case of the right-arrow key, we set the application to edit mode and the edit index to the maximum of the first and last marked index. However, if the maximum index is located at the end of the text, we do nothing:

```
          case Qt::Key_Right: {
            int maxIndex = qMax(m_firstIndex, m_lastIndex);

            if (maxIndex < m_editorText.size()) {
              m_mode = Edit;
              m_caret.show();
              m_editIndex = maxIndex;
```

```
      }
    }
    break;
```

In case of the up and down arrows, we simulate a mouse click one line above or below the current line, just as in the previous edit case:

```
case Qt::Key_Up: {
  QRect charRect = m_rectList[m_editIndex];

  if (charRect.top() > 0) {
    int x = charRect.left() + (charRect.width() / 2),
        y = charRect.top() - 1;
    simulateMouseClick(x, y);
  }
}
break;

case Qt::Key_Down: {
  QRect charRect = m_rectList[m_editIndex];
  int x = charRect.left() + (charRect.width() / 2),
      y = charRect.bottom() + 1;
  simulateMouseClick(x, y);
}
break;
```

In the mark mode, the delete and backspace keys perform the same task—they delete the marked text:

```
case Qt::Key_Delete:
case Qt::Key_Backspace: {
    int minIndex = qMin(m_firstIndex, m_lastIndex),
        maxIndex = qMax(m_firstIndex, m_lastIndex);
```

We remove the marked text from the edit text, set the modified flag, set the application to edit mode, set the edit index to the minimum of the first and last marked index, and show the caret:

```
    m_editorText.remove(minIndex, maxIndex - minIndex);
    setModifiedFlag(true);
    m_mode = Edit;
    m_editIndex = minIndex;
    m_caret.show();
  }
  break;
```

The return key case is similar to the previous edit mode case, with the difference that we first delete the marked text. We then add a new line to the editor text:

```
case Qt::Key_Return:
    onDelete();
    m_editorText.insert(m_editIndex++, 'n');
    setModifiedFlag(true);
    break;
```

If the key is not a special key, we check if it is a regular key by calling text on the key event pointer. If the text is not empty, the user has printed a regular key, and we insert the first character in the editor text:

```
default: {
    QString text = eventPtr->text();

    if (!text.isEmpty()) {
        onDelete();
        m_editorText.insert(m_editIndex++, text[0]);
        setModifiedFlag(true);
    }
}
break;
}
```

Finally, we calculate the new rectangles enclosing the characters, set the caret, and force an eventual call to paintEvent by calling update:

```
    calculate();
    setCaret();
    update();
}
```

The simulateMouseClick method is called when the user moves the caret up or down. It simulates a mouse click by calling mousePressEvent and mouseReleaseEvent, with suitably prepared event objects:

```
void EditorWidget::simulateMouseClick(int x, int y) {
    QMouseEvent pressEvent(QEvent::MouseButtonPress, QPointF(x, y),
        Qt::LeftButton, Qt::NoButton, Qt::NoModifier);
    mousePressEvent(&pressEvent);
    QMouseEvent releaseEvent(QEvent::MouseButtonRelease,
                QPointF(x, y), Qt::LeftButton,
                Qt::NoButton, Qt::NoModifier);
    mousePressEvent(&releaseEvent);
}
```

The `setCaret` method sets the caret to the appropriate size and position in edit mode. Firstly, we use `m_editIndex` to find the rectangle of the correct character. We then create a new rectangle that is of only one-pixel width, in order for the caret to appear as a thin vertical line:

```
void EditorWidget::setCaret() {
  QRect charRect = m_rectList[m_editIndex];
  QRect caretRect(charRect.left(), charRect.top(),
           1, charRect.height());
  m_caret.set(caretRect);
}
```

The `mouseToIndex` method takes a mouse point and returns the index of the character at that point. Unlike the version of Chapter 5, *Qt Graphical Applications*, we need to take into consideration that the text may be center or right-aligned:

```
int EditorWidget::mouseToIndex(QPoint point) {
    int x = point.x(), y = point.y();
```

If the mouse point is below the text of the editor, the index of the last character is returned:

```
if (y > (m_fontHeight * m_lineList.size())) {
  return m_editorText.size();
}
```

Otherwise, we start by finding the line of the mouse point, and obtain the indexes of the first and last character on the line:

```
else {
  int lineIndex = y / m_fontHeight;
  QPair<int,int> lineInfo = m_lineList[lineIndex];
  int firstIndex = lineInfo.first, lastIndex = lineInfo.second;
```

If the mouse point is located to the left of the first character on the line (which it may be if the text is center or right-aligned), we return the index of the first character of the line:

```
if (x < m_rectList[firstIndex].left()) {
    return firstIndex;
}
```

If the mouse point, on the other hand, is located to the right of the line, we return the index of the character next to the last character of the line:

```
else if (x >= m_rectList[lastIndex].right()) {
  return (lastIndex + 1);
}
```

Otherwise, we iterate through the character on the line and, for each character, we check whether the mouse point is located inside the character's enclosing rectangle:

```
else {
  for (int charIndex = firstIndex + 1;
       charIndex <= lastIndex; ++charIndex){
     int left = m_rectList[charIndex].left();
```

If the mouse point is located inside the rectangle, we check if it is closest to the left or right border of the rectangle. If it is closest to the left border, we return the index of the character. If it is closest to the right border, we instead return the index of the next character:

```
if (x < left) {
  int last = m_rectList[charIndex - 1].left();
  int leftSize = x - last, rightSize = left - x;
  return (leftSize < rightSize) ? (charIndex - 1)
                               : charIndex;
    }
  }
 }
}
```

We are not supposed to reach this point. The `assert` macro is added for debugging purposes only:

```
assert(false);
return 0;
}
```

The `resizeEvent` method is called when the user resizes the window. We calculate the rectangles enclosing the characters, since the width of the window may have changed, which may cause the lines to hold fewer or more characters:

```
void EditorWidget::resizeEvent(QResizeEvent* eventPtr) {
  calculate();
  DocumentWidget::resizeEvent(eventPtr);
}
```

The `calculate` method divides the text into lines, and calculates the rectangles enclosing every character of the text. The indexes of the first and last character of each line are stored in `m_lineList`, and the enclosing rectangles are stored in `m_rectList`:

```
void EditorWidget::calculate() {
  m_lineList.clear();
  m_rectList.clear();
```

We use the Qt `QFontMetrics` class to obtain the height of a character of the editor font. The height is stored in `m_fontHeight`. The `width` method gives the width of the window content, in pixels:

```
QFontMetrics metrics(m_textFont);
m_fontHeight = metrics.height();
QList<int> charWidthList, lineWidthList;
int windowWidth = width();
```

We start by iterating through the editor text in order to divide the text into lines:

```
{ int firstIndex = 0, lineWidth = 0;
  for (int charIndex = 0; charIndex < m_editorText.size();
      ++charIndex) {
    QChar c = m_editorText[charIndex];
```

When we encounter a new line, we add the first and last index of the current line to `m_lineList`:

```
if (c == 'n') {
  charWidthList.push_back(1);
  lineWidthList.push_back(lineWidth);
  m_lineList.push_back
            (QPair<int,int>(firstIndex, charIndex));
  firstIndex = charIndex + 1;
  lineWidth = 0;
}
```

Otherwise, we call the `width` method of the Qt `QMetrics` object to obtain the width of the character, in pixels:

```
else {
  int charWidth = metrics.width(c);
  charWidthList.push_back(charWidth);
```

If the character makes the width of the line exceed the width of the window content, we add the first and last index to `m_lineList` and start a new line.

However, we have two different cases to consider. If the current character is the first character of the line, we have the (rather unlikely) situation that the width of that character exceeds the width of the window content. In that case, we add the index of that character as both the first and last index to `m_lineList`. The first index of the next line is the character next to that character:

```
if ((lineWidth + charWidth) > windowWidth) {
  if (firstIndex == charIndex) {
```

```
        lineWidthList.push_back(windowWidth);
        m_lineList.push_back
            (QPair<int,int>(firstIndex, charIndex));
        firstIndex = charIndex + 1;
    }
```

If the current character is not the first character of the line, we add the indexes of the first character and the character preceding the current character to `m_lineList`. The index of the next line becomes the index of the current character:

```
    else {
        lineWidthList.push_back(lineWidth);
        m_lineList.push_back(QPair<int,int>(firstIndex,
            charIndex - 1));
        firstIndex = charIndex;
    }
    lineWidth = 0;
}
```

If the character does not make the width of the line exceed the width of the window content, we simply add the width of the character to the width of the line:

```
    else {
        lineWidth += charWidth;
    }
    }
}
```

Finally, we need to add the last line to `m_lineList`:

```
    m_lineList.push_back(QPair<int,int>(firstIndex,
        m_editorText.size() - 1));
    lineWidthList.push_back(lineWidth);
}
```

When we have divided the text into lines, we continue to calculate the enclosing rectangles of the individual characters. We start by setting `top` to zero, since it holds the top position of the line. It will be increased by the line height for each line:

```
{ int top = 0, left;
  for (int lineIndex = 0; lineIndex < m_lineList.size();
      ++lineIndex) {
    QPair<int,int> lineInfo = m_lineList[lineIndex];
    int lineWidth = lineWidthList[lineIndex];
    int firstIndex = lineInfo.first,
        lastIndex = lineInfo.second;
```

Depending on the alignment of the text, we need to decide where the line starts. In the case of left alignment, we set the left position of the line to zero:

```
switch (m_alignment) {
  case Left:
    left = 0;
    break;
```

In case of center alignment, we set the left position to half of the difference between the width of the window content and the line. In this way, the line will appear at the center of the window:

```
  case Center:
    left = (windowWidth - lineWidth) / 2;
    break;
```

In case of right alignment, we set the left position to the difference between the width of the window content and the line. In this way, the line will appear to the right in the window:

```
  case Right:
    left = windowWidth - lineWidth;
    break;
}
```

Finally, when we have decided the starting left position of the line and the width of each individual character of the text, we iterate through the line and calculate the enclosing rectangle for each character:

```
for (int charIndex = firstIndex;
     charIndex <= lastIndex; ++charIndex) {
  int charWidth = charWidthList[charIndex];
  QRect charRect(left, top, charWidth, m_fontHeight);
  m_rectList.push_back(charRect);
  left += charWidth;
}
```

For the very last line of the text, we add a rectangle holding the position beyond the last character:

```
if (lastIndex == (m_editorText.size() - 1)) {
  QRect lastRect(left, top, 1, m_fontHeight);
  m_rectList.push_back(lastRect);
}
```

The top field is increased by the height of the line for each new line:

```
            top += m_fontHeight;
        }
    }
}
```

The `paintEvent` method is called by the framework every time the window needs to be repainted, or when we force a repainting by calling `update`. The framework clears the content of the window before the call to `paintEvent`:

First, we create a `QPinter` object that we then use to write on. We set some rendering and the font of the text:

```
void EditorWidget::paintEvent(QPaintEvent* /* eventPtr */) {
    QPainter painter(this);
    painter.setRenderHint(QPainter::Antialiasing);
    painter.setRenderHint(QPainter::TextAntialiasing);
    painter.setFont(m_textFont);
```

We calculate the minimum and maximum index of the marked text (even though we do not yet know if the application holds mark mode):

```
int minIndex = qMin(m_firstIndex, m_lastIndex),
    maxIndex = qMax(m_firstIndex, m_lastIndex);
```

We iterate through the text of the editor. We write every character except a new line:

```
for (int index = 0; index < m_editorText.length(); ++index) {
    QChar c = m_editorText[index];
```

If the character is marked, we write it with white text on a black background:

```
if (c != 'n') {
    if ((m_mode == Mark) &&
        (index >= minIndex) && (index < maxIndex)) {
        painter.setPen(Qt::white);
        painter.setBackground(Qt::black);
    }
```

If the character is not marked, we write it with black text on a white background:

```
    else {
        painter.setPen(Qt::black);
        painter.setBrush(Qt::white);
    }
```

When the colors of the text and background have been set, we look up the rectangle enclosing the character and write the character itself:

```
    QRect rect = m_rectList[index];
    painter.drawText(rect, c);
  }
}
```

Finally, we also paint the caret:

```
    m_caret.paint(&painter);
  }
```

The main function

The `main` function is similar to the main function of the previous applications: it creates an application, shows the drawing window, and starts the execution of the application.

Main.cpp:

```
#include "EditorWindow.h"
#include <QApplication>

int main(int argc, char *argv[]) {
  QApplication application(argc, argv);
  EditorWindow editorWindow;
  editorWindow.show();
  return application.exec();
}
```

The output is shown in the following screenshot:

Summary

In this chapter, we have developed more advanced versions of the analog clock, the drawing program, and the editor. The clock shows the current hour, minute, and second. The drawing program, allows the user to draw lines, rectangles, and ellipses. The editor allows the user to input and edit text. The clock face has digits instead of lines. In the drawing program we can mark, modify, and cut and paste figures, and in the editor, we can change font and alignment and mark a text block.

In Chapter 7, *The Games*, we will start developing the games Othello and Nought and Crosses.

7

The Games

In Chapter 6, *Enhancing the QT Graphical Applications*, we developed an analog clock, a drawing program, and an editor with the Qt graphical library. In this chapter, we continue by developing the Othello and Noughts and Crosses games with the Qt library. You will find a description of these games after this introduction. We start in this chapter with basic versions, where two players play against each other. In Chapter 8, *The Computer Plays*, we improve the games so that the computer plays against the human.

Topics we will cover in this chapter include:

- Introduction to game theory. We develop a game grid where the players take turns to add their marks to the game grid.
- We announce the winner. In Othello, after each move, we calculate how many of the opponent's marks can be changed. When every position of the game grid has been occupied, we declare the winner or a draw.
- In Noughts and Crosses, we count the number of marks in a row. If there are five marks in a row, we declare the winner.
- We continue to use C++ features such as classes, fields, and methods. We also continue to use Qt features such as windows and widgets.

Othello

In Othello, the game grid is empty at the beginning of the game. During the game, two players take turns adding marks, colored in black and white, to the game grid. Each time a player adds a mark, we look at the other marks and see if the new mark causes any of the opponent's marks to be enclosed. In that case, we swap the color of the opponent's enclosed marks.

For instance, if the black player adds a black mark in a position where the three marks to the left are white and the fourth mark is black, the three white marks are being enclosed by the two black marks, and they are swapped to black marks. When every position on the game grid has been occupied by white and black marks, we count the marks and the player with the most marks is the winner. If there is an equal number of black and white marks, it is a draw.

Here's what our game should look like:

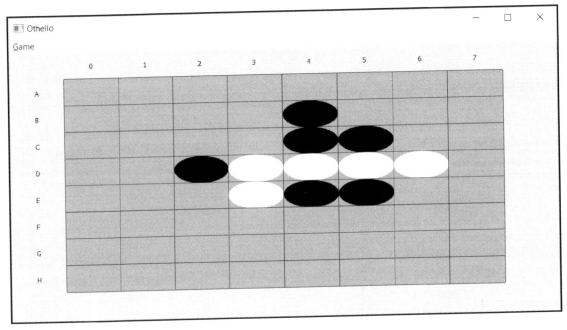

The game widget

First of all, we need a game grid. The GameWidget class is common to all the applications of this chapter and of Chapter 8, *The Computer Plays*. In Chapter 5, *Qt Graphical Applications* and Chapter 6, *Enhancing the QT Graphical Applications*, we developed the DocumentWidget class, since we worked with document-based applications. In this chapter and Chapter 8, *The Computer Plays*, we instead develop the GameWidget class.

The `DocumentWidget` class of the two previous chapters and the `GameWidget` class of this chapter and the next chapter have both similarities and differences. They are both subclasses of the Qt class `QWidget`, and they are both intended to be embedded in a window. However, while `DocumentWidget` was intended to hold a document, `GameWidget` is intended to hold a game grid. It draws the grid and catches mouse clicks in the positions of the grid. `GameWidget` is an abstract class that lets it its subclass define methods that are called when the user clicks the mouse or when a mark in one of the positions of the game grid needs to be repainted.

However, we reuse the `MainWindow` class from the previous chapters to hold the main window of the application, with its menu bar.

GameWidget.h

```
#ifndef GAMEWIDGET_H
#define GAMEWIDGET_H

#include <QPainter>
#include <QMouseEvent>
#include <QMessageBox>

#include "..\MainWindow\MainWindow.h"

class GameWidget : public QWidget {
  Q_OBJECT
```

The constructor initializes the number of rows and columns of the game grid:

```
public:
    GameWidget(int rows, int columns, QWidget* parentWidget);
```

The `clearGrid` method sets every position in the game grid to zero, which is assumed to represent an empty position. Therefore, every class that inherits `GameWidget` shall let the value zero represent an empty position:

```
void clearGrid();
```

The `resizeEvent` method is called when the user changes the size of the window. Since the number of rows and columns is constant, the width and height of each position is changed in accordance with the new size of the window:

```
void resizeEvent(QResizeEvent *eventPtr);
```

The `mousePressEvent` is called when the user presses one of the mouse buttons, `paintEvent` is called when the window needs to be repainted, and `closeEvent` is called when the user clicks on the close box at the top-right corner of the window:

```
void mousePressEvent(QMouseEvent *eventPtr);
void paintEvent(QPaintEvent *eventPtr);
void closeEvent(QCloseEvent *eventPtr);
```

The `mouseMark` and `drawMark` methods are pure virtual methods intended to be overridden by subclasses; `mouseMark` is called when the user clicks at a position in the grid, and `drawMark` is called when a position needs to be repainted. They are pure virtual methods, whereas `GameWidget` is abstract, which means that it is only possible to use `GameWidget` as a base class. The subclasses of `GameWidget` must override the methods to become non-abstract:

```
virtual void mouseMark(int row, int column) = 0;
virtual void drawMark(QPainter& painter,
                      const QRect& markRect, int mark) = 0;
```

The `isQuitOk` method displays a message box that asks the user if they really want to quit the game:

```
private:
    bool isQuitOk();
```

The `isQuitEnabled` method is called before the `Game` menu becomes visible. The `Quit` item is enabled when a game is in progress:

```
public slots:
    DEFINE_LISTENER(GameWidget, isQuitEnabled);
```

The `onQuit` and `onExit` methods are called when the user selects the **Quit** or **Exit** menu items:

```
void onQuit();
void onExit();
```

The `isGameInProgress` and `setGameInProgress` methods return and set the value of the `m_gameInProgress` field:

```
protected:
    bool isGameInProgress() const {return m_gameInProgress;}
    void setGameInProgress(bool active)
                          {m_gameInProgress = active;}
```

The `get` and `set` methods get and set a value at a position in the game grid. The value is an integer; remember that an empty position is assumed to hold the value zero:

```
protected:
   int get(int row, int column) const;
   void set(int row, int column, int value);
```

The `m_gameInProgress` field is true as long as a game is in progress. The `m_rows` and `m_columns` fields hold the number of rows and columns of the game grid; `m_rowHeight` and `m_columnWidth` hold the height and width in pixels of each position in the game grid. Finally, `m_gameGrid` is a pointer to a buffer holding the values of the positions of the game grid:

```
private:
   bool m_gameInProgress = false;
   int m_rows, m_columns;
   int m_rowHeight, m_columnWidth;
   int* m_gameGrid;
};


#endif // GAMEWIDGET_H
```

The `GameWidget.cpp` file holds the definitions of the methods of the `GameWidget` class, the mouse event methods, and the menu methods, as well as the drawings and settings of the marks.

GameWidget.cpp

```
#include "GameWidget.h"
#include <QApplication>
#include <CAssert>
```

The constructor initializes the number of rows and columns of the grid, dynamically allocates its memory, and calls `clearGrid` to clear the grid:

```
GameWidget::GameWidget(int rows, int columns,
                       QWidget* parentWidget)
 :QWidget(parentWidget),
  m_rows(rows),
  m_columns(columns),
  m_gameGrid(new int[rows * columns]) {
  assert(rows > 0);
  assert(columns > 0);
  clearGrid();
}
```

The `get` method returns the value at the position indicated by the row and column and `set` sets the value. The buffer holding the values is organized in rows. That is, the first part of the buffer holds the first row, and then the second row, and so on:

```
int GameWidget::get(int row, int column) const {
  return m_gameGrid[(row * m_columns) + column];
}

void GameWidget::set(int row, int column, int value) {
  m_gameGrid[(row * m_columns) + column] = value;
}
```

The `clearGrid` method sets every position to zero, since zero is assumed to represent an empty position:

```
void GameWidget::clearGrid() {
  for (int row = 0; row < m_rows; ++row) {
    for (int column = 0; column < m_columns; ++column) {
      set(row, column, 0);
    }
  }
}
```

The `Quit` menu item is enabled as long as a game is in progress:

```
bool GameWidget::isQuitEnabled() {
  return m_gameInProgress;
}
```

If a game is in progress when the user selects to quit the game, a message box with a confirmation question is displayed:

```
bool GameWidget::isQuitOk() {
  if (m_gameInProgress) {
    QMessageBox messageBox(QMessageBox::Warning,
                           tr("Quit"), QString());
    messageBox.setText(tr("Quit the Game."));
    messageBox.setInformativeText
                  (tr("Do you really want to quit the game?"));
    messageBox.setStandardButtons(QMessageBox::Yes |
                                  QMessageBox::No);
    messageBox.setDefaultButton(QMessageBox::No);
```

If the user presses the `Yes` button, `true` is returned:

```
    return (messageBox.exec() == QMessageBox::Yes);
  }
```

```
      return true;
  }
```

The onQuit method is called when the user selects the **Quit** menu item. If the call to isQuitOk returns true, m_gameInProgress is set to false and update is called, which eventually forces a repaint of the window where the game grid is cleared.

```
void GameWidget::onQuit() {
  if (isQuitOk()) {
    m_gameInProgress = false;
    update();
  }
}
```

The onExit method is called when the user selects the **Exit** menu item. If the call to isQuitOk returns true, the application is exited. This is shown in the following code:

```
void GameWidget::onExit() {
  if (isQuitOk()) {
    qApp->exit(0);
  }
}
```

The resizeEvent method is called when the user resizes the window. The row height and column width are recalculated since the number of rows and columns is constant regardless of the size of the window. We divide the height and width of the window by the number of rows and columns plus two, since we add extra rows and columns as margins. Consider the following code:

```
void GameWidget::resizeEvent(QResizeEvent* eventPtr) {
  m_rowHeight = height() / (m_rows + 2);
  m_columnWidth = width() / (m_columns + 2);
  QWidget::resizeEvent(eventPtr);
  update();
}
```

The mousePressEvent method is called when the user clicks on the window:

```
void GameWidget::mousePressEvent(QMouseEvent* eventPtr) {
  if (m_gameInProgress &&
        (eventPtr->button() == Qt::LeftButton)) {
    QPoint mousePoint = eventPtr->pos();
```

The column width and row height are subtracted from the mouse point, since the game grid is enclosed by margins:

```
mousePoint.setX(mousePoint.x() - m_columnWidth);
mousePoint.setY(mousePoint.y() - m_rowHeight);
```

If the mouse point is located inside one of the game grid positions, and that position is empty (zero), the pure virtual method `mouseMark` is called, which takes care of the actual action of the mouse click. In the next section, black and white marks are added to the game grid, and in the Noughts and Crosses application later on. Noughts and crosses are added to the game grid:

```
int row = mousePoint.y() / m_rowHeight,
    column = mousePoint.x() / m_columnWidth;
```

If the rows and columns clicked are located in the game grid (rather than in the margins outside the game grid) and the position is empty (zero), we call the `mouseMark`, which is a pure virtual method, with the row and column:

```
if ((row < m_rows) && (column < m_columns) &&
    (get(row, column) == 0)) {
  mouseMark(row, column);
  update();
}
  }
}
```

The `paintEvent` method is called when the window needs to be repainted. If a game is in progress (`m_gameInProgress` is true), the rows and columns are written, and then for each position in the game grid, the pure virtual method `drawMark` is called, which takes care of the actual painting of each position:

```
void GameWidget::paintEvent(QPaintEvent* /*eventPtr*/) {
  if (m_gameInProgress) {
    QPainter painter(this);
    painter.setRenderHint(QPainter::Antialiasing);
    painter.setRenderHint(QPainter::TextAntialiasing);
```

First, we iterate through the rows and for each row, we write a letter from A to Z. There are 26 letters of the alphabet, and we assume there are no more than 26 rows:

```
for (int row = 0; row < m_rows; ++row) {
  QString text;
  text.sprintf("%c", (char) (((int) 'A') + row));
  QRect charRect(0, (row + 1) * m_rowHeight,
                 m_columnWidth, m_rowHeight);
```

```
        painter.drawText(charRect, Qt::AlignCenter |
                        Qt::AlignHCenter, text);
    }
```

Then we iterate through the columns, and for each column, we write its number:

```
    for (int column = 0; column < m_columns; ++column) {
        QString text;
        text.sprintf("%i", column);
        QRect charRect((column + 1) * m_columnWidth, 0,
                    m_columnWidth, m_rowHeight);
        painter.drawText(charRect, Qt::AlignCenter |
                        Qt::AlignHCenter, text);
    }

    painter.save();
    painter.translate(m_columnWidth, m_rowHeight);
```

 A pure virtual method is a method that is not intended to be defined in the class, only in its subclasses. A class holding at least one pure virtual method becomes abstract, which means that it is not possible to create objects of the class. The class can only be used as a base class in a class hierarchy. A class that inherits an abstract class must define each pure virtual method of the base class, or become abstract itself.

Finally, we iterate through the game grid, and for each position, we call the pure virtual method `drawMark` with the rectangle of the position and its current mark:

```
    for (int row = 0; row < m_rows; ++row) {
        for (int column = 0; column < m_columns; ++column) {
            QRect markRect(column * m_columnWidth, row * m_rowHeight,
                        m_columnWidth, m_rowHeight);
            painter.setPen(Qt::black);
            painter.drawRect(markRect);
            painter.fillRect(markRect, Qt::lightGray);
            drawMark(painter, markRect, get(row, column));
        }
    }

    painter.restore();
    }
}
```

The `closeEvent` method is called when the user clicks on the close box at the top-right corner of the window. If the call to `isQuitOk` returns true, the window is closed, and the application is exited:

```
void GameWidget::closeEvent(QCloseEvent* eventPtr) {
  if (isQuitOk()) {
    eventPtr->accept();
    qApp->exit(0);
  }
  else {
    eventPtr->ignore();
  }
}
```

The OthelloWindow class

The `Othello` class is a subclass of `MainWindow` from Chapter 6, *Enhancing the QT Graphical Applications*. It adds menus to the window and sets the `OthelloWidget` class here, which is a subclass of `GameWidget`, to its central widget.

OthelloWindow.h

```
#ifndef OTHELLOWINDOW_H
#define OTHELLOWINDOW_H

#include "..\MainWindow\MainWindow.h"
#include "OthelloWidget.h"

class OthelloWindow : public MainWindow {
  Q_OBJECT

  public:
    OthelloWindow(QWidget *parentWidget = nullptr);
    ~OthelloWindow();

    void closeEvent(QCloseEvent *eventPtr)
      {m_othelloWidgetPtr->closeEvent(eventPtr);}
```

The `m_othelloWidgetPtr` field holds a pointer to the widget located in the center of the window. It points at an object of the `OthelloWidget` class. This is shown in the following code:

```
  private:
    OthelloWidget* m_othelloWidgetPtr;
};
```

```
#endif // OTHELLOWINDOW_H
```

The `OthelloWindow.cpp` file defines the methods of the `OthelloWIndow` class.

OthelloWindow.cpp

```
#include "OthelloWidget.h"
#include "OthelloWindow.h"
#include <QtWidgets>
```

The constructor sets the title of the window to `Othello` and the size to *1000 x 500* pixels:

```
OthelloWindow::OthelloWindow(QWidget *parentWidget /*= nullptr*/)
 :MainWindow(parentWidget) {
  setWindowTitle(tr("Othello"));
  resize(1000, 500);
```

An `OthelloWidget` object is dynamically created and placed at the center of the window:

```
  m_othelloWidgetPtr = new OthelloWidget(this);
  setCentralWidget(m_othelloWidgetPtr);
```

We add the menu `Game` to the menu bar and connect the `onMenuShow` method to the menu, which causes it to be called before the menu becomes visible:

```
  { QMenu* gameMenuPtr = menuBar()->addMenu(tr("&Game"));
    connect(gameMenuPtr, SIGNAL(aboutToShow()),
            this, SLOT(onMenuShow()));
```

The user can choose the black or white color to make the first move. The `isBlackStartsEnabled` and `isWhiteStartsEnabled` methods are called before the items become visible. The items become disabled when a game is in progress:

```
    addAction(gameMenuPtr, tr("&Black Starts"),
            SLOT(onBlackStarts()), 0,
            tr("Black Starts"), nullptr,tr("Black Starts"),
            LISTENER(isBlackStartsEnabled));

    addAction(gameMenuPtr, tr("&White Starts"),
            SLOT(onWhiteStarts()), 0,
            tr("White Starts"), nullptr, tr("White Starts"),
            LISTENER(isWhiteStartsEnabled));

    gameMenuPtr->addSeparator();
```

When a game is in progress, the user can quit the game. The item becomes disabled when no game is in progress:

```
addAction(gameMenuPtr, tr("&Quit the Game"),
          SLOT(onQuit()),
          QKeySequence(Qt::CTRL + Qt::Key_Q),
          tr("Quit Game"), nullptr, tr("Quit the Game"),
          LISTENER(isQuitEnabled));
```

The user can exit the application at any time:

```
    addAction(gameMenuPtr, tr("E&xit"),
              SLOT(onExit()), QKeySequence::Quit);
  }
}
```

The destructor deallocates the `Othello` widget in the center of the window:

```
OthelloWindow::~OthelloWindow() {
  delete m_othelloWidgetPtr;
}
```

The OthelloWidget class

`OthelloWidget` is a subclass of the `GameWidget` class we defined at the beginning of this chapter. It becomes a non-abstract class by overriding `mouseMark` and `drawMark`, which are called when the user clicks at a position in the game grid and when a position needs to be repainted.

OthelloWidget.h

```
#ifndef OTHELLOWIDGET_H
#define OTHELLOWIDGET_H

#include "..\MainWindow\GameWidget.h"

#define ROWS     8
#define COLUMNS  8
```

A mark in Othello can be black or white. We use the `Mark` enumeration to store values on the game grid. The `Empty` item holds a value of zero, which is assumed to be `GameWidget` to represent an empty position:

```
enum Mark {Empty = 0, Black, White};

class OthelloWidget : public GameWidget {
```

```
Q_OBJECT

public:
  OthelloWidget(QWidget* parentWidget);

  void mouseMark(int row, int column);
  void drawMark(QPainter& painter,
                const QRect& markRect, int mark);
```

The `isBlackStartsEnabled` and `isWhiteStartsEnabled` listeners are called before the `BlackStarts` and `WhiteStarts` menu items become visible in order to enable them. Note that the listeners and methods must be marked as public slots for the menu framework to allow them as listeners:

```
public slots:
  DEFINE_LISTENER(OthelloWidget, isBlackStartsEnabled);
  DEFINE_LISTENER(OthelloWidget, isWhiteStartsEnabled);
```

The `onBlackStarts` and `onWhiteStarts` methods are called when the `BlackStarts` and `WhiteStarts` menu items are selected by the user:

```
  void onBlackStarts();
  void onWhiteStarts();
```

The `checkWinner` method checks if every position on the game grid has been occupied by a black or white mark. If it has, the marks are counted, and the winner is announced unless it is a draw:

```
private:
  void checkWinner();
```

The `turn` method is called when one of the players has made a move. It calculates the positions to be turned as a result of the move:

```
  void turn(int row, int column, Mark mark);
```

The `calculateMark` method calculates the set of marks to be turned if the player places the mark in the position given by the row and column:

```
  void calculateMark(int row, int column, Mark mark,
                     QSet<QPair<int,int>>& resultSet);
```

The `m_nextMark` field is alternatively given the values `Black` and `White` of the preceding `Mark` enumeration, depending on which player is about to do the next move.

It is initialized by `onBlackStarts` or `onWhiteStarts`, as shown in the previous code:

```
        Mark m_nextMark;
    };


    #endif // OTHELLOWIDGET_H
```

The `OthelloWidget` class holds the functionality of the game. It allows the player to add black and white marks to the game grid, turn marks, and announce the winner.

OthelloWidget.cpp

```
        #include "OthelloWidget.h"
        #include "OthelloWindow.h"

        #include <QTime>
        #include <CTime>
        #include <CAssert>
        using namespace std;

        OthelloWidget::OthelloWidget(QWidget* parentWidget)
         :GameWidget(ROWS, COLUMNS, parentWidget) {
          // Empty.
        }
```

The `BlackStarts` and `WhiteStarts` menu items are enabled when there is not already a game in progress:

```
        bool OthelloWidget::isBlackStartsEnabled() {
          return !isGameInProgress();
        }

        bool OthelloWidget::isWhiteStartsEnabled() {
          return !isGameInProgress();
        }
```

The `onBlackStarts` and `onWhiteStarts` methods set a new game in progress, set the mark to make the first move (black or white), clear the grid, and update the window to paint an empty game grid:

```
        void OthelloWidget::onBlackStarts() {
          setGameInProgress(true);
          m_nextMark = Black;
          update();
        }

        void OthelloWidget::onWhiteStarts() {
```

```
    setGameInProgress(true);
    m_nextMark = White;
    update();
}
```

The `onMouseMark` is called when the player clicks an empty position on the game grid. We set the position with the next mark, turn every mark that is affected by the move, and update the window to reflect the change:

```
void OthelloWidget::mouseMark(int row, int column) {
    set(row, column, m_nextMark);
    turn(row, column, m_nextMark);
    update();
```

We check if the move has caused the game grid to become full and switch the next mark:

```
    checkWinner();
    m_nextMark = (m_nextMark == Black) ? White : Black;
}
```

The `drawMark` method is called when a position in the game grid needs to be repainted. We draw a black or white ellipse with black borders if the position is not empty. If the position is empty, we do nothing. Note that the framework clears the window before the call to repaint:

```
void OthelloWidget::drawMark(QPainter& painter,
        const QRect& markRect, int mark) {
    painter.setPen(Qt::black);
    painter.drawRect(markRect);
    painter.fillRect(markRect, Qt::lightGray);

    switch (mark) {
      case Black:
        painter.setPen(Qt::black);
        painter.setBrush(Qt::black);
        painter.drawEllipse(markRect);
        break;

      case White:
        painter.setPen(Qt::white);
        painter.setBrush(Qt::white);
        painter.drawEllipse(markRect);
        break;

      case Empty:
        break;
```

```
        }
    }
```

The `checkWinner` method counts the number of positions that are occupied by black and white marks or are empty:

```
void OthelloWidget::checkWinner() {
  int blacks = 0, whites = 0, empties = 0;

  for (int row = 0; row < ROWS; ++row) {
    for (int column = 0; column < COLUMNS; ++column) {
      switch (get(row, column)) {
        case Black:
          ++blacks;
          break;

        case White:
          ++whites;
          break;

        case Empty:
          ++empties;
          break;
      }
    }
  }
```

If there are no empty positions left, the game is over, and we announce the winner, unless it is a draw. The winner is the player with the most marks in their color:

```
if (empties == 0) {
  QMessageBox messageBox(QMessageBox::Information,
      tr("Victory"), QString());
  QString text;

  if (blacks == whites) {
    text.sprintf("A Draw.");
  }
  else if (blacks > whites) {
    text.sprintf("The Winner: Black");
  }
  else {
    text.sprintf("The Winner: White");
  }

  messageBox.setText(text);
  messageBox.setStandardButtons(QMessageBox::Ok);
```

```
        messageBox.exec();
        setGameInProgress(false);

        clearGrid();
        update();
      }
    }
```

The `turn` method calls `calculateMark` to obtain the set of positions where the mark shall be turned. Then each position in the set is set to the mark in question.

In this application, `turn` is the only method that calls `calculateMark`. However, in Chapter 8, *The Computer Plays*, `calculateMark` will also be called to calculate the move of the computer player. Therefore, the functionality of `turn` and `calculateMark` are divided into two methods:

```
    void OthelloWidget::turn(int row, int column, Mark mark) {
      QSet<QPair<int,int>> totalSet;
      calculateMark(row, column, mark, totalSet);

      for (QPair<int,int> pair : totalSet) {
        int row = pair.first, column = pair.second;
        set(row, column, mark);
      }
    }
```

The `calculateMark` method counts the number of marks that will be turned for each position on the game grid, in all eight directions:

```
    void OthelloWidget::calculateMark(int row, int column,
        Mark playerMark, QSet<QPair<int,int>>& totalSet){
```

Each integer pair in `directionArray` refers to a direction in accordance with the compass rising:

```
    QPair<int,int> directionArray[] =
      {QPair<int,int>(-1, 0),    // North
       QPair<int,int>(-1, 1),    // Northeast
       QPair<int,int>(0, 1),     // East
       QPair<int,int>(1, 1),     // Southeast
       QPair<int,int>(1, 0),     // South
       QPair<int,int>(1, -1),    // Southwest
       QPair<int,int>(0, -1),    // West
       QPair<int,int>(-1, -1)};  // Northwest
```

The size of an array can be decided by dividing its total size (in bytes) by the size of its first value:

```
int arraySize =
    (sizeof directionArray) / (sizeof directionArray[0]);
```

We iterate through the directions and, for each direction, keep moving as long as we find the mark of the opponent:

```
for (int index = 0; index < arraySize; ++index) {
    QPair<int,int> pair = directionArray[index];
```

The `row` and `column` fields hold the current row and column as long as we iterate in that direction:

```
int rowStep = pair.first, columnStep = pair.second,
    currRow = row, currColumn = column;
```

We gather the marks we find during the iteration in `directionSet`:

```
QSet<QPair<int,int>> directionSet;

while (true) {
    currRow += rowStep;
    currColumn += columnStep;
```

If we reach one of the borders of the game grid, or if we find an empty position, we break the iteration:

```
if ((currRow < 0) || (currRow == ROWS) ||
        (currColumn < 0) || (currColumn == COLUMNS) ||
        (get(currRow, currColumn) == Empty)) {
    break;
}
```

If we find the player's mark, we add the direction set to the total set and break the iteration:

```
else if (get(currRow, currColumn) == playerMark) {
    totalSet += directionSet;
    break;
}
```

If we do not find the player's mark or an empty position, we have found the opponent's mark, and we add its position to the direction set:

```
      else {
         directionSet.insert(QPair<int,int>(row, column));
      }
    }
  }
}
```

The main function

The `main` function works in the same way as in the previous Qt applications. It creates an application, shows the Othello window, and executes the applications. The execution continues until the `exit` method is called, which it is when the user closes the window or selects the **Exit** menu item.

Main.cpp

```
#include "OthelloWidget.h"
#include "OthelloWindow.h"
#include <QApplication>

int main(int argc, char *argv[]) {
  QApplication application(argc, argv);
  OthelloWindow othelloWindow;
  othelloWindow.show();
  return application.exec();
}
```

Noughts and crosses

The Noughts and Crosses application sets up a game grid and allows two players to play each other. In Noughts and Crosses, two players take turns adding noughts and crosses to a game grid. The player that first manages to place five marks in a row wins the game. The marks can be placed horizontally, vertically, or diagonally. While each player tries to place five of their own marks in a row, they must also try to prevent the opponent from placing five marks in a row.

In Chapter 8, *The Computer Plays,* the computer plays against the human.

The NaCWindow class

We reuse the GameWidget from the game widget section. The NaCWindow class is similar to OthelloWindow. It adds the Nought Begins and Cross Begins menu items to the window's menu bar.

NaCWindow.h

```
#ifndef NACWINDOW_H
#define NACWINDOW_H

#include "..\MainWindow\MainWindow.h"
#include "NaCWidget.h"

class NaCWindow : public MainWindow {
  Q_OBJECT

  public:
    NaCWindow(QWidget *parentWidget = nullptr);
    ~NaCWindow();

  public:
    void closeEvent(QCloseEvent *eventPtr) override
                   {m_nacWidgetPtr->closeEvent(eventPtr);}

  private:
    NaCWidget* m_nacWidgetPtr;
};

#endif // NACWINDOW_H
```

The NaCWindow.cpp file holds the definitions of the methods of the NacWindow class.

NaCWindow.cpp

```
#include "NaCWindow.h"
#include <QtWidgets>

NaCWindow::NaCWindow(QWidget *parentWidget /*= nullptr*/)
 :MainWindow(parentWidget) {
  setWindowTitle(tr("Noughts and Crosses"));
  resize(1000, 500);

  m_nacWidgetPtr = new NaCWidget(this);
  setCentralWidget(m_nacWidgetPtr);

  { QMenu* gameMenuPtr = menuBar()->addMenu(tr("&Game"));
```

```
        connect(gameMenuPtr, SIGNAL(aboutToShow()),
                this, SLOT(onMenuShow()));

        addAction(gameMenuPtr, tr("&Nought Starts"),
                SLOT(onNoughtStarts()), 0,
                tr("Nought Starts"), nullptr, tr("Nought Starts"),
                LISTENER(isNoughtStartsEnabled));

        addAction(gameMenuPtr, tr("&Cross Starts"),
                SLOT(onCrossStarts()), 0,
                tr("Cross Starts"), nullptr, tr("Cross Starts"),
                LISTENER(isCrossStartsEnabled));

        gameMenuPtr->addSeparator();

        addAction(gameMenuPtr, tr("&Quit the Game"),
                SLOT(onQuit()),
                QKeySequence(Qt::CTRL + Qt::Key_Q), tr("Quit Game"),
                nullptr, tr("Quit the Game"),
                LISTENER(isQuitEnabled));

        addAction(gameMenuPtr, tr("E&xit"),
                SLOT(onExit()), QKeySequence::Quit);
    }
}

NaCWindow::~NaCWindow() {
    delete m_nacWidgetPtr;
}
```

The NaCWidget class

The NaCWidget class handles the functionality of Noughts and Crosses. It allows two players to play each other. In Chapter 8, *The Computer Plays*, we will write a game where the computer plays the human.

NaCWidget.h

```
#ifndef NACWIDGET_H
#define NACWIDGET_H

#include "..\MainWindow\GameWidget.h"

#define ROWS      26
#define COLUMNS   26
```

Similar to the Othello application, a position in the game grid can hold one of three values:

- `Empty` (which is zero)
- `Nought`
- `Cross`

The `Mark` enumeration corresponds to the `Empty`, `Nought`, and `Cross` values:

```
enum Mark {Empty = 0, Nought, Cross};

class NaCWidget : public GameWidget {
  Q_OBJECT

  public:
    NaCWidget(QWidget* parentWidget);

    void mouseMark(int row, int column);
    void drawMark(QPainter& painter,
                  const QRect& markRect, int mark);

  public slots:
    DEFINE_LISTENER(NaCWidget, isNoughtStartsEnabled);
    void onNoughtStarts();

    DEFINE_LISTENER(NaCWidget, isCrossStartsEnabled);
    void onCrossStarts();

  private:
    void checkWinner(int row, int column, Mark mark);
    int countMarks(int row, int column, int rowStep,
                   int columnStep, Mark mark);

    Mark m_nextMark;
};

#endif // NACWIDGET_H
```

The `NaCWidget.cpp` file holds the definitions of the methods of the `NaCWidget` class.

NaCWidget.cpp

```
#include "NaCWidget.h"
#include <CTime>

NaCWidget::NaCWidget(QWidget* parentWidget)
  :GameWidget(ROWS, COLUMNS, parentWidget) {
```

```
    // Empty.
  }
```

The isNoughtStartsEnabled and isCrossStartsEnabled methods are called before the Game menu becomes visible. The Noughts Begins and Cross Begins menu items are enabled if there is no game in progress:

```
bool NaCWidget::isCrossStartsEnabled() {
  return !isGameInProgress();
}

bool NaCWidget::isNoughtStartsEnabled() {
  return !isGameInProgress();
}
```

The onNoughtBegins and onCrossBegins methods are called when the user selects the Nought Begins and Cross Begins menu items. They set the game in progress, set the first mark to make the first move (m_nextMark), and force a repainting of the game grid by calling update:

```
void NaCWidget::onNoughtStarts() {
  setGameInProgress(true);
  m_nextMark = Nought;
  update();
}

void NaCWidget::onCrossStarts() {
  setGameInProgress(true);
  m_nextMark = Cross;
  update();
}
```

The mouseMark method is called when the players click a position in the game grid. We set the next mark at the position, check if one of the players has won the game, swap the next move, and repaint the window by calling update:

```
void NaCWidget::mouseMark(int row, int column) {
  set(row, column, m_nextMark);
  checkWinner(row, column, m_nextMark);
  m_nextMark = (m_nextMark == Nought) ? Cross : Nought;
  update();
}
```

The `drawMark` method is called when a position in the game grid needs to be repainted:

```
void NaCWidget::drawMark(QPainter& painter,
    const QRect& markRect, int mark) {
```

We set the pen color to black, and in the case of a nought, we draw an ellipse, as follows:

```
painter.setPen(Qt::black);
switch (mark) {
  case Nought:
    painter.drawEllipse(markRect);
    break;
```

In the case of a cross, we draw two lines between the top-left and bottom-right corners and between the top-right and bottom-left corners:

```
case Cross:
  painter.drawLine(markRect.topLeft(),
                   markRect.bottomRight());
  painter.drawLine(markRect.topRight(),
                   markRect.bottomLeft());
  break;
```

In the case of an empty position, we do nothing. Remember that the framework clears the window before the repainting:

```
    case Empty:
      break;
  }
}
```

When a player has made a move, we check if the move has led to victory. We call `countMarks` in four directions to `checkWinner` and see if the move has caused five marks in a row:

```
void NaCWidget::checkWinner(int row, int column, Mark mark) {
```

For the north and south directions, the code would be:

```
if ((countMarks(row, column, -1, 0, mark) >= 5) ||
```

For the west and east directions, the code would be:

```
(countMarks(row, column, 0, -1, mark) >= 5) ||
```

For the northwest and southeast directions, the code would be:

```
(countMarks(row, column, -1, 1, mark) >=5)||
```

For southeast and northwest, it would be:

```
(countMarks(row, column, 1, 1, mark) >= 5)) {
```

If the move has caused five marks in a row, we display a message box with the winner (black or white). In Noughts and Crosses, there can be no draw:

```
QMessageBox messageBox(QMessageBox::Information,
                       tr("Victory"), QString());
QString text;
text.sprintf("The Winner: %s.",
             (mark == Nought) ? "Nought" : "Cross");

messageBox.setText(text);
messageBox.setStandardButtons(QMessageBox::Ok);
messageBox.exec();
setGameInProgress(false);
```

The game grid is cleared, and is thereby ready for another game:

```
    clearGrid();
    update();
  }
}
```

The countMarks method counts the number of marks in a row. We countMarks the number of marks in both directions. For instance, if both rowStep and columnStep are minus one, we decrease the current row and column by one for each iteration. That means that we call countMarks in the northeast direction in the first iteration. In the second iteration, we call countMarks in the opposite direction, that is, in the southwest direction:

```
int NaCWidget::countMarks(int row, int column, int rowStep,
                          int columnStep, Mark mark) {
    int countMarks = 0;
```

We keep counting until we encounter one of the game grid borders, or we find a mark that is not the mark we are counting, that is, the mark of the opposite player or an empty mark:

```
{ int currentRow = row, currentColumn = column;
  while ((currentRow >= 0) && (currentRow < ROWS) &&
         (currentColumn >= 0) && (currentColumn < COLUMNS) &&
         (get(currentRow, currentColumn) == mark)) {
    ++countMarks;
```

```
                    currentRow += rowStep;
                    currentColumn += columnStep;
                }
        }
```

In the second iteration, we subtract the row and column steps instead of adding them. In this way, we call `countMarks` in the opposite direction. We also initialize the current rows and columns by adding the steps in order, so we do not `countMarks` the middle mark twice:

```
        { int currentRow = row + rowStep,
              currentColumn = column + columnStep;
          while ((currentRow >= 0) && (currentRow < ROWS) &&
                 (currentColumn >= 0) && (currentColumn < COLUMNS) &&
                 (get(currentRow, currentColumn) == mark)) {
            ++countMarks;
            currentRow -= rowStep;
            currentColumn -= columnStep;
          }
        }

     return countMarks;
   }
```

The main function

The `main` function creates the application, shows the window, and executes the application until the user closes the window or selects the **Exit** menu item.

Main.cpp

```
        #include "NaCWidget.h"
        #include "NaCWindow.h"
        #include <QApplication>

        int main(int argc, char *argv[]) {
          QApplication application(argc, argv);
          NaCWindow mainWindow;
          mainWindow.show();
          return application.exec();
        }
```

The output for the preceding code is as follows:

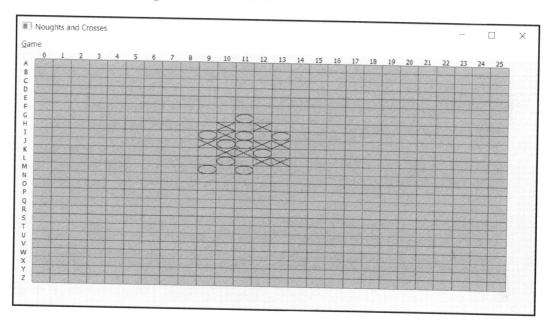

Summary

In this chapter, we developed the two games, Othello and Noughts and Crosses. We were introduced to game theory, and we developed a game grid where the players take turns to add their marks. In Othello, we developed methods to count the number of marks to change for each move, and in Noughts and Crosses, we developed methods to recognize if one of the players had managed to place five marks in a row—if they had, we declared them the winner.

In Chapter 8, *The Computer Plays*, we will develop more advanced versions of these games, where the computer plays against a human.

8

The Computer Plays

In this chapter, we continue to work on the Othello and Noughts and Crosses games. The new part of this chapter is the computer playing against the human; instead of two human players, the computer plays against a human.

Topics we will cover in this chapter include:

- Game-theory reasoning. In both games, the human or the computer can make the first move, and we add code for the computer to play against the human.
- In Othello, for each move, we scan the game grid and try to find the move that causes the highest number of the human's marks to be swapped.
- In Noughts and Crosses, we try to find the position in the game grid that gives us the highest number of marks in a row, or, if the human is about to get five in row, we have to place the computer's mark in a position that prevents that.
- An introduction to random number generation. If the computer can choose between several equivalent moves, it shall randomly select one of the moves.
- We continue to use C++ features such as classes, fields, and methods. We also continue to use Qt features such as windows and widgets.

Othello

In the Othello application of this chapter, we reuse the `MainWindow` and `GameWidget` classes of the previous chapter.

The OthelloWindow class

The OthelloWindow class is rather similar to its counterpart in the previous chapter. However, in addition to the menus and items, the window of this version also holds submenus. The submenus will be added by calling the addAction method in the OthelloWindow.cpp file.

OthelloWindow.h

```
#ifndef OTHELLOWINDOW_H
#define OTHELLOWINDOW_H

#include "..\MainWindow\MainWindow.h"
#include "OthelloWidget.h"

class OthelloWindow : public MainWindow {
  Q_OBJECT

  public:
    OthelloWindow(QWidget *parentWidget = nullptr);
    ~OthelloWindow();

    void closeEvent(QCloseEvent *eventPtr)
                {m_othelloWidgetPtr->closeEvent(eventPtr);}

  private:
    OthelloWidget* m_othelloWidgetPtr;
};

#endif // OTHELLOWINDOW_H
```

The OthelloWindow.cpp file holds the definitions of the methods of the OthelloWindow class.

OthelloWindow.cpp

```
#include "OthelloWidget.h"
#include "OthelloWindow.h"
#include <QtWidgets>
```

The title of the window has been changed to Othello Advanced:

```
OthelloWindow::OthelloWindow(QWidget *parentWidget /*= nullptr*/)
 :MainWindow(parentWidget) {
  setWindowTitle(tr("Othello Advanced"));
  resize(1000, 500);
```

```
        m_othelloWidgetPtr = new OthelloWidget(this);
        setCentralWidget(m_othelloWidgetPtr);

        { QMenu* gameMenuPtr = menuBar()->addMenu(tr("&Game"));
          connect(gameMenuPtr, SIGNAL(aboutToShow()),
                  this, SLOT(onMenuShow()));
```

There are two submenus of the Game menu, Computer Starts and Human Starts:

```
          { QMenu* computerStartsMenuPtr =
              gameMenuPtr->addMenu(tr("&Computer Starts"));
            connect(computerStartsMenuPtr, SIGNAL(aboutToShow()),
                    this, SLOT(onMenuShow()));
```

The Computer Starts submenu holds the two items Computer Black and Computer White:

```
        addAction(computerStartsMenuPtr, tr("Computer &Black"),
                  SLOT(onComputerStartsBlack()), 0,
                  tr("Computer Black"), nullptr,
                  tr("Computer Black"),
                  LISTENER(isComputerStartsBlackEnabled));

        addAction(computerStartsMenuPtr, tr("Computer &White"),
                  SLOT(onComputerStartsWhite()), 0,
                  tr("Computer White"), nullptr,
                  tr("Computer White"),
                  LISTENER(isComputerStartsWhiteEnabled));
        }
```

The Human Starts submenu holds two items, Human Black and Human White:

```
          { QMenu* humanStartsMenuPtr =
              gameMenuPtr->addMenu(tr("&Human Starts"));
            connect(humanStartsMenuPtr, SIGNAL(aboutToShow()),
                    this, SLOT(onMenuShow()));

          addAction(humanStartsMenuPtr, tr("Human &Black"),
                    SLOT(onHumanStartsBlack()), 0, tr("Human Black"),
                    nullptr, tr("Human Black"),
                    LISTENER(isHumanStartsBlackEnabled));

          addAction(humanStartsMenuPtr, tr("Human &White"),
                    SLOT(onHumanStartsWhite()), 0, tr("Human White"),
                    nullptr, tr("Human White"),
                    LISTENER(isHumanStartsWhiteEnabled));
          }
```

```
          gameMenuPtr->addSeparator();

      addAction(gameMenuPtr, tr("&Quit the Game"),
                SLOT(onQuit()),
                QKeySequence(Qt::CTRL + Qt::Key_Q), tr("Quit Game"),
                nullptr, tr("Quit the Game"),
                LISTENER(isQuitEnabled));

      addAction(gameMenuPtr, tr("E&xit"),i
                SLOT(onExit()), QKeySequence::Quit);
    }
  }

  OthelloWindow::~OthelloWindow() {
    delete m_othelloWidgetPtr;
  }
```

The OthelloWidget Class

The OthelloWidget class holds the functionality of Othello. It allows the computer to play against a human:

OthelloWidget.h

```
          #ifndef OTHELLOWIDGET_H
          #define OTHELLOWIDGET_H

          #include "..\MainWindow\GameWidget.h"

          #define ROWS     8
          #define COLUMNS 8

          enum Mark {Empty = 0, Black, White};

          class OthelloWidget : public GameWidget {
            Q_OBJECT

            public:
              OthelloWidget(QWidget* parentWidget);

              void mouseMark(int row, int column);
              void drawMark(QPainter& painter,
                            const QRect& markRect, int mark);

            public slots:
              DEFINE_LISTENER(OthelloWidget, isComputerStartsBlackEnabled);
```

```
        DEFINE_LISTENER(OthelloWidget, isComputerStartsWhiteEnabled);
        DEFINE_LISTENER(OthelloWidget, isHumanStartsBlackEnabled);
        DEFINE_LISTENER(OthelloWidget, isHumanStartsWhiteEnabled);

        void onComputerStartsBlack();
        void onComputerStartsWhite();
        void onHumanStartsBlack();
        void onHumanStartsWhite();

    private:
        bool checkWinner();
        void turn(int row, int column, Mark mark);
        void calculateComputerMove();
        void calculateTurns(int row, int column, Mark mark,
                            QSet<QPair<int,int>>& totalSet,
                            int& neighbours);
        Mark m_humanMark, m_computerMark;
    };

    #endif // OTHELLOWIDGET_H
```

The `OthelloWidget.cpp` file holds the definitions of the methods of the
`OthelloWidget` class:

OthelloWidget.cpp

```
        #include "OthelloWidget.h"
        #include "OthelloWindow.h"

        #include <QTime>
        #include <CTime>
        #include <CAssert>
        using namespace std;

        OthelloWidget::OthelloWidget(QWidget* parentWidget)
         :GameWidget(ROWS, COLUMNS, parentWidget) {
           // Empty.
        }
```

The `isComputerStartsBlackEnabled`, `isComputerStartsWhiteEnabled`,
`isHumanStartsBlackEnabled`, and `isHumanStartsWhiteEnabled` methods are called
before the `Computer Starts` and `Human Starts` submenus. They become enabled if there
is no game in progress:

```
        bool OthelloWidget::isComputerStartsBlackEnabled() {
           return !isGameInProgress();
        }
```

```
bool OthelloWidget::isComputerStartsWhiteEnabled() {
  return !isGameInProgress();
}

bool OthelloWidget::isHumanStartsBlackEnabled() {
  return !isGameInProgress();
}

bool OthelloWidget::isHumanStartsWhiteEnabled() {
  return !isGameInProgress();
}
```

The `onComputerStartsBlack` and `onComputerStartsWhite` methods are called when the user selects one of the items of the `Computer Starts` submenu. They set the computer mark to black or white, start the game by setting the mark in the middle of the game grid, and update the window:

```
void OthelloWidget::onComputerStartsBlack() {
  setGameInProgress(true);
  set(ROWS / 2, COLUMNS / 2, m_computerMark = Black);
  m_humanMark = White;
  update();
}

void OthelloWidget::onComputerStartsWhite() {
  setGameInProgress(true);
  set(ROWS / 2, COLUMNS / 2, m_computerMark = White);
  m_humanMark = Black;
  update();
}
```

The `onHumanStartsBlack` and `onHumanStartsWhite` methods are called when the user selects one of the items of the `Human Starts` submenu. They set the computer mark to black or white and update the window. They do not set any mark in the game grid. Instead, the human is to make the first move:

```
void OthelloWidget::onHumanStartsBlack() {
  setGameInProgress(true);
  m_humanMark = Black;
  m_computerMark = White;
  update();
}

void OthelloWidget::onHumanStartsWhite() {
  setGameInProgress(true);
  m_humanMark = White;
  m_computerMark = Black;
```

```
      update();
  }
```

The `mouseMark` method is called when the user clicks one empty position in the game grid. We start by setting the next mark at the position, and turn the marks as a result of the move:

```
void OthelloWidget::mouseMark(int row, int column) {
    set(row, column, m_humanMark);
    turn(row, column, m_humanMark);
    update();
```

If the human's move did not cause the game grid to become full, we call to `calculateComputerMove` to set the computer mark to the position, causing the maximum number of opposite marks to be turned. We then update the window and call `checkWinner` again to decide if the computer move caused the game grid to become full:

```
    if (!checkWinner()) {
      calculateComputerMove();
      update();
      checkWinner();
    }
  }
```

The `drawMark` method is called when a position in the game grid needs to be repainted. It draws the mark in the same way as in the previous chapter:

```
void OthelloWidget::drawMark(QPainter& painter,
                             const QRect& markRect, int mark) {
    painter.setPen(Qt::black);
    painter.drawRect(markRect);
    painter.fillRect(markRect, Qt::lightGray);

    switch (mark) {
      case Black:
        painter.setPen(Qt::black);
        painter.setBrush(Qt::black);
        painter.drawEllipse(markRect);
        break;

      case White:
        painter.setPen(Qt::white);
        painter.setBrush(Qt::white);
        painter.drawEllipse(markRect);
        break;

      case Empty:
        break;
```

```
        }
    }
```

The `checkWinner` method of this chapter is also similar to its counterpart in the previous chapter. It checks whether the game grid is full. If it is full, the winner is announced, or else it is a draw:

```
bool OthelloWidget::checkWinner() {
  int blacks = 0, whites = 0, empties = 0;

  for (int row = 0; row < ROWS; ++row) {
    for (int column = 0; column < COLUMNS; ++column) {
      switch (get(row, column)) {
        case Black:
          ++blacks;
          break;

        case White:
          ++whites;
          break;

        case Empty:
          ++empties;
          break;
      }
    }
  }

  if (empties == 0) {
    QMessageBox messageBox(QMessageBox::Information,
                           tr("Victory"), QString());
    QString text;

    if (blacks > whites) {
      text.sprintf("The Winner: %s.", (m_computerMark == Black)
                                      ? "Computer" : "Human");
    }
    else if (whites > blacks) {
      text.sprintf("The Winner: %s.", (m_computerMark == White)
                                      ? "Computer" : "Human");
    }
    else {
      text.sprintf("A Draw.");
    }

    messageBox.setText(text);
    messageBox.setStandardButtons(QMessageBox::Ok);
```

```
        messageBox.exec();
        setGameInProgress(false);
        clearGrid();
        update();

        return true;
    }

    return false;
}
```

The `calculateComputerMove` method calculates the move of the computer that generates the highest number of turned opposite marks. We iterate through the computer marks and, for each mark, call `calculateTurns` to obtain the maximum number of opposite marks that would be turned if we placed the marks at that position. For each mark, we also obtain the number of neighbours, which is valuable if we do not find any marks to turn.

The `maxTurnSetSize` and `maxNeighbours` fields hold the maximum number of turnable marks and neighbours; `maxTurnSetList` holds a list of the maximum sets of positions of turnable marks, and `maxNeighboursList` holds a list of the maximum number of neighbours:

```
void OthelloWidget::calculateComputerMove() {
    int maxTurnSetSize = 0, maxNeighbours = 0;
    QList<QSet<QPair<int,int>>> maxTurnSetList;
    QList<QPair<int,int>> maxNeighboursList;
```

We iterate through all the positions in the game grid. For each empty position, we obtain the number of opposite marks to be turned if we were to place our mark in that position. We also obtain the number of opposite neighbours:

```
for (int row = 0; row < ROWS; ++row) {
    for (int column = 0; column < COLUMNS; ++column) {
        if (get(row, column) == Empty) {
            QSet<QPair<int,int>> turnSet;
            int neighbours = 0;
            calculateTurns(row, column, m_computerMark,
                           turnSet, neighbours);
            int turnSetSize = turnSet.size();
```

If we find a set of turnable marks that is larger than the current maximum set, we set the `maxTurnSetSize` field to the size of the new turnable set, insert the current position in the set, clear `maxTurnSetList` (since we do not want its previous smaller sets), and add the new set.

We add the current set for the sake of simplicity; it is easier to add it to the set than to store it in any other way:

```
if (turnSetSize > maxTurnSetSize) {
  maxTurnSetSize = turnSetSize;
  turnSet.insert(QPair<int,int>(row, column));
  maxTurnSetList.clear();
  maxTurnSetList.append(turnSet);
}
```

If the new set is not empty and of equal size to the maximum set, then we simply add it to maxTurnSetList:

```
else if ((turnSetSize > 0) &&
         (turnSetSize == maxTurnSetSize)) {
  turnSet.insert(QPair<int,int>(row, column));
  maxTurnSetList.append(turnSet);
}
```

We also check the number of neighbours of the current position. We work in the same way as in the turnable set case. If the neighbours are more than the maximum number of neighbours, we clear maxNeighboursList and add the new position:

```
if (neighbours > maxNeighbours) {
  maxNeighbours = neighbours;
  maxNeighboursList.clear();
  maxNeighboursList.append(QPair<int,int>(row, column));
}
```

If there is at least one neighbour, and the neighbours is equal to the maximum number of neighbours, we add it to the maxNeighboursList list:

```
        else if ((neighbours > 0) &&
                 (neighbours == maxNeighbours)) {
          maxNeighboursList.append(QPair<int,int>(row, column));
        }
      }
    }
  }
```

If there is at least one position where we will turn at least one opposite mark, we choose it. If there are several positions that will turn the same amount of opposite marks, we randomly select one of them. We use the C standard functions srand, rand, and time to obtain a random integer number.

The random number generator algorithm takes a start value and then generates a sequence of random numbers. The `srand` function initializes the generator with a start value, and then `rand` is called repeatedly in order to obtain new random numbers. In order to not call `srand` with the same start value every time (which would result in the same random number sequence), we call `srand` with the result of a call to the `time` standard C function, which returns the number of seconds since January 1, 1970. In this way, the random number generator is initialized with a new value for each game, and we obtain a new sequence of random numbers by repeatedly calling `rand`:

```
if (maxTurnSetSize > 0) {
    srand(time(NULL));
    int index = rand() % maxTurnSetList.size();
    QSet<QPair<int,int>> maxTurnSet = maxTurnSetList[index];
```

When we have obtained the set of positions to be turned, we iterate through the set and set the computer mark to all its positions:

```
    for (QPair<int,int> position : maxTurnSet) {
        int row = position.first, column = position.second;
        set(row, column, m_computerMark);
    }
}
```

If there is no position that would cause opposite marks to be turned, we look at the neighbours instead. In the same way, we randomly select one of the positions with the maximum number of neighbours. Note that we do not need to iterate through any set; in this case, we only set one mark:

```
else {
    assert(!maxNeighboursList.empty());
    srand(time(NULL));
    int index = rand() % maxNeighboursList.size();
    QPair<int,int> position = maxNeighboursList[index];
    int row = position.first, column = position.second;
    set(row, column, m_computerMark);
}
}
```

The `turn` method is called when the human has made a move. It calls `calculateMark` to obtain a set of turnable opposite marks, and then iterates through the set and sets each position in the game grid:

```
void OthelloWidget::turn(int row, int column, Mark mark) {
    QSet<QPair<int,int>> turnSet;
    calculateMark(row, column, mark, turnSet);
```

```
        for (QPair<int,int> pair : turnSet) {
          int row = pair.first, column = pair.second;
          set(row, column, mark);
        }
      }
```

The `calculateTurns` method calculates the set of turnable opposite marks and number of neighbours of the given position:

```
void OthelloWidget::calculateTurns(int row, int column,
              Mark playerMark,QSet<QPair<int,int>>& totalSet,
              int& neighbours) {
```

Each integer pair in `directionArray` refers to a direction in accordance with the compass rising:

```
QPair<int,int> directionArray[] =
  {QPair<int,int>(-1, 0),    // North
   QPair<int,int>(-1, 1),    // Northeast
   QPair<int,int>(0, 1),     // East
   QPair<int,int>(1, 1),     // Southeast
   QPair<int,int>(1, 0),     // South
   QPair<int,int>(1, -1),    // Southwest
   QPair<int,int>(0, -1),    // West
   QPair<int,int>(-1, -1)};  // Northwest
```

The size of an array can be decided by dividing its total size (in bytes) by the size of its first value:

```
int arraySize =
  (sizeof directionArray) / (sizeof directionArray[0]);

neighbours = 0;
int opponentMark = (playerMark == Black) ? White : Black;
```

We iterate through the directions and, for each direction, keep moving as long as we find the mark of the opponent:

```
for (int index = 0; index < arraySize; ++index) {
  QPair<int,int> pair = directionArray[index];
```

The `row` and `column` fields hold the current row and column as long as we iterate through a direction:

```
int rowStep = pair.first, columnStep = pair.second,
  currRow = row, currColumn = column;
```

First, we check if we have a neighbor of the opponent mark in the closest position. If we have not reached one of the borders of the game grid, and if there is an opponent mark in the position, we increase `neighbours`:

```
if (((row + rowStep) >= 0) && ((row + rowStep) < ROWS) &&
    ((column + rowStep) >= 0) &&
    ((column + columnStep) < COLUMNS) &&
    (get(row + rowStep, column + rowStep) == opponentMark)) {
  ++neighbours;
}
```

We gather the marks we find during the iteration in `directionSet`:

```
QSet<QPair<int,int>> directionSet;

while (true) {
  currRow += rowStep;
  currColumn += columnStep;
```

If we reach one of the borders of the game grid, or if we find an empty position, we break the iteration:

```
if ((currRow < 0) || (currRow == ROWS) ||
    (currColumn < 0) || (currColumn == COLUMNS) ||
    (get(currRow, currColumn) == Empty)) {
  break;
}
```

If we find the player's mark, we add the `directionSet` to the total set and break the iterations:

```
else if (get(currRow, currColumn) == playerMark) {
  totalSet += directionSet;
  break;
}
```

If we do find the player's mark or an empty position, we have found the opponent's mark, and we add its position to the direction set:

```
else {
  directionSet.insert(QPair<int,int>(row, column));
}
}
}
```

The main function

As always, the `main` function creates an application, shows the window, and executes the application until the user closes the window or selects the **Exit** menu item.

Main.cpp

```
#include "OthelloWidget.h"
#include "OthelloWindow.h"
#include <QApplication>

int main(int argc, char *argv[]) {
  QApplication application(argc, argv);
  OthelloWindow othelloWindow;
  othelloWindow.show();
  return application.exec();
}
```

Noughts and Crosses

The Noughts and Crosses application of this chapter is based on the version in the previous chapter. The difference is that in this version the computer plays against a human.

The NaCWindow class

The `NaCWindow` class is similar to the `OthelloWindow` class in the previous section (NaC is an abbreviation for Noughts and Crosses). It adds two submenus to the game menu, where the computer or human makes the first move and selects a nought or cross:

NaCWindow.h

```
#ifndef NACWINDOW_H
#define NACWINDOW_H

#include "..\MainWindow\MainWindow.h"
#include "NaCWidget.h"

class NaCWindow : public MainWindow {
  Q_OBJECT

  public:
    NaCWindow(QWidget *parentWidget = nullptr);
    ~NaCWindow();
```

```
  public:
    void closeEvent(QCloseEvent *eventPtr)
                  {m_nacWidgetPtr->closeEvent(eventPtr);}

  private:
    NaCWidget* m_nacWidgetPtr;
};


#endif // NACWINDOW_H
```

The `NaCWindow.cpp` file holds the definitions of the methods of the `NaCWindow` class:

NaCWindow.cpp

```
#include "NaCWindow.h"
#include <QtWidgets>
```

The title has been changed to `Noughts and Crosses Advanced`:

```
NaCWindow::NaCWindow(QWidget *parentWidget /*= nullptr*/)
 :MainWindow(parentWidget) {
  setWindowTitle(tr("Noughts and Crosses Advanced"));
  resize(1000, 500);

  m_nacWidgetPtr = new NaCWidget(this);
  setCentralWidget(m_nacWidgetPtr);

  { QMenu* gameMenuPtr = menuBar()->addMenu(tr("&Game"));
    connect(gameMenuPtr, SIGNAL(aboutToShow()),
          this, SLOT(onMenuShow()));

    { QMenu* computerStartsMenuPtr =
        gameMenuPtr->addMenu(tr("&Computer Starts"));
      connect(computerStartsMenuPtr, SIGNAL(aboutToShow()),
            this, SLOT(onMenuShow()));

    addAction(computerStartsMenuPtr, tr("Computer &Nought"),
            SLOT(onComputerStartsNought()), 0,
            tr("Computer Nought"), nullptr,
            tr("Computer Nought"),
            LISTENER(isComputerStartsNoughtEnabled));

      addAction(computerStartsMenuPtr, tr("Computer &Cross"),
            SLOT(onComputerStartsCross()), 0,
            tr("Computer Cross"), nullptr,
            tr("Computer Cross"),
            LISTENER(isComputerStartsCrossEnabled));
    }
```

```
      { QMenu* humanStartsMenuPtr =
          gameMenuPtr->addMenu(tr("&Human Starts"));
        connect(humanStartsMenuPtr, SIGNAL(aboutToShow()),
                this, SLOT(onMenuShow()));

        addAction(humanStartsMenuPtr, tr("Human &Nought"),
                SLOT(onHumanNought()), 0, tr("Human Nought"),
                nullptr, tr("Human Nought"),
                LISTENER(isHumanNoughtEnabled));

        addAction(humanStartsMenuPtr, tr("Human &Cross"),
                SLOT(onHumanCross()), 0, tr("Human Cross"),
                nullptr, tr("Human Cross"),
                LISTENER(isHumanCrossEnabled));
      }

    gameMenuPtr->addSeparator();

    addAction(gameMenuPtr, tr("&Quit the Game"),
            SLOT(onQuit()),
            QKeySequence(Qt::CTRL + Qt::Key_Q), tr("Quit Game"),
            nullptr, tr("Quit the Game"),
            LISTENER(isQuitEnabled));

    addAction(gameMenuPtr, tr("E&xit"),
            SLOT(onExit()), QKeySequence::Quit);
    }
}

NaCWindow::~NaCWindow() {
  delete m_nacWidgetPtr;
}
```

The NaCWidget class

The NaCWidget class has been improved compared to the version in the previous chapter.
It holds the calculateComputerMove and calculateMarkValue methods for the
computer to play against the human:

NaCWidget.h

```
#ifndef NACWIDGET_H
#define NACWIDGET_H

#include "..\MainWindow\GameWidget.h"
```

```
#define ROWS     26
#define COLUMNS 26

enum Mark {Empty = 0, Nought, Cross};

class NaCWidget : public GameWidget {
  Q_OBJECT

  public:
    NaCWidget(QWidget* parentWidget);

    void mouseMark(int row, int column);
    void drawMark(QPainter& painter,
                  const QRect& markRect, int mark);

  public slots:
    DEFINE_LISTENER(NaCWidget, isComputerStartsNoughtEnabled);
    DEFINE_LISTENER(NaCWidget, isComputerStartsCrossEnabled);
    DEFINE_LISTENER(NaCWidget, isHumanStartsNoughtEnabled);
    DEFINE_LISTENER(NaCWidget, isHumanStartsCrossEnabled);

    void onComputerStartsNought();
    void onComputerStartsCross();
    void onHumanStartsNought();
    void onHumanStartsCross();

  private:
    bool checkWinner(int row, int column, Mark mark);
    int countMarks(int row, int column, int rowStep,
                   int columnStep, Mark mark);
    void calculateComputerMove(int& row, int &column);
    double calculateMarkValue(int row, int column, Mark mark);

    Mark m_humanMark, m_computerMark;
};

#endif // NACWIDGET_H
```

The NaCWidget.cpp file holds the definitions of the methods of the NaCWidget class:

NaCWidget.cpp

```
#include "NaCWidget.h"
#include <CTime>
#include <CAssert>

NaCWidget::NaCWidget(QWidget* parentWidget)
  :GameWidget(ROWS, COLUMNS, parentWidget) {
```

```
      // Empty.
   }
```

The isComputerStartsNoughtEnabled, isComputerStartsCrossEnabled, isHumanStartsNoughtEnabled, and isHumanStartsCrossEnabled methods decide whether to enable the Computer Nought, Computer Cross, Human Nought, and Human cross menu items. They are all enabled when there is no game in progress:

```
bool NaCWidget::isComputerStartsNoughtEnabled() {
  return !isGameInProgress();
}

bool NaCWidget::isComputerStartsCrossEnabled() {
  return !isGameInProgress();
}

bool NaCWidget::isHumanStartsNoughtEnabled() {
  return !isGameInProgress();
}

bool NaCWidget::isHumanStartsCrossEnabled() {
  return !isGameInProgress();
}
```

The onComputerStartsNought, onComputerStartsCross, onHumanStartsNought, and onHumanStartsCross are called when the user selects the Computer Noughts, Computer Cross, Human Noughts, and Human Cross menu items. They set the game in progress, set the computer and human marks to nought and cross, and update the window. In cases where the computer makes the first move, it is placed in the middle of the game grid in order to use the game grid as effectively as possible:

```
void NaCWidget::onComputerStartsNought() {
  setGameInProgress(true);
  set(ROWS /2, COLUMNS / 2, m_computerMark = Nought);
  m_humanMark = Cross;
  update();
}

void NaCWidget::onComputerStartsCross() {
  setGameInProgress(true);
  set(ROWS /2, COLUMNS / 2, m_computerMark = Cross);
  m_humanMark = Nought;
  update();
}

void NaCWidget::onHumanStartsNought() {
```

```
      setGameInProgress(true);
      m_computerMark = Cross;
      m_humanMark = Nought;
      update();
   }

   void NaCWidget::onHumanStartsCross() {
      setGameInProgress(true);
      m_computerMark = Nought;
      m_humanMark = Cross;
      update();
   }
```

The `mouseMark` method is called when the human player clicks an empty position in the game grid. We start by setting the mark to the position and updating the window:

```
   void NaCWidget::mouseMark(int row, int column) {
      set(row, column, m_humanMark);
      update();
```

If the human's move did not cause them to win the game, we calculate the next move of the computer, set the position, check if the move has caused the computer to win the game, and update the window:

```
      if (!checkWinner(row, column, m_humanMark)) {
         calculateComputerMove(row, column);
         set(row, column, m_computerMark);
         checkWinner(row, column, m_computerMark);
         update();
      }
   }
```

The `drawMark` method is called when a position needs to be repainted. It is similar to its counterpart in the previous chapter. It draws a nought or a cross:

```
   void NaCWidget::drawMark(QPainter& painter,
                            const QRect& markRect, int mark) {
      painter.setPen(Qt::black);

      switch (mark) {
         case Nought:
            painter.drawEllipse(markRect);
            break;

         case Cross:
            painter.drawLine(markRect.topLeft(),
                             markRect.bottomRight());
```

```
        painter.drawLine(markRect.topRight(),
                         markRect.bottomLeft());
      break;

    case Empty:
      break;
    }
  }
```

The `checkWinner` method is also similar to its counterpart in the previous chapter. It decides if the latest move has caused five marks in a row. If it has, the winner is announced:

```
bool NaCWidget::checkWinner(int row, int column, Mark mark) {
  if ((countMarks(row, column, -1, 0, mark) >= 5) ||
      (countMarks(row, column, 0, -1, mark) >= 5) ||
      (countMarks(row, column, -1, 1, mark) >= 5) ||
      (countMarks(row, column, 1, 1, mark) >= 5)) {
    QMessageBox messageBox(QMessageBox::Information,
                           tr("Victory"), QString());
    QString text;
    text.sprintf("The Winner: %s.",
                 (mark == m_computerMark) ? "Computer" : "Human");

    messageBox.setText(text);
    messageBox.setStandardButtons(QMessageBox::Ok);
    messageBox.exec();
    setGameInProgress(false);
    clearGrid();
    update();
    return true;
  }

  return false;
}
```

The `countMarks` method counts the number of marks in a row. It has been improved compared to its counterpart in the previous chapter. In this version, we also count the highest possible number of marks in a row that the move can lead to. Since `countMarks` is called by `calculateComputerMove`, we need to know how many marks in a row the move may lead to:

```
double NaCWidget::countMarks(int row, int column, int rowStep,
                             int columnStep, Mark mark) {
```

The `markCount` field holds the number of marks in a row that we would get if we placed our mark at the given position; `freeCount` holds the number of marks in a row we possibly can get if we continue to add marks in that row. The reason is that the computer will not add marks to a row that cannot become five in a row:

```
double markCount = 0;
int freeCount = 0;
```

We iterate through the game grid in the given direction:

```
{ bool marked = true;
  int currentRow = row, currentColumn = column;

  while ((currentRow >= 0) && (currentRow < ROWS) &&
         (currentColumn >= 0) && (currentColumn < COLUMNS)) {
```

As long as we find the mark, we increase both `markCount` and `freeCount`:

```
if (get(currentRow, currentColumn) == mark) {
  if (marked) {
    ++markCount;
  }

  ++freeCount;
}
```

If we find an empty position, we add 0.4 (since a free row is better than a closed row) to the `markCount`, and continue to increase the `freeCount`:

```
else if (get(currentRow, currentColumn) == Empty) {
  if (marked) {
    markCount += 0.4;
  }

  marked = false;
  ++freeCount;
}
```

If we find neither the computer mark nor an empty position, we must have found the human's mark, and we break the iteration:

```
else {
  break;
}
```

At the end of each iteration, we add the row and columns steps to the current row and column:

```
        currentRow += rowStep;
        currentColumn += columnStep;
    }
}
```

We perform a similar iteration in the opposite direction. The only difference is that we subtract the row and columns steps at the end of each iteration, instead of adding to them:

```
{ bool marked = true;
  int currentRow = row + rowStep,
      currentColumn = column + columnStep;

  while ((currentRow >= 0) && (currentRow < ROWS) &&
         (currentColumn >= 0) && (currentColumn < COLUMNS)) {
    if (get(currentRow, currentColumn) == mark) {
      if (marked) {
        ++markCount;
      }
    }
    else if (get(currentRow, currentColumn) == Empty) {
      if (marked) {
        markCount += 0.4;
      }

      marked = false;
      ++freeCount;
    }
    else {
      break;
    }

    currentRow -= rowStep;
    currentColumn -= columnStep;
  }
}
```

If the free count is at least five, we return the mark count. If it is less than five, we return zero, since we cannot obtain five in a row in this direction:

```
        return (freeCount >= 5) ? markCount : 0;
    }
```

The `calculateComputerMove` method calculates the computer move that causes the maximum numbers of marks in a row. We count both the computer and human's rows, since we may be facing a situation where we need to stop the human from winning instead of maximizing the computer's chance to win.

The `maxComputerValue` and `maxHumanValue` fields hold the maximum number of marks in a row that we have found so far. The `maxComputerList` and `maxHumanList` hold the position that causes the maximum number of marks in a row for the computer and the human:

```
void NaCWidget::calculateComputerMove(int& maxRow, int &maxColumn){
    double maxComputerValue = 0, maxHumanValue = 0;
    QList<QPair<int,int>> maxComputerList, maxHumanList;
```

We iterate through the game grid. For each empty position, we try to set the computer and human mark and see how many marks in a row that would cause:

```
for (int row = 0; row < ROWS; ++row) {
    for (int column = 0; column < COLUMNS; ++column)   {
        if (get(row, column) == Empty) {
            set(row, column, m_computerMark);
```

We obtain the maximum number of marks in a row for the computer and human mark. If it is larger than the previous maximum number, we clear the list and add the position to the list:

```
{ double computerValue =
    calculateMarkValue(row, column, m_computerMark);

  if (computerValue > maxComputerValue) {
    maxComputerValue = computerValue;
    maxComputerList.clear();
    maxComputerList.append(QPair<int,int>(row, column));
  }
```

If the new number of marks in a row is greater than zero or equals the maximum number, we just add the position:

```
  else if ((computerValue > 0) &&
           (computerValue == maxComputerValue)) {
    maxComputerList.append(QPair<int,int>(row, column));
  }
}
```

We do the same for the human mark as the computer mark:

```
set(row, column, m_humanMark);

{ double humanValue =
    calculateMarkValue(row, column, m_humanMark);

  if (humanValue > maxHumanValue) {
    maxHumanValue = humanValue;
    maxHumanList.clear();
    maxHumanList.append(QPair<int,int>(row, column));
  }
  else if ((humanValue > 0) &&
            (humanValue == maxHumanValue)) {
    maxHumanList.append(QPair<int,int>(row, column));
  }
}
```

Finally, we reset the position to the empty value:

```
    set(row, column, Empty);
  }
 }
}
```

The computer or human must have at least one in a row for a position:

```
assert(!maxComputerList.empty() && !maxHumanList.empty());
```

If the computer's value is at least two and larger the human value, or if the human value is less the four, we randomly select one of the computer's maximum moves:

```
if ((maxComputerValue >= 2) &&
    ((maxComputerValue >= maxHumanValue) ||
     (maxHumanValue < 3.8))) {
  srand(time(NULL));
  QPair<int,int> pair =
    maxComputerList[rand() % maxComputerList.size()];
  maxRow = pair.first;
  maxColumn = pair.second;
}
```

However, if the computer cannot make at least two in a row, or if the human is about to get five in a row, we randomly select one of the human's maximum moves:

```
else {
  srand(time(NULL));
  QPair<int,int> pair =
    maxHumanList[rand() % maxHumanList.size()];
  maxRow = pair.first;
  maxColumn = pair.second;
  }
}
```

The `calculateMarkValue` method calculates the maximum number of marks in a row that the given position may cause by calculating the larger value of its four directions:

```
double NaCWidget::calculateMarkValue(int row, int column,
                                          Mark mark) {
  return qMax(qMax(countMarks(row, column, -1, 0, mark),
                   countMarks(row, column, 0, -1, mark)),
              qMax(countMarks(row, column, -1, 1, mark),
                   countMarks(row, column, 1, 1, mark)));
}
```

The main function

Finally, the `main` function works at it always does in the Qt applications:

Main.cpp

```
#include "NaCWidget.h"
#include "NaCWindow.h"
#include <QApplication>

int main(int argc, char *argv[]) {
  QApplication application(argc, argv);
  NaCWindow mainWindow;
  mainWindow.show();
  return application.exec();
}
```

Summary

In this chapter, we have developed more advanced versions of the games of the previous chapter. In both Othello and Noughts and Crosses, we have added code that lets the computer play against the human. In Othello, we looked for the position in the game grid that would cause the highest number of the opponent's marks to be changed. In Noughts and Crosses, we searched for the move that gave the computer the highest possible number of marks in a row, preferably five in a row. However, we also had to search for the potential number of marks in a row for the opponent, and prevent their next move if it led to victory. Now, I suggest that you sit back and enjoy a couple of rounds with the computer before moving on to the next chapter.

In the next chapter, we will start developing a **Domain-Specific Language (DSL)**, which is a language intended for a specific domain. We will develop a DSL for specifying the drawings of graphical objects, such as lines, rectangles, ellipses, and text, as well as the settings for color, font, pen and brush style, and alignment. We will also write a viewer that displays the graphical objects.

9

Domain-Specific Language

In the previous chapters, we developed the games Othello and Noughts and Crosses with the Qt library. In this chapter, we will start to develop a **Domain-Specific Language** (DSL), which is a language intended for a specific domain. More specifically, we will develop a language for writing graphical objects in a Qt widget. The language allows us to draw lines, rectangles, ellipses, and to write text. Moreover, it does allow us to choose color as well as pen and brush style for the graphical objects. It also allows us to choose font and alignment for the text.

Topics we will cover in this chapter include:

- First, we will informally look into the source code of our DSL by looking at an example. We will draw graphical objects and set their color, style, and font.
- We will formally define our language with grammar.
- When we have defined the grammar, we write the scanner. The scanner reads the source code and recognizes meaningful sequences of characters, called **tokens**.
- When we have written the scanner, we write the parser. The parser can be considered the heart of our DSL. It requests new tokens from the scanner, when needed. It checks that the source code complies with the grammar, and it generates a sequence of actions. Each action holds an instruction, such as setting the color or drawing a line.
- Finally, we write a viewer that reads the action sequence generated by the parser and displays the graphical objects in a Qt widget.

Introducing the source language – a simple example

The source language of our DSL is made up by a sequence of instructions. There are instructions for drawing graphical objects such as lines, rectangles, ellipses, and text. We also have instructions for setting the color and style of the objects as well as font and alignment of the text. Finally, there is instruction for assigning values to a name.

Let us look at an example. The following code draws a rectangle and writes text. Note that the language is not case-sensitive, that is, it does not matter whether we use small or capital letters in our code. We start by defining the top-left corner of a rectangle:

```
topLeft = point(100, 100);
```

We use the coordinate operators to extract the *x* and *y* coordinates of the top-left point and define the bottom-right corner:

```
left = xCoordinate(topleft);
top = yCoordinate(topLeft);
bottomRight = point(left + 100, top + 100);
```

We use the predefined values `DashLine` and `CrossPatterns` to set the style of the pen and brush:

```
SetPenStyle(DashLine);
SetBrushStyle(CrossPattern);
```

We use the predefined color `Black` for the pen and create our own color `Purple` for the brush. We can create a new color with three values corresponding to their red, green, and blue components. Each component can hold a value between 0 and 255, inclusive:

```
SetPenColor(Black);
PurpleColor = color(128, 0, 128);
SetBrushColor(PurpleColor);
DrawRectangle(topLeft, bottomRight);
```

We continue to add a text, with font and alignment. We choose 12 point `Times New Roman` with left horizontal alignment and top vertical alignment:

```
SetFont(font("Times New Roman", 12));
SetHorizontalAlignment(AlignLeft);
SetVerticalAlignment(AlignTop);
DrawText(point(300, 150), "Hello, DSL!");
```

The instructions of this example will be divided into meaningful parts by the scanner; the parser will check that the instructions comply with the grammar and generate a sequence of actions read by the viewer and display the following Qt widget:

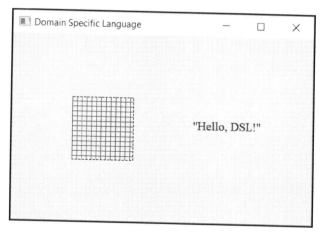

The grammar of the source language

The source language of our DSL needs to be exactly defined. We do that by defining grammar for the language. Grammar is made up by rules (in *italic* style), keywords (in **bold** style), separations, and punctuations.

The `program` rule is the start rule. The arrow (->) means that a program is made up by an instructions list. The arrow can be read as:

```
program -> instructionList
```

In the grammar, an asterisk (*) means **zero** or **more**. Hence, an instruction list is made up by zero or more instructions:

```
instructionList -> instruction*
```

The assignment instruction takes a name followed by the assignment operator (=), an expression, and a semicolon. The instructions for setting the pen and brush color and style take one expression, so do the settings of the font and alignment. The instructions for drawing lines, rectangles, and text take two expressions. Note that every instruction is terminated by a semicolon (;).

The vertical bar (|) can be read as **or**. An instruction is an assignment or the setting of the pen color or the setting of the brush color, and so on:

```
instruction -> name = expression;
             | SetPenColor(expression);
             | SetPenStyle(expression);
             | SetBrushColor(expression);
             | SetBrushStyle(expression);
             | SetFont(expression);
             | SetHorizontalAlignment(expression);
             | SetVerticalAlignment(expression);
             | DrawLine(expression, expression);
             | DrawRectangle(expression, expression);
             | DrawEllipse(expression, expression);
             | DrawText(expression, expression);
```

The next part of the parser to define is the expressions. First, we look at the operators of the expressions. We also have to look into the priority of the operators. For instance, multiplication and division have higher priority than addition and subtraction. The operators of the grammar have the following priorities:

Expression	Operator	Priority
Addition Subtraction	+ −	Lowest
Multiplication Division	* /	
Primary	point xCoordinate yCoordinate color font (expression) name value	Highest

We define two rules each for addition and subtraction, as well as for multiplication and division. We start with the lowest priority level, which is addition and subtraction. In the `expression` rule we call the `mulDivExpression` rule, which handles multiplication and division expressions, and we call the `expressionRest` rule to examine the rest of the expression:

```
expression -> mulDivExpression expressionRest
```

In the `expressionRest` rule we look into the next token. If it is a plus or a minus, we have an addition or subtraction expression. We call `mulDivExpression` to handle expressions of higher priority. Finally, we call the `expressionRest` rule again in case of another plus or minus. However, if the first token is neither a plus nor a minus, we do nothing:

```
expressionRest -> + mulDivExpression expressionRest
               | - mulDivExpression expressionRest
               | /* empty */
```

`mulDivExpression` and `mulDivExpressionRest` work in the same way as `expression` and `expressionRest` shown previously:

```
mulDivExpression -> primaryExpression mulDivExpressionRest
mulDivExpressionRest -> * primaryExpression mulDivExpressionRest
                     | / primaryExpression mulDivExpressionRest
                     | /* empty */
```

The primary expression is a point, an *x* or *y* coordinate, a color, a font, a name, or a value. A point is made up by two expressions holding the *x* and *y* coordinate of the point. A coordinate takes an expression holding a point and gives it an *x* or *y* coordinate:

```
primaryExpression -> point(expression, expression)
                  | xCoordinate(expression)
                  | yCoordinate(expression)
```

A color expression is made up by its red, green, and blue components, while a font expression is made up by the name and size of the font:

```
| color(expression, expression, expression)
| font(expression, expression)
```

An expression can be enclosed in parentheses in order to change the priority of the expression. For instance, in the expression 2 + 3 x 4, multiplication takes precedence over addition, but in the expression (2 + 3) x 4, addition takes precedence over multiplication:

```
| (expression)
```

Finally, an expression can be a name earlier associated with a value, or simply a value:

```
| name
| value
```

The target language

The target language is defined by a sequence of actions. Informally, the actions correspond to the instructions of the grammar. We have actions for setting the color or style of a pen or a brush, and for setting the horizontal or vertical alignment of the text, as well as actually drawing the lines, rectangles, ellipses, and text of the drawing. Later in this chapter, we will write a parser that generates a sequence of actions, and a viewer that reads the actions and displays graphical objects in a Qt widget.

An `Action` object holds the identity of the action (which is defined by the `TokenId` enumeration in the `Token` class, as follows) together with, at most, two values.

Action.h:

```
#ifndef ACTION_H
#define ACTION_H

#include "Token.h"
#include "Value.h"

class Action {
  public:
    Action(TokenId actionId, const Value& value1 = Value(),
           const Value& value2 = Value());

    Action(const Action& action);
    Action operator=(const Action& action);

    TokenId id() const {return m_actionId;}
    const Value& value1() const {return m_value1;}
    const Value& value2() const {return m_value2;}

  private:
    TokenId m_actionId;
    Value m_value1, m_value2;
};

#endif // ACTION_H
```

The `Action.cpp` file holds the definitions of the methods of the `Action` class.

Action.cpp:

```
#include "Action.h"
```

The constructor takes the action identity and at most two values:

```
Action::Action(TokenId actionId,
               const Value& value1 /*= Value()*/,
               const Value& value2 /*= Value()*/ )
  :m_actionId(actionId),
   m_value1(value1),
   m_value2(value2) {
   // Empty.
}
```

The colors

When setting the color of the pen or brush, we need to submit the color with the instruction. We can use the color rule in the preceding grammar to create our own color. However, there is a set of predefined colors of the Qt class `QColor`. The following scanner defines a set of predefined `QColor` objects (`Aqua`, `Black`, ...) and maps them to their names. For instance, the user can write the following instruction in the source code:

```
SetPenColor(Aqua);
```

In that case, since the name `Aqua` is associated with the `QColor` object `Aqua`, the pen color is set to `Aqua`.

Colors.h:

```
#ifndef COLOR_H
#define COLOR_H

#include <QWidget>

extern QColor
  Aqua, Black, Blue, Brown, Cyan, Gray, Green, Lime, Magenta,
  Navyblue, Orange, Orchid, Pink, Purple, Red, Silver, Snow,
  SteelBlue, SystemColor, Turquoise, Violet, White, Yellow;

#endif // COLOR_H
```

The `Colors.cpp` file holds the definitions of the colors in the `Colors.h` file.

Colors.cpp:

```
#include "Colors.h"
```

Each color is defined by its red, green, and blue component. Each component holds a value from 0 to 255, inclusive. For instance, the `Blue` color holds the full value of the blue component and zero of the other components, while `Yellow` is a blend of red and green:

```
QColor
    Aqua(0, 255, 255), Black(0, 0, 0), Blue(0, 0, 255),
    Brown(165, 42, 42), Cyan(0, 255, 255), Gray(127, 127, 127),
    Green(0, 128, 0), Lime(0, 255, 0), Magenta(255, 0, 255),
    Navyblue(159, 175, 223), Orange(255, 165, 0),
    Orchid(218, 112, 214), Pink(255, 192, 203),
    Purple(128, 0, 128), Red(255, 0, 0), Silver(192, 192, 192),
    Snow(255, 250, 250), SteelBlue(70, 130, 180),
    SystemColor(0, 0, 0), Turquoise(64, 224, 208),
    Violet(238, 130, 238), White(255, 255, 255),
    Yellow(255, 255, 0);
```

Error handling

There are some functions for error handling: `check` checks whether a condition is true and reports an error if it is not. The `syntaxError` and `semanticError` functions report a syntactic and semantic error, while `error` throws an exception that is caught and reported by the `main` function.

Error.h:

```
#ifndef ERROR_H
#define ERROR_H

#include <QString>

void error(const QString& message);
void syntaxError();
void syntaxError(const QString& message);
void semanticError(const QString& message);
void check(bool condition, const QString& message);

#endif // ERROR_H
```

The `Error.cpp` file holds the definitions of the `Error.h` file.

Error.cpp:

```
#include <SStream>
#include <Exception>
using namespace std;
```

```
#include "Error.h"

extern int g_lineNo = 1;

void error(const QString& message) {
  throw exception(message.toStdString().c_str());
}
```

We use the C++ `stringstream` standard class to compound the error message:

```
void syntaxError() {
  stringstream stringStream;
  stringStream << "Syntax error at line " << g_lineNo << ".";
```

The `str` method returns an object of the C++ `string` standard class, and `c_str` returns a character pointer that is converted to a `QString` object in the `error` call:

```
  error(stringStream.str().c_str());
}
```

A syntax error occurs when the scanner finds a character sequence that does not constitute a token, or when the parser detects that the token sequence does not comply with the grammar. We will cover the topic soon; for now, just remember that a scanner can report errors too:

```
void syntaxError(const QString& message) {
  stringstream stringStream;
  stringStream << "Syntax error at line " << g_lineNo
               << ": " << message.toStdString() << ".";
  error(stringStream.str().c_str());
}
```

A semantic error occurs when an unknown name is found, or when the types of an expression do not comply:

```
void semanticError(const QString& message) {
  stringstream stringStream;
  stringStream << "Sematic error: "
               << message.toStdString() << ".";
  error(stringStream.str().c_str());
}
```

The check method has a similar effect to the assert macro. It checks whether the condition is true. If it is not true, semanticError is called, which eventually throws an error exception:

```
void check(bool condition, const QString& message) {
  if (!condition) {
    semanticError(message);
  }
}
```

The value

There are several kinds of values in the language, which are used to set the color or style of the pen or brush, or to set the end-points of a line, or to set the name of the font, or the alignment of the text: numerical (double), string (QString), color (QColor), font (QFont), point (QPoint), pen style (Qt::PenStyle), brush style (Qt::BrushStyle), and horizontal or vertical alignment (Qt::AlignmentFlag).

Value.h:

```
#ifndef VALUE_H
#define VALUE_H

#include <IOStream>
using namespace std;

#include <QtWidgets>

enum TypeId {NumericalTypeId, StringTypeId, ColorTypeId,
             PenStyleTypeId, BrushStyleId, AlignmentTypeId,
             FontTypeId, PointTypeId};

class Value {
  public:
    Value();
    Value(double numericalValue);
    Value(const QString& stringValue);
    Value(const QPoint& pointValue);
    Value(const QColor& colorValue);
    Value(const QFont& fontValue);
    Value(const Qt::PenStyle& penStyleValue);
    Value(const Qt::BrushStyle& brushStyleValue);
    Value(const Qt::AlignmentFlag& alignment);

    Value(const Value& value);
```

```
    Value& operator=(const Value& value);

    bool isNumerical() const {return (m_typeId==NumericalTypeId);}
    bool isString() const { return (m_typeId == StringTypeId); }
    bool isColor() const { return (m_typeId == ColorTypeId); }
    bool isFont() const { return (m_typeId == FontTypeId); }
    bool isPoint() const { return (m_typeId == PointTypeId); }
    bool isPenStyle() const {return (m_typeId == PenStyleTypeId);}
    bool isBrushStyle() const {return (m_typeId == BrushStyleId);}
    bool isAlignment() const {return (m_typeId==AlignmentTypeId);}

    double numericalValue() const { return m_numericalValue; }
    const QString& stringValue() const { return m_stringValue; }
    const QColor& colorValue() const { return m_colorValue; }
    const QFont& fontValue() const { return m_fontValue; }
    const QPoint& pointValue() const { return m_pointValue; }
    const Qt::PenStyle& penStyleValue() const
                        { return m_penStyleValue; }
    const Qt::BrushStyle& brushStyleValue() const
                           { return m_brushStyleValue; }
    const Qt::AlignmentFlag& alignmentValue() const
                              { return m_alignmentValue; }

private:
    TypeId m_typeId;
    double m_numericalValue;
    QString m_stringValue;
    QPoint m_pointValue;
    QColor m_colorValue;
    QFont m_fontValue;
    Qt::PenStyle m_penStyleValue;
    Qt::BrushStyle m_brushStyleValue;
    Qt::AlignmentFlag m_alignmentValue;
};

#endif // VALUE_H
```

The `Value.cpp` file holds the definitions of the methods of the `Value` class.

Value.cpp:

```
#include <CAssert>
using namespace std;

#include "Value.h"

Value::Value() {
  // Empty.
```

```
  }
```

The non-default constructors initialize the `Value` object with appropriate values:

```
Value::Value(double numericalValue)
 :m_typeId(NumericalTypeId),
  m_numericalValue(numericalValue) {
  // Empty.
}

Value::Value(const QPoint& pointValue)
 :m_typeId(PointTypeId),
  m_pointValue(pointValue) {
  // Empty.
}
```

The scanner

The **scanner** is a part of the application that accepts the source code and generates a sequence of tokens. A **token** is the smallest meaningful part of the source code. For instance, the characters **f**, **o**, **n**, and **t** make up the keyword **font**, and the characters **1**, **2**, and **3** constitute the numerical value **123**.

However, first we need the `Token` class to keep track of the tokens. The `m_tokenId` field is set to a value of the enumeration `TokenId`. In the case of a name, the `m_name` field holds the name, and in the case of a value, the `m_value` field holds the value.

Token.h:

```
#ifndef TOKEN_H
#define TOKEN_H

#include <QWidget>
#include "Value.h"
```

The `TokenId` enumeration holds all the tokens of the scanner. They are divided into keywords, operators, punctuation, and separators, as well as names and values. In order to avoid converting between different enumerations, the `TokenId` enumeration is used by the scanner, parser, and viewer. The `TokenId` enumeration is used by the scanner to distinguish between the different tokens by the parser when type checking and evaluating expressions, and by the `Action` class to distinguish between different actions.

The first part (`ColorId` to `YCoordinateId`) is keywords of the language:

```
enum TokenId {ColorId, DrawEllipseId, DrawLineId,
              DrawRectangleId, DrawTextId, FontId,
              PointId, SetBrushColorId, SetBrushStyleId,
              SetFontId, SetHorizontalAlignmentId,
              SetPenColorId, SetPenStyleId,
              SetVerticalAlignmentId,
              XCoordinateId, YCoordinateId,
```

The second part (`AddId` to `DivideId`) is operators:

```
AddId, SubtractId, MultiplyId, DivideId,
```

The next part is parentheses, assignment (=), comma, and semicolon:

```
LeftParenthesisId, RightParenthesisId,
AssignId, CommaId, SemicolonId,
```

Finally, the last part is the name, value, and end-of-file marking:

```
NameId, ValueId, EndOfFileId};

class Token{
  public:
    Token();
    Token(TokenId tokenId);
    Token(TokenId tokenId, const QString& name);
    Token(TokenId tokenId, const Value& value);
```

Each token can be annotated with a name or a value:

```
    TokenId id() const {return m_tokenId;}
    const QString& name() const { return m_name; }
    const Value& value() const { return m_value; }

  private:
    TokenId m_tokenId;
    QString m_name;
    Value m_value;
};

#endif // TOKEN_H
```

The `Token.cpp` file holds the definitions of the methods of the `Token` class.

Token.cpp:

```cpp
#include "Token.h"
```

The default token is initialized with an end-of-file token:

```cpp
Token::Token()
 :m_tokenId(EndOfFileId) {
   // Empty.
}
```

Most tokens hold only a value of the `TokenId` enumeration:

```cpp
Token::Token(TokenId tokenId)
 :m_tokenId(tokenId) {
   // Empty.
}
```

Tokens can also hold a name or a value:

```cpp
Token::Token(TokenId tokenId, const QString& name)
 :m_tokenId(tokenId),
  m_name(name) {
   // Empty.
}

Token::Token(TokenId tokenId, const Value& value)
 :m_tokenId(tokenId),
  m_value(value) {
   // Empty.
}
```

The `Scanner` class takes the source code and divides it into tokens. A token can also be associated by a name or a value.

Scanner.h:

```cpp
#ifndef SCANNER_H
#define SCANNER_H

#include "Token.h"
#include "Colors.h"
```

The `init` method initializes the names of the keywords and operators:

```
class Scanner {
  public:
    static void init();
    Scanner(QString& buffer);
```

The `nextToken` method scans the buffer and returns the next token. If there is no recognizable token, an error exception is thrown that is later caught by the `main` function:

```
  public:
    Token nextToken();
```

The `m_buffer` field holds the source code; `m_bufferIndex` holds the index of the next character in the buffer to be examined (the index is initialized to zero); `m_keywordMap` holds the names of the keywords; `m_valueMap` holds a map of color, alignment, and pen and brush style values, and `m_operatorList` hold a list of operators:

```
  private:
    QString m_buffer;
    int m_bufferIndex = 0;
```

In previous chapters, we have used the C++ standard classes `map`, `set`, `list`, `vector`, and `stack`. In this chapter, we will use the Qt classes `QMap`, `QSet`, `QList`, `QVector`, and `QStack` instead. They work approximately in the same way:

```
    static QMap<QString,TokenId> m_keywordMap;
    static QMap<QString,Value> m_valueMap;
    static QList<pair<QString,TokenId>> m_operatorList;
};

#endif // SCANNER_H
```

The `Scanner.cpp` file holds the definitions of the methods of the `Scanner` class.

Scanner.cpp:

```
#include <SStream>
#include <IOStream>
#include <Exception>
using namespace std;

#include "Error.h"
#include "Scanner.h"

QMap<QString,Value> Scanner::m_valueMap;
QMap<QString,TokenId> Scanner::m_keywordMap;
```

```
QList<pair<QString, TokenId>> Scanner::m_operatorList;
```

The `g_lineNo` global field keeps track of the current line in the source code, in order for the error messages to state the line number:

```
extern int g_lineNo;
```

The `ADD_TO_OPERATOR_LIST` macro adds a token to the operator list. For instance, `ADD_TO_OPERATOR_LIST("+", AddId)` adds the pair of "+" and `AddId` to the list:

```
#define ADD_TO_OPERATOR_LIST(text, token)
  m_operatorList.push_back(pair<QString,TokenId>(text, token));

void Scanner::init() {
  ADD_TO_OPERATOR_LIST("+", AddId)
  ADD_TO_OPERATOR_LIST("-", SubtractId)
  ADD_TO_OPERATOR_LIST("*", MultiplyId)
  ADD_TO_OPERATOR_LIST("/", DivideId)
  ADD_TO_OPERATOR_LIST("(", LeftParenthesisId)
  ADD_TO_OPERATOR_LIST(")", RightParenthesisId)
  ADD_TO_OPERATOR_LIST("=", AssignId)
  ADD_TO_OPERATOR_LIST(",", CommaId)
  ADD_TO_OPERATOR_LIST(";", SemicolonId)
```

The `ADD_TO_KEYWORD_MAP` macro adds a keyword to the keyword map. For instance, `ADD_TO_KEYWORD_MAP(ColorId)` adds the pair of `Color` and `ColorId` to the map. Note that the `Id` part of the keyword (the last two characters) text is removed:

```
#define ADD_TO_KEYWORD_MAP(x) {
  QString s(#x);
  m_keywordMap[s.toLower().left(s.length() - 2)] = x; }

  ADD_TO_KEYWORD_MAP(ColorId)
  ADD_TO_KEYWORD_MAP(DrawEllipseId)
  ADD_TO_KEYWORD_MAP(DrawLineId)
  ADD_TO_KEYWORD_MAP(DrawRectangleId)
  ADD_TO_KEYWORD_MAP(DrawTextId)
  ADD_TO_KEYWORD_MAP(FontId)
  ADD_TO_KEYWORD_MAP(PointId)
  ADD_TO_KEYWORD_MAP(SetBrushColorId)
  ADD_TO_KEYWORD_MAP(SetBrushStyleId)
  ADD_TO_KEYWORD_MAP(SetFontId)
  ADD_TO_KEYWORD_MAP(SetHorizontalAlignmentId)
  ADD_TO_KEYWORD_MAP(SetPenColorId)
  ADD_TO_KEYWORD_MAP(SetPenStyleId)
  ADD_TO_KEYWORD_MAP(SetVerticalAlignmentId)
  ADD_TO_KEYWORD_MAP(XCoordinateId)
```

```
                ADD_TO_KEYWORD_MAP(YCoordinateId)
```

The `ADD_TO_VALUE_MAP` macro adds a value to the value map. For instance, `ADD_TO_VALUE_MAP(Aqua)` adds the pair of aqua and the `QColor` object Aqua to the map. Note that the text is converted to lower case. Also note that only the last part after the last potential pair of colons (: :) is included:

```
#define ADD_TO_VALUE_MAP(x) {
    QString s(#x);
    QString t = s.toLower();
    int i = t.lastIndexOf("::");
    m_valueMap[(i == -1) ? t : t.mid(i + 2)] = Value(x); }
```

`ADD_TO_VALUE_MAP(Qt::AlignLeft)` adds the pair of align left and the `Qt::PenStyle` value to the map. Again, note that only the last segment of the value's name is stored as text:

```
        ADD_TO_VALUE_MAP(Qt::AlignLeft)
        ADD_TO_VALUE_MAP(Qt::AlignTop)

        ADD_TO_VALUE_MAP(Qt::PenStyle::NoPen)
        ADD_TO_VALUE_MAP(Qt::PenStyle::SolidLine)

        ADD_TO_VALUE_MAP(Qt::BrushStyle::NoBrush)
        ADD_TO_VALUE_MAP(Qt::BrushStyle::SolidPattern)

        ADD_TO_VALUE_MAP(Aqua)
        ADD_TO_VALUE_MAP(Black)
    }
```

In the constructor, we load the buffer into the `m_buffer` field. We also add the null-character (' ') in order to find the end of the buffer in an easier way:

```
    Scanner::Scanner(QString& buffer)
     :m_buffer(buffer)  {
      m_buffer.append('');
    }
```

The `nextToken` method scans the buffer and returns the token found. First, we iterate as long as we find new-line, white-space, or line comment. In case of a new line, we increase the line count:

```
    Token Scanner::nextToken()  {
      while (true)  {
        if (m_buffer[m_bufferIndex] == 'n')  {
          ++g_lineNo;
```

```
        ++m_bufferIndex;
    }
```

A white-space is regular space, a horizontal or vertical tabulator, a return character, or new line. We use the `isSpace` method to check whether the character is a white-space:

```
else if (m_buffer[m_bufferIndex].isSpace()) {
    ++m_bufferIndex;
}
```

If we encounter the beginning of a line comment (`//`), we continue until we find the end of the line (`'n'`) or the end of the buffer (`' '`):

```
else if (m_buffer.indexOf("//", m_bufferIndex) ==
            m_bufferIndex) {
    while ((m_buffer[m_bufferIndex] != QChar('n')) &&
            (m_buffer[m_bufferIndex] != QChar(''))) {
        ++m_bufferIndex;
    }
}
```

If we do not find a new line, white-space, or line comment, we break the iteration and continue looking for the next token:

```
else {
    break;
}
    }
```

When we have scanned through the potential white-spaces and comments, we start looking for the real tokens. We start by checking if the next character in the buffer is a null character (`' '`). If it is a null character, we have found the end of the source code and return end-of-file. Remember that we added a null character at the end of the buffer in the constructor, just to be able to recognize the end of the file:

```
if (m_buffer[m_bufferIndex] == QChar('')) {
    return Token(EndOfFileId);
}
```

If the next token is not end-of-file, we check if it is an operator. We iterate through the operator list and check if the buffer begins with any of the operator's text. For instance, the add operator holds the text +:

```
for (const pair<QString,TokenId>& pair : m_operatorList) {
    const QString& operatorText = pair.first;
    TokenId tokenId = pair.second;
```

When we have found the operator, we increment the buffer index, and return the token:

```
if (m_buffer.indexOf(operatorText, m_bufferIndex) ==
    m_bufferIndex) {
  m_bufferIndex += operatorText.length();
  return Token(tokenId);
}
}
```

If the buffer does not begin with an operator, we look after a name representing a keyword, a value, or simply a name. We start by checking if the buffer begins with a letter or the underscore character ('_'), since a name is allowed to start with a letter or an underscore. However, the remaining characters can be digits besides the letters and underscores:

```
if (m_buffer[m_bufferIndex].isLetter() ||
    (m_buffer[m_bufferIndex] == '_')) {
  int index = m_bufferIndex;
```

We iterate until we find a character that is not a letter, digit, or underscore:

```
while (m_buffer[index].isLetterOrNumber() ||
       (m_buffer[index] == '_')) {
  ++index;
}
```

We extract the text and increase the buffer index:

```
int size = index - m_bufferIndex;
QString text = m_buffer.mid(m_bufferIndex, size).toLower();
m_bufferIndex += size;
```

The text can hold a keyword, a value, or a name. First, we check whether the text is present in the keyword map. If it is present, we just return the token associated with the keyword text:

```
if (m_keywordMap.contains(text)) {
  return Token(m_keywordMap[text]);
}
```

We then check whether the text is present in the value map. If it is present, we return a value token with the value annotated to the token. The value can later be obtained by the parser:

```
else if (m_valueMap.contains(text)) {
  return Token(ValueId, m_valueMap[text]);
}
```

If the text is neither a keyword nor a value, we assume that it is a name and return a name token with the name annotated to the token. The name can later be obtained by the parser:

```
else {
   return Token(NameId, text);
   }
}
```

When we have looked for a name without finding it, we start looking for a string instead. A string is a text enclosed by double quotes (' " '). If the next character in the buffer is a double quote, it is the beginning of a text. We remove the double quote from the buffer and iterate until we find the end quote of the text:

```
if (m_buffer[m_bufferIndex] == '"') {
   int index = m_bufferIndex + 1;

   while (m_buffer[index] != '"') {
```

If we find a null character before the end of the text, a syntax error is reported since we have found the end of the file inside the text:

```
if (m_buffer[index] == QChar('')) {
   syntaxError("unfinished string");
   }

   ++index;
   }
```

When we have found the end quote, we increase the buffer index and return a value token with the text as its annotated value. The text can later be obtained by the parser:

```
int size = index - m_bufferIndex + 1;
QString text = m_buffer.mid(m_bufferIndex, size);
m_bufferIndex += size;
return Token(ValueId, Value(text));
}
```

If the next character in the buffer is a digit, we have found a numerical value, with or without decimals. First, we iterate as long as we find digits in the buffer:

```
if (m_buffer[m_bufferIndex].isDigit()) {
   int index = m_bufferIndex;
   while (m_buffer[index].isDigit()) {
      ++index;
   }
```

When we no longer find any digits, we check whether the next character in the buffer is a dot ('.'). If it is a dot, we continue to iterate as long as we find digits:

```
if (m_buffer[index] == '.') {
  ++index;

  while (m_buffer[index].isDigit()) {
    ++index;
  }
}
```

When we no longer find any digits, we increase the buffer index and return a value token with the annotated value. The value can later be obtained by the parser:

```
int size = index - m_bufferIndex;
QString text = m_buffer.mid(m_bufferIndex, size);
m_bufferIndex += size;
return Token(ValueId, Value(text.toDouble()));
}
```

Finally, if none of the preceding cases apply, the source code is syntactically incorrect, and we report a syntax error:

```
syntaxError();
```

We return an end-of-file token, simply because we have to return a value. However, we will never reach this point of the code since the `syntaxError` call caused an exception to be thrown:

```
  return Token(EndOfFileId);
}
```

Now that we have looked at the scanner, we will continue to look at the parser in the next section.

Building the parser

Now that we have looked into the scanner, it is time to move on to the parser. The parser checks that the source code complies with the grammar. It also performs type checking and generates the action list, which is later displayed by the viewer, as follows. The `Parser` class mirrors the grammar in that way the it holds one method for each grammar rule.

Parser.h:

```
#ifndef PARSER_H
#define PARSER_H

#include "Action.h"
#include "Scanner.h"
```

The constructor takes a grammar object and the action list, which is empty at the beginning. The parser calls the scanner each time it needs a new token:

```
class Parser {
  public:
    Parser(Scanner& m_scanner, QList<Action>& actionList);
```

The `match` method checks whether the given token equals the next token obtained by the scanner. If it does not, a syntax error is reported:

```
  private:
    void match(TokenId tokenId);
```

The remaining methods of the `Parser` class are divided into methods for instructions and expressions in the grammar, as well as methods for type checking and evaluation of expressions:

```
    void instructionList();
    void instruction();
```

We also add a method to the parser for each expression rule in the grammar:

```
    Value expression();
    Value expressionRest(Value leftValue);
    Value mulDivExpression();
    Value mulDivExpressionRest(Value leftValue);
    Value primaryExpression();
    Value primaryExpression();
```

When evaluating the values of expressions, we need to check the types of the values. For instance, when adding two values, both of the operands shall have numerical values:

```
    void checkType(TokenId operatorId, const Value& value);
    void checkType(TokenId operatorId, const Value& leftValue,
                   const Value& rightValue);
    Value evaluate(TokenId operatorId, const Value& value);
    Value evaluate(TokenId operatorId, const Value& leftValue,
                   const Value& rightValue);
```

The `m_lookAhead` field holds the next token obtained by the scanner, and `m_scanner` holds the scanner itself. The `m_actionList` field holds a reference to the action list given in the constructor. Finally, `m_assignMap` holds a map for the names assigned to values by the assignment rule:

```
private:
    Token m_lookAHead;
    Scanner& m_scanner;
    QList<Action>& m_actionList;
    QMap<QString,Value> m_assignMap;
};

#endif // PARSER_H
```

The `Parser.cpp` file holds the definitions of the methods of the `Parser` class.

Parser.cpp:

```
#include <CAssert>
using namespace std;

#include "Value.h"
#include "Token.h"
#include "Scanner.h"
#include "Parser.h"
#include "Error.h"
```

The constructor initializes the references to the scanner and the action list, and sets the `m_lookAHead` field to the first token obtained by the scanner. Then the parsing process begins by calling `instructionList`. When the instruction list has been parsed, the only remaining token shall be the end-of-file token:

```
Parser::Parser(Scanner& m_scanner, QList<Action>& actionList)
   :m_scanner(m_scanner),
    m_actionList(actionList) {
    m_lookAHead = m_scanner.nextToken();
    instructionList();
    match(EndOfFileId);
}
```

The `g_lineNo` field keeps track of the current line of the source code so that a syntax error can be reported with the correct line number:

```
extern int g_lineNo;
```

The `instructionList` method keeps iterating until it encounters the end-of-file token:

```
void Parser::instructionList() {
  while (m_lookAHead.id() != EndOfFileId) {
    instruction();
  }
}
```

The `match` method compares the next token obtained by the scanner with the given token. If they do not comply, a syntax error is reported. If they do comply, the next token is obtained by the scanner:

```
void Parser::match(TokenId tokenId) {
  if (m_lookAHead.id() != tokenId) {
    syntaxError();
  }

  m_lookAHead = m_scanner.nextToken();
}
```

Parsing the instructions of the language

The `instruction` method holds a sequence of switch cases, one case for each category of instructions. We will look into the next token obtained by the scanner:

```
void Parser::instruction() {
  TokenId tokenId = m_lookAHead.id();
```

In the case of a name, we parse the name, assignment (=), the following expression, and a semicolon:

```
switch (tokenId) {
  case NameId: {
      QString assignName = m_lookAHead.name();
      match(NameId);
      match(AssignId);
      Value assignValue = expression();
      match(SemicolonId);
```

If the name is already associated with a value, a semantic error is reported:

```
      check(!m_assignMap.contains(assignName),
          "the name "" + assignName + "" defined twiced");
      m_assignMap[assignName] = assignValue;

    }
    break;
```

The settings of pen and brush colors and styles, as well as fonts and alignments, are a little bit more complicated. We call `expression` to parse and evaluate the value of an expression. The type of the expression is checked, and an `Action` object is added to the action list:

```
case SetPenColorId:
case SetPenStyleId:
case SetBrushColorId:
case SetBrushStyleId:
case SetFontId:
case SetHorizontalAlignmentId:
case SetVerticalAlignmentId: {
    match(tokenId);
    match(LeftParenthesisId);
    Value value = expression();
    match(RightParenthesisId);
    match(SemicolonId);
    checkType(tokenId, value);
    m_actionList.push_back(Action(tokenId, value));
}
break;
```

The drawing of lines, rectangles, ellipses, and text takes two expressions, whose values are evaluated and type checked:

```
case DrawLineId:
case DrawRectangleId:
case DrawEllipseId:
case DrawTextId: {
    match(tokenId);
    match(LeftParenthesisId);
    Value firstValue = expression();
    match(CommaId);
    Value secondValue = expression();
    match(RightParenthesisId);
    match(SemicolonId);
    checkType(tokenId, firstValue, secondValue);
    m_actionList.push_back(Action(tokenId, firstValue,
                                  secondValue));
}
break;
```

If none of the preceding tokens apply, a syntax error is reported:

```
default:
    syntaxError();
}
```

```
    }
```

Parsing the expressions of the language

An expression, at its lowest priority level, is made up by two multiplication or division expressions. First, we call `mulDivExpression`, which is the next expression in increasing priority order, to obtain the left value of a possible addition or subtraction expression, and then `expressionRest`, which checks if there actually is such an expression:

```
Value Parser::expression () {
    Value leftValue = mulDivExpression ();
    return expressionRest(leftValue);
}
```

The `expressionRest` method checks whether the next token is a plus or a minus. In that case, we have an addition or subtraction expression, the token is matched, the left and right values are type checked, and the resulting expression is evaluated and returned:

```
Value Parser::expressionRest(Value leftValue) {
    TokenId tokenId = m_lookAHead.id();

    switch (tokenId) {
      case AddId:
      case SubtractId: {
          match(tokenId);
          Value rightValue = mulDivExpression();
          check(leftValue.isNumerical() && rightValue.isNumerical(),
                "non-numerical values in arithmetic expression");
          Value resultValue =
              evaluate(tokenId, leftValue, rightValue);
          return expressionRest(resultValue);
      }

      default:
        return leftValue;
    }
}
```

The `mulDivExpression` method works in a way similar to `expression` shown previously. It calls `primaryExpression` and `mulDivExpressionRest`, which look for multiplication and division. Multiplication and division have higher priority than addition and subtraction. As stated in *The grammar of source language* section previously, we need a new pair of rules in the grammar, with two pairs of methods in the parser for the addition/subtraction and multiplication/division expressions:

```
Value Parser::mulDivExpression() {
  Value leftValue = primaryExpression();
  return mulDivExpressionRest(leftValue);
}

Value Parser::mulDivExpressionRest(Value leftValue) {
  TokenId tokenId = m_lookAHead.id();

  switch (tokenId) {
    case MultiplyId:
    case DivideId: {
        match(tokenId);
        Value rightValue = primaryExpression();
        check(leftValue.isNumerical() && rightValue.isNumerical(),
            "non-numerical values in arithmetic expression");
        Value resultValue =
          evaluate(tokenId, leftValue, rightValue);
        return mulDivExpressionRest (resultValue);
    }

    default:
      return leftValue;
  }
}
```

Finally, the primary expression is made up by a point, coordinate, color, or font expression. It can also be made up by an expression enclosed in parentheses, a name (in which case we look up its value), or a value:

```
Value Parser::primaryExpression() {
  TokenId tokenId = m_lookAHead.id();
```

The coordinate expression takes a point and returns its x or y coordinate. We match the keyword and the parentheses and call expressions in between. We then check that the value of the expression is a point, and finally call evaluate to extract the *x* or *y* coordinate:

```
switch (tokenId) {
  case XCoordinateId:
  case YCoordinateId: {
      match(tokenId);
      match(LeftParenthesisId);
      Value value = expression();
      match(RightParenthesisId);
      check(value.isPoint(),
          "not a point in coordinate expression");
      checkType(tokenId, value);
      return evaluate(tokenId, value);
```

```
        }
      break;
```

A point expression is made up by the keyword `point` and two numerical expressions: the *x* and *y* coordinate:

```
case PointId: {
    match(PointId);
    match(LeftParenthesisId);
    Value xValue = expression();
    match(CommaId);
    Value yValue = expression();
    match(RightParenthesisId);
    check(xValue.isNumerical() && yValue.isNumerical(),
            "non-numerical values in point expression");
    return Value(QPoint(xValue.numericalValue(),
                        yValue.numericalValue())));
}
```

A color expression is made up by the keyword `color` and three numerical expressions: the red, green, and blue components:

```
case ColorId: {
    match(ColorId);
    match(LeftParenthesisId);
    Value redValue = expression();
    match(CommaId);
    Value greenValue = expression();
    match(CommaId);
    Value blueValue = expression();
    match(RightParenthesisId);
    check(redValue.isNumerical() && greenValue.isNumerical()
            && blueValue.isNumerical(),
            "non-numerical values in color expression");
    return Value(QColor(redValue.numericalValue(),
                        greenValue.numericalValue(),
                        blueValue.numericalValue())));
}
```

A font expression is made up by the keyword `font` and two expressions: the name of the font (string) and its size (numerical):

```
case FontId: {
    match(FontId);
    match(LeftParenthesisId);
    Value nameValue = expression();
    match(CommaId);
```

```
        Value sizeValue = expression();
        match(RightParenthesisId);
        check(nameValue.isString() && sizeValue.isNumerical(),
              "invalid types in font expression");
        return Value(QFont(nameValue.stringValue(),
                           sizeValue.numericalValue())));
    }
```

An expression can be enclosed by parentheses. In that case, we match the parentheses and call `expression` in between to obtain the value of the expression:

```
case LeftParenthesisId: {
    match(LeftParenthesisId);
    Value value = expression();
    match(RightParenthesisId);
    return value;
}
```

In case of a name, we look up its value in the assignment map and return the value. If there is no value, a semantic error is reported:

```
case NameId: {
    QString lookupName = m_lookAHead.name();
    match(NameId);
    check(m_assignMap.contains(lookupName ),
          "unknown name: "" + lookupName + ""."); 
    return m_assignMap[lookupName ];
}
```

In the case of a value, we simply return the value:

```
case ValueId: {
    Value value = m_lookAHead.value();
    match(ValueId);
    return value;
}
```

In any other case, a syntax error is reported:

```
default:
    syntaxError();
    return Value();
    }
}
```

Type checking the expression

The first `checkType` method checks the type of an expression with one value. When setting a pen or brush style, the type must be a pen or brush style, respectively:

```
void Parser::checkType(TokenId codeId, const Value& value) {
  switch (codeId) {
    case SetPenStyleId:
      check(value.isPenStyle(), "not a pen-style value");
      break;

    case SetBrushStyleId:
      check(value.isBrushStyle(), "not a brush-style value");
      break;
```

When setting a color or a font, the value must be a color or a font, respectively:

```
    case SetPenColorId:
    case SetBrushColorId:
      check(value.isColor(), "not a color value");
      break;

    case SetFontId:
      check(value.isFont(), "not a font value");
      break;
```

When setting an alignment, the value must be an alignment:

```
    case SetHorizontalAlignmentId:
    case SetVerticalAlignmentId:
      check(value.isAlignment(), "not an alignment value");
      break;
```

When extracting the *x* or *y* coordinate from a point, the value must be a point:

```
    case XCoordinateId:
    case YCoordinateId:
      check(value.isPoint(), "not a point value");
      break;
  }
}
```

The second `checkType` method takes two values. The drawing instructions must take two points:

```
void Parser::checkType(TokenId codeId, const Value& leftValue,
                       const Value& rightValue) {
```

```
switch (codeId) {
  case DrawLineId:
  case DrawRectangleId:
  case DrawEllipseId:
    check(leftValue.isPoint() && rightValue.isPoint(),
        "non-point values in draw expression");
    break;
```

The drawing of text instructions must take a point and a string:

```
  case DrawTextId:
    check(leftValue.isPoint() && rightValue.isString(),
        "invalid values in text-drawing expression");
    break;
  }
}
```

Evaluating the values of the expressions

The first `evaluate` method returns the value of an expression with one value. The *x* and *y* coordinate operators return the *x* or *y* coordinate of the point:

```
Value Parser::evaluate(TokenId codeId, const Value& value) {
  switch (codeId) {
    case XCoordinateId:
      return Value((double) value.pointValue().x());

    case YCoordinateId:
      return Value((double) value.pointValue().y());
```

The assertion is for debugging purposes only, and we return false simply because the method has to return a value:

```
    default:
      assert(false);
      return false;
  }
}
```

Finally, the second `evaluate` method evaluates the value of expressions with two values. First, we extract numerical values and evaluate the arithmetic expressions:

```
Value Parser::evaluate(TokenId codeId, const Value& leftValue,
                       const Value& rightValue) {
  double leftNumericalValue = leftValue.numericalValue(),
         rightNumericalValue = rightValue.numericalValue();
```

```
switch (codeId) {
  case AddId:
    return Value(leftNumericalValue + rightNumericalValue);

  case SubtractId:
    return Value(leftNumericalValue - rightNumericalValue);

  case MultiplyId:
    return Value(leftNumericalValue * rightNumericalValue);
```

In case of division by zero, a semantic error is reported:

```
  case DivideId:
    if (rightNumericalValue == 0) {
      semanticError("division by zero");
    }

    return Value(leftNumericalValue / rightNumericalValue);
```

Finally, in the point expression, we return a point value holding the two numerical values holding its *x* and *y* coordinates:

```
  case PointId:
    return Value(QPoint(leftNumericalValue,
                        rightNumericalValue));
```

As in the first evaluate case previously, the assertion is for debugging purposes only, and we return false simply because the method has to return a value:

```
  default:
    assert(false);
    return Value();
  }
}
```

The viewer

Finally, it is time to write the viewer, the last part of our DSL. The viewer iterates through the actions and displays the graphical objects. The `ViewerWidget` class inherits the Qt class `QWidget`, which displays a widget on the screen.

ViewerWidget.h:

```
#ifndef MAINWIDGET_H
#define MAINWIDGET_H
```

```
#include <QWidget>
#include <QtWidgets>
#include "Value.h"
#include "Colors.h"
#include "Action.h"

class ViewerWidget : public QWidget {
    Q_OBJECT
```

The constructor calls the constructor of the base class `QWidget` and stores a reference to the action list:

```
public:
    ViewerWidget(const QList<Action>& actionList,
                 QWidget *parentWidget = nullptr);
```

The main part of the class is the `paintEvent` method. It gets called every time the widget needs to be repainted and iterates through the actions list:

```
void paintEvent(QPaintEvent *eventPtr);
```

The default constructor of `QFont` is called, which initializes the font to an appropriate system font. Both the horizontal and vertical alignment is centered. Finally, `m_actionList` holds a reference to the action list generated by the parser:

```
private:
    Qt::Alignment m_horizontalAlignment = Qt::AlignHCenter,
                  m_verticalAlignment = Qt::AlignVCenter;
    const QList<Action>& m_actionList;
};

#endif // MAINWIDGET_H
```

The `ViewerWidget.cpp` file holds the definitions of the methods of the `ViewerWidget` class.

ViewerWidget.cpp:

```
#include <QtWidgets>
#include "ViewerWidget.h"
```

The constructor calls the constructor of the base class `QWidget` with the parent widget, initializes the `m_actionList` reference, sets the title of the widget, and sets an appropriate size:

```
ViewerWidget::ViewerWidget(const QList<Action>& actionList,
                           QWidget *parentWidget)
```

```
  :QWidget(parentWidget),
   m_actionList(actionList) {
   setWindowTitle(tr("Domain Specific Language"));
   resize(500, 300);
}
```

The `paintEvent` method is called every time the widget needs to be repainted. First, the `QPainter` object `painter` is defined, we then iterate through the action list:

```
void ViewerWidget::paintEvent(QPaintEvent* /*event*/) {
  QPainter painter(this);

  for (const Action& action : m_actionList) {
    switch (action.id()) {
```

The `SetPenColor` action creates a new pen with the new color and current style, which is added to `painter`. In the same way, the `SetPenStyle` action creates a pen with the new style and the current color:

```
case SetPenColorId: {
    QColor penColor = action.value1().colorValue();
    QPen pen(penColor);
    pen.setStyle(painter.pen().style());
    painter.setPen(pen);
  }
  break;

case SetPenStyleId: {
    Qt::PenStyle penStyle = action.value1().penStyleValue();
    QPen pen(penStyle);
    pen.setColor(painter.pen().color());
    painter.setPen(pen);
  }
  break;
```

We set the color and style of the brush in the same way as we set the pen previously. The only difference is that we create a brush instead of a pen:

```
case SetBrushColorId: {
    QColor brushColor = action.value1().colorValue();
    QBrush brush(brushColor);
    brush.setStyle(painter.brush().style());
    painter.setBrush(brush);
  }
  break;

case SetBrushStyleId: {
```

```
    Qt::BrushStyle brushStyle =
        action.value1().brushStyleValue();
    QBrush brush(brushStyle);
    brush.setColor(painter.brush().color());
    painter.setBrush(brush);
}
break;
```

In the case of the font, we call `setFont` on `painter`. Thereafter, the font is associated to `painter`, and will be used when writing text:

```
case SetFontId: {
    QFont font = action.value1().fontValue();
    painter.setFont(font);
}
break;
```

The horizontal and vertical alignment are stored in `m_horizontalAlignment` and `m_verticalAlignment`, which are values that are later used when writing text:

```
case SetHorizontalAlignmentId:
    m_horizontalAlignment = action.value1().alignmentValue();
    break;

case SetVerticalAlignmentId:
    m_verticalAlignment = action.value1().alignmentValue();
    break;
```

Now, it is time to actually draw some graphical objects. A line is simply drawn between two points, while a rectangle or ellipse has top-left and bottom-right corners, which are placed in a rectangle that is used as a parameter to the calls to `drawRect` and `drawEllipse`:

```
case DrawLineId:
    painter.drawLine(action.value1().pointValue(),
                     action.value2().pointValue());
    break;

case DrawRectangleId: {
    QRect rect(action.value1().pointValue(),
               action.value2().pointValue());

    painter.drawRect(rect);
}
break;

case DrawEllipseId: {
```

```
        QRect rect(action.value1().pointValue(),
                   action.value2().pointValue());

        painter.drawEllipse(rect);
    }
    break;
```

Finally, we write text. We start by extracting the point to center the text around and the text to draw. We then obtain the size of the text (in pixels) with the Qt QFontMetrics class:

```
case DrawTextId: {
    QPoint point = action.value1().pointValue();
    const QString& text = action.value2().stringValue();
    QFontMetrics metrics(painter.font());
    QSize size = metrics.size(0, text);
```

In the case of left horizontal alignment, the left side of the text is the *x* coordinate of the point. In the case of center alignment, the left side of the text is moved to the left with half the text width, and in the case of right alignment, the left side is moved to the left with the whole text width:

```
    switch (m_horizontalAlignment) {
      case Qt::AlignHCenter:
        point.rx() -= size.width() / 2;
        break;

      case Qt::AlignRight:
        point.rx() -= size.width();
        break;
    }
```

In the same way: in the case of top vertical alignment, the top side of the text is the *y* coordinate of the point. In the case of center alignment, the top side of the text is moved upwards with half of the text height, and in the case of bottom alignment, the top side is moved upwards with the whole text height:

```
    switch (m_verticalAlignment) {
      case Qt::AlignVCenter:
        point.ry() -= size.height() / 2;
        break;

      case Qt::AlignBottom:
        point.ry() -= size.height();
        break;
    }

    painter.drawText(point, text);
```

```
        }
      break;
    }
  }
}
```

The main function

Finally, the main function calls the `init` static method on the scanner in order to initialize its tokens, keywords, and values. A `QApplication` object is created, the source code is read and parsed, and the viewer widget is created. It executes the action list and displays the graphical objects. The application executes until the user presses the close button in the top-right corner.

Main.cpp:

```cpp
#include <QApplication>
#include <QMessageBox>

#include "Action.h"
#include "Error.h"
#include "Scanner.h"
#include "Parser.h"
#include "ViewerWidget.h"

int main(int argc, char *argv[]) {
  Scanner::init();
  QApplication application(argc, argv);

  try {
    QString path = "C:\Input.dsl";
    QFile file(path);
    if (!file.open(QIODevice::ReadOnly)) {
      error("Cannot open file "" + path + "" for reading.");
    }

    QString buffer(file.readAll());
    Scanner scanner(buffer);

    QList<Action> actionList;
    Parser(scanner, actionList);

    ViewerWidget mainWidget(actionList);
    mainWidget.show();
    return application.exec();
```

```
        }
```

In the case of a syntactic or semantic error, its message is displayed in a message box:

```
        catch (exception e) {
          QMessageBox messageBox(QMessageBox::Information,
                          QString("Error"), QString(e.what()));
          messageBox.exec();
        }
      }
```

Summary

In this chapter, we started to develop a DSL that generates a sequence of actions creating graphical objects, which are viewed in a widget. Our DSL supports instructions for drawing graphical objects such as lines, rectangles, ellipses, and text, and for setting the color, style, and alignment of the objects. It also supports expressions with arithmetic operators.

The language of our DSL is defined by grammar and is made up by a scanner that scans the text for meaningful parts, the parser checks that the source code complies with the grammar and generates a sequence of actions, which is read and executed by the viewer.

In the next chapter, we will continue to develop our DSL. The DSL of this chapter only supports code executed in straight sequence. However, in the next chapter, we will add function calls as well as selection and iteration (the `if` and `while` instructions).

10
Advanced Domain-Specific Language

In the previous chapter, we developed a **domain-specific language** (DSL). In this chapter, we will improve the language in several ways:

- We will add **selection** and **iteration**. More specifically, we will add the `if` and `while` instructions. In the language of the previous chapter, the actions were executed in a straightforward manner. In this chapter, it is possible to select between alternatives and to iterate over a part of the code.
- We will add **variables**. In the previous chapter, we could assign values to a name once. In this chapter, however, values are assigned to names that can be reassigned during the execution of the program.
- We add **functions**, with parameters and return values. In the previous chapter, a program was made up of a sequence of instructions. In this chapter, it is a sequence of functions. Similar to C++, there must be a `main` function where the execution starts.
- Finally, we will add another module in the process from the source code to the viewer. In the previous chapter, the parser generated a sequence of actions that were displayed by the viewer. In this chapter, the parser generates a sequence of **directives**, which in turn are evaluated to actions by the **evaluator**.
- Since the language of this chapter supports selection, iteration, variables, and functions calls, it starts to look like a traditional programming language.

Topics we will cover in this chapter include:

- Just as in the previous chapter, we will informally look into the source code of our DSL by looking at an example. However, in this example we will use variables and function calls, we will also use the `if` and `while` instructions.

- We will then formally define our language with **grammar**. The grammar is an extension of the grammar of the last chapter. We will add instructions for functions definitions, calls, and returns, as well as selection (`if`) and iteration (`while`).

- When we have defined the grammar, we will write the **scanner**. The scanner of this chapter is almost identical to the scanner of the previous chapter. The only difference is that we will add a few keywords.

- When we have written the scanner, we will write the **parser**. The parser is an extension of the parser of the previous chapter, we add methods for functions, selection, and iteration. However, the parser of the previous chapter generated a sequence of **actions**, which were read and executed by the **viewer**. In this chapter, however, the parser instead generates a sequence of directives that are read by the evaluator.

- In this chapter, the next step is the evaluator rather than the viewer. The evaluator takes the directive sequence generated by the parser, and generates a sequence of actions which are read and executed by the viewer. The evaluator works with maps that assign values to names. There is a **stack of value maps** that make sure that each called function gets its own fresh value map. There is also a **value stack** that stores temporary values when evaluating expressions. Finally, there is the **call stack**, holding return addresses for function calls.

- Finally, the viewer works in the same way as in the previous chapter. It iterates through the action list generated by the evaluator and displays the graphical objects in a Qt widget.

Improving the source language – an example

Let's look at a new example, where we define and call a function named `triangle` that draws a triangle with different pens in different sizes. Note that the functions do not have to occur in any particular order.

We start by setting the `left` and `length` variables to 50. They hold the *x* coordinate of the left-most corner of the first triangle, and its base length. We also set the `index` variable to zero; its value will be used in the `while` iteration:

```
function main() {
  left = 50;
  length = 50;
  index = 0;
```

We continue to iterate as long as `index` is less than four. Note that in this chapter we add Boolean values to the `Value` class. When `index` holds an even value, we set the pen style to a solid line, and when it holds an odd value, we set the pen style to a dashed line. Note that we have extended the language with relational expressions and the modulus (%) operator:

```
while (index < 4) {
  if ((index % 2) == 0) {
    SetPenStyle(SolidLine);
  }
  else {
    SetPenStyle(DashLine);
  }
```

We set the top-left point of the triangle, and call the `drawTriangle` function to perform the actual drawing of the triangle:

```
topLeft = point(left, 25);
call drawTriangle(topLeft, length);
```

After the call to `triangle`, we increase the base length of the next triangle, and the left-most corner:

```
  length = length + 25;
  left = left + length;
  index = index + 1;
  }
}
```

In the `drawTriangle` function, we call `getTopRight` and `getBottomMiddle` functions to obtain the top-right and bottom-middle points of the triangle. Finally, we draw the three lines of the triangle by calling `drawLine`:

```
function drawTriangle(topLeft, length) {
  topRight = call getTopRight(topLeft, length);
  bottomMiddle = call getBottomMiddle(topLeft, length);
  drawLine(topLeft, topRight);
  drawLine(topRight, bottomMiddle);
```

```
        drawLine(bottomMiddle, topLeft);
    }
```

The `getTopRight` function extracts the *x* and *y* coordinate of the top-left point, and returns a point where the *x* coordinate has been increased by the length of the base of the triangle:

```
function getTopRight(topLeft, length) {
    return point(xCoordinate(topLeft) + length,
                 yCoordinate(topLeft));
}
```

The `getBottomMiddle` function also extracts the *x* and *y* coordinates of the top-left point. Then it calculates the *x* and *y* coordinates of the middle-bottom point and returns `point`:

```
function getBottomMiddle(topLeft, length) {
    left = xCoordinate(topLeft);
    top = yCoordinate(topLeft);
    middle = left + length / 2;
    bottom = top + length;
    return point(middle, bottom);
}
```

The output of the execution of the code is shown in the following screenshot:

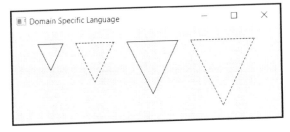

Improving the grammar

In this chapter, we will improve the grammar of our language. To begin with, a program is made up by a sequence of functions rather than instructions. Technically, a program can hold zero functions. However, a semantic error will report that the `main` function is missing:

```
program -> functionDefinitionList
functionDefinitionList -> functionDefinition*
```

The definition of a function is made up by the keyword `function`, a list of names enclosed by parentheses and a list of instructions enclosed by brackets. The `nameList` is made up of zero or more names, separated by commas:

```
functionDefinition -> function name(nameList) { instructionList }
```

When it comes to instructions, we add the calling of a function. We can either call the function directly, as an instruction (`calldrawTriangle` in the preceding example), or as a part of an expression (`callgetTopRight` and `callgetBottomMiddle`).

We also add the `while` instruction and the `if` instructions, with or without the `else` part. Finally, there is also the block instruction: a list of instructions enclosed by brackets:

```
instruction -> callExpression ;
            | while (expression) instruction
            | if (expression) instruction
            | if (expression) instruction else instruction
            | { instructionList }
            | ...

callInstruction -> callExpression ;
```

When it comes to expressions, the only difference is that we have added function calls. The `expressionList` is a list of zero or more expressions, separated by commas:

```
primaryExpression -> call name(expressionList)
                  |
```

The Token and the Scanner

Similar to the previous chapter, the final target code of the language is the actions, even though they are generated by an evaluator rather than the parser. The `Action` class is identical to the class of the previous chapter. So are the `Value` and `ViewerWidget` classes, as well as the colors and error handling. However, the `Token` and `Scanner` classes have been extended. The `TokenId` enumeration has been extended with more token identities.

Token.h:

```
class Token {
  // ...
  enum TokenId {BlockId, CallId, ElseId, FunctionId, GotoId,
                IfId, IfNotGotoId, ReturnId, WhileId, // ...
                };
  // ...
```

```
    };
```

In the same way, `init` in `Scanner` has been extended with the keywords.

Scanner.cpp:

```
void Scanner::init() {
   ADD_TO_KEYWORD_MAP(CallId)
   ADD_TO_KEYWORD_MAP(ElseId)
   ADD_TO_KEYWORD_MAP(FunctionId)
   ADD_TO_KEYWORD_MAP(IfId)
   ADD_TO_KEYWORD_MAP(ReturnId)
   ADD_TO_KEYWORD_MAP(WhileId)
// ...
}
```

The parser

The parser has been extended with methods corresponding to the new rules of the grammar. Moreover, the parser of this chapter does not generate actions; instead, it generates **directives**. The reason for this is that, while the source code of the previous chapter holds instructions that were executed from the beginning to the end, the source code of this chapter holds selection, iteration, and function calls that can alter the flow of the instructions. Therefore, it makes sense to introduce a middle layer—the parser generates directives that are evaluated to become actions.

Since the language of this chapter supports functions, we need the `Function` class to store the functions. It stores the names of the formal parameters and the start address of the function.

Function.h:

```
#ifndef FUNCTION_H
#define FUNCTION_H

#include <QtWidgets>

#include "Value.h"
#include "Action.h"

class Function {
  public:
    Function() {}
    Function(const QList<QString>& nameList, int address);
```

```
    const QList<QString>& nameList() const {return m_nameList;}
    int address() {return m_address;}

    Function(const Function& function);
    Function operator=(const Function& function);

  private:
    QList<QString> m_nameList;
    int m_address;
};

#endif // FUNCTION_H
```

The `Function.cpp` file holds the definitions of the methods of the `Function` class.

Function.cpp:

```
#include "Function.h"

Function::Function(const QList<QString>& nameList, int address)
 :m_nameList(nameList),
  m_address(address) {
  // Empty.
}

Function::Function(const Function& function)
 :m_nameList(function.m_nameList),
  m_address(function.m_address) {
  // Empty.
}

Function Function::operator=(const Function& function) {
  m_nameList = function.m_nameList;
  m_address = function.m_address;
  return *this;
}
```

Since the parser in this chapter generates a sequence of directives rather than actions, we also need the `Directive` class to hold the directives. In most cases, a `Directive` object only holds its identity of the `TokenId` enumeration. However, in the case of a function call, we need to store the name of the function and the number of actual parameters. In the case of a function definition, we store a reference to the `Function` object. In the case of an expression made up by a name of a value, we need to store the name or value. Finally, there are several kinds of jump directives, in which case we need to store the address.

Directive.h:

```
#ifndef DIRECTIVE_H
#define DIRECTIVE_H

#include <QtWidgets>

#include "Token.h"
#include "Value.h"
#include "Function.h"

class Directive {
  public:
    Directive(TokenId tokenId);
    Directive(TokenId tokenId, int address);
    Directive(TokenId tokenId, const QString& name);
    Directive(TokenId tokenId, const QString& name,
              int parameters);
    Directive(TokenId tokenId, const Value& value);
    Directive(TokenId tokenId, const Function& function);

    Directive(const Directive& directive);
    Directive operator=(const Directive& directive);

    TokenId directiveId() {return m_directiveId;}
    const QString& name() {return m_name;}
    const Value& value() {return m_value;}
    const Function& function() {return m_function;}

    int parameters() const {return m_parameters;}
    int address() const {return m_address;}
    void setAddress(int address) {m_address = address;}

  private:
    TokenId m_directiveId;
    QString m_name;
    int m_parameters, m_address;
    Value m_value;
    Function m_function;
};

#endif // DIRECTIVE_H
```

The `Directive.cpp` file holds the definitions of the methods of the `Directive` class.

Directive.cpp:

```
#include "Directive.h"
```

In most cases, we only create an object of the `Directive` class with a directive identity:

```
Directive::Directive(TokenId directiveId)
 :m_directiveId(directiveId) {
   // Empty.
 }
```

The jump directives need the jump address:

```
Directive::Directive(TokenId directiveId, int address)
 :m_directiveId(directiveId),
  m_address(address) {
   // Empty.
 }
```

When assigning a value to a variable, we need the name of the variable. However, we do not need the value since it will be stored on a stack. Also, when an expression is made up of a name, we need to store the name:

```
Directive::Directive(TokenId directiveId, const QString& name)
 :m_directiveId(directiveId),
  m_name(name) {
   // Empty.
 }
```

The directive for function calls needs the name of the function and the number of actual parameters:

```
Directive::Directive(TokenId directiveId, const QString& name,
                     int parameters)
 :m_directiveId(directiveId),
  m_name(name),
  m_parameters(parameters) {
   // Empty.
 }
```

When an expression is made up simply of a value, we just store the value in the directive:

```
Directive::Directive(TokenId directiveId, const Value& value)
 :m_directiveId(directiveId),
  m_value(value) {
   // Empty.
 }
```

Finally, in a function definition we store an object of the `Function` class:

```
Directive::Directive(TokenId directiveId,
                     const Function& function)
```

```
    :m_directiveId(directiveId),
     m_function(function) {
     // Empty.
    }
```

The `Parser` class has been extended with the methods for the new rules in the grammar: function definitions and the `if`, `while`, `call`, and `return` instructions.

Parser.h:

```
// ...

class Parser {
  private:
     void functionDefinitionList();
     void functionDefinition();
```

The `nameList` method gathers the formal parameters of the function, while `expressionList` gathers the actual parameters of the function call:

```
     QList<QString> nameList();
     int expressionList();
```

The `callExpression` method has also been added to the `Parser` class, since a function can be explicitly called as an **instruction**, or as a part of an expression:

```
     void callExpression();
     // ...
};
```

The `Parser.cpp` file holds the definitions of the methods of the `Parser` class.

The start method of the parser of this chapter is `functionDefinitionList`. It calls `functionDefinition` as long as it does not reach end-of-file.

Parser.cpp:

```
    void Parser::functionDefinitionList() {
      while (m_lookAHead.id() != EndOfFileId) {
        functionDefinition();
      }
    }
```

The `functionDefinition` method parses a function definition. We start by matching the `function` keyword and store the name of the function:

```
    void Parser::functionDefinition() {
```

```
match(FunctionId);
QString name = m_lookAHead.name();
match(NameId);
```

The function name is followed by the parameter name list enclosed by parenthesis. We store the name list in the `nList` field. We cannot call the field `nameList`, since that name has already been taken by the method:

```
match(LeftParenthesisId);
QList<QString> nList = nameList();
match(RightParenthesisId);
```

We store the current size of the directive list size as the start address of the function, create a `Function` object with the name list and start address, and add a `Directive` object with the function to the directive list:

```
int startAddress = (int) m_directiveList.size();
Function function(nList, startAddress);
m_directiveList.push_back(Directive(FunctionId, function));
```

The name list is followed by a list of instructions enclosed by brackets:

```
match(LeftBracketId);
instructionList();
match(RightBracketId);
```

Just to be sure the function really returns the controls back to the calling function, we add a `Directive` object with the `return` token identity:

```
m_directiveList.push_back(Directive(ReturnId));
```

When the function has been defined, we check that there is no other function with the same name:

```
check(!m_functionMap.contains(name),
    "function "" + name + "" already defined");
```

If the function is named `"main"`, it is the start function of the program and it cannot have parameters:

```
check(!((name == "main") && (nList.size() > 0)),
    "function "main" cannot have parameters");
```

Finally, we add the function to the `functionMap`:

```
m_functionMap[name] = function;
}
```

The `nameList` method parses a comma-separated list of names enclosed in parentheses:

```
QList<QString> Parser::nameList() {
  QList <QString> nameList;
```

We continue as long as we do not encounter a right parenthesis:

```
while (m_lookAHead.id() != RightParenthesisId) {
  QString name = m_lookAHead.name();
  nameList.push_back(name);
  match(NameId);
```

After we have matched the name, we check whether the next token is a right parenthesis. If it is, we have reached the end of the name list and break the iteration:

```
if (m_lookAHead.id() == RightParenthesisId) {
  break;
}
```

If the next token is not a right parenthesis, we instead assume that it is a comma, match it, and continue to iterate with the next expression:

```
    match(CommaId);
  }
```

Finally, before we return the name list, we need to check that no name occurs twice in the name list. We iterate through the name list and add the names to a set:

```
QSet<QString> nameSet;
for (const QString& name : nameList) {
  if (nameSet.contains(name)) {
    semanticError("parameter "" + name + "" defined twice");
  }

  nameSet.insert(name);
}

return nameList;
}
```

The `instructionList` method looks a little bit different in this chapter since it is placed inside a block of instructions. We iterate as long as we do not encounter a right bracket:

```
void Parser::instructionList() {
  while (m_lookAHead.id() != RightBracketId) {
    instruction();
  }
}
```

As a function can be explicitly called as an instruction, or as part of an expression, we simply call `callExpression` and match the semicolon in the case of a call instruction:

```
void Parser::instruction() {
  switch (m_lookAHead.id()) {
    case CallId:
      callExpression();
      match(SemicolonId);
      break;
```

In the return instruction, we match the `return` keyword and check whether it is followed by a semicolon. If it is not followed by a semicolon, we parse an expression and then assume that the next token is a semicolon. Note that we do not store the result of the expression. The evaluator will place its value on a stack later in the process:

```
    case ReturnId:
      match(ReturnId);

      if (m_lookAHead.id() != SemicolonId) {
        expression();
      }

      m_directiveList.push_back(Directive(ReturnId));
      match(SemicolonId);
      break;
```

In the case of the `if` keyword, we match it and parse an expression enclosed by parentheses:

```
    case IfId: {
      match(IfId);
      match(LeftParenthesisId);
      expression();
      match(RightParenthesisId);
```

If the expression becomes evaluated to a false value, we shall jump over the instruction following the `if` expression. Therefore, we add a `IfNotGoto` directive, intending to jump over the instruction following the `if` keyword:

```
      int ifNotIndex = (int) m_directiveList.size();
      m_directiveList.push_back(Directive(IfNotGotoId, 0));
      instruction();
```

If the instruction is followed by the `else` keyword, we match it and add a `Goto` directive, that is intended to jump over the `else` part in the case of a true value of the expression of the `if` instruction:

```
if (m_lookAHead.id() == ElseId) {
  match(ElseId);
  int elseIndex = (int) m_directiveList.size();
  m_directiveList.push_back(Directive(GotoId, 0));
```

We then set the jump address of the preceding `IfNotTrue` directive. If the expression is not true, the program shall jump to this point:

```
m_directiveList[ifNotIndex].
  setAddress((int) m_directiveList.size());
instruction();
```

On the other hand, if the expression of the `if` instruction is true, the program shall jump over the `else` part to this point:

```
m_directiveList[elseIndex].
  setAddress((int) m_directiveList.size());
}
```

If the `if` instruction is not followed by the `else` keyword, it shall jump to this point in the program if the expression is not true:

```
else {
  m_directiveList[ifNotIndex].
    setAddress((int) m_directiveList.size());
  }
}
break;
```

In the case of the `while` keyword, we match it and store the current index of the directive list in order for the program to jump back to this point after every iteration:

```
case WhileId: {
  match(WhileId);
  int whileIndex = (int) m_directiveList.size();
```

We then parse the expression and its enclosing parentheses:

```
match(LeftParenthesisId);
expression();
match(RightParenthesisId);
```

In the case that the expression is not true, we add an IfNotGoto directive in order for the program to jump out of the iteration:

```
int ifNotIndex = (int) m_directiveList.size();
m_directiveList.push_back(Directive(IfNotGotoId, 0));
instruction();
```

We add a Goto directive after the instruction following the while expression, so that the program can jump back to the expression at the end of each iteration:

```
m_directiveList.push_back(Directive(GotoId, whileIndex));
```

Finally, we set the address of the IfNotTrue directive at the beginning of the while instruction, so that it can jump to this point in the program if the expression is not true:

```
m_directiveList[ifNotIndex].
    setAddress((int) m_directiveList.size());
}
break;
```

In the case of a left bracket, we have a sequence of instructions enclosed by brackets. We parse the pair of brackets and call instructionList:

```
case LeftBracketId:
    match(LeftBracketId);
    instructionList();
    match(RightBracketId);
    break;
```

Finally, in the case of a name, we have an assignment. We match the name keyword, and the assignment operator (=), parse the expression, and match the semicolon. We then add an Assign object to the directive list holding the name to be assigned a value. Note that we do not store the value of the expression, since it will be pushed on a value stack by the evaluator:

```
case NameId: {
    QString name = m_lookAHead.name();
    match(NameId);
    match(AssignId);
    expression();
    match(SemicolonId);
    m_directiveList.push_back(Directive(AssignId, name));
}
break;
// ...
}
```

```
}
```

The `callExpression` method matches the `call` keyword, stores the name of the function, parses the parameter expressions, and adds a `Directive` object holding the call to the directive list. Note that we do not check whether the function exists or count the number of parameters at this point, since the function may be not yet defined. All type checking is taken care of by the evaluator later in the process:

```
void Parser::callExpression() {
  match(CallId);
  QString name = m_lookAHead.name();
  match(NameId);
  match(LeftParenthesisId);
  int size = expressionList();
  match(RightParenthesisId);
  m_directiveList.push_back(Directive(CallId, name, size));
}
```

The `expressionList` method parses a list of expressions. Unlike the preceding name list case, we do not return the list itself, only its size. The expressions generate directives of their own, their values are stored on a stack by the evaluator later in the process:

```
int Parser::expressionList() {
  int size = 0;
```

We iterate as long as we do not encounter a right parenthesis:

```
while (m_lookAHead.id() != RightParenthesisId) {
  expression();
  ++size;
```

After parsing the expression, we check whether the next token is a right parenthesis. If it is, the expression list is finished and we break the iteration:

```
if (m_lookAHead.id() == RightParenthesisId) {
  break;
}
```

If the next token is not a right parenthesis, we assume it is a comma, match it, and continue the iteration:

```
match(CommaId);
}
```

Finally, after the iteration, we return the number of expressions:

```
      return size;
   }
```

The evaluator

The **evaluator** evaluates a sequence of directives and generates a list of actions that are later read and executed by the viewer. The evaluation starts with the directive on the first line, which is a jump to the start address of the `main` function. The evaluation stops when it encounters a `return` directive without a return address. In that case, we have reached the end of `main` and the execution shall be finished.

The evaluator works against a stack of values. Each time a value has been evaluated it is pushed on the stack, and each time values are needed to evaluate an expression they are popped from the stack.

Evaluator.h:

```
      #ifndef EVALUATOR_H
      #define EVALUATOR_H

      #include <QtWidgets>

      #include "Error.h"
      #include "Directive.h"
      #include "Action.h"
      #include "Function.h"
```

The constructor of the `Evaluator` class evaluates the directive list with the help of the functions map:

```
      class Evaluator {
        public:
          Evaluator(const QList<Directive>& directiveList,
                    QList<Action>& actionList,
                    QMap<QString,Function> functionMap);
```

The checkType and evaluate methods are identical to the previous chapter. They have been moved from Parser to Evaluator. The checkType methods check that the expressions associated with the token have the correct types, and the evaluate methods evaluates the expressions:

```
private:
  void checkType(TokenId tokenId, const Value& value);
  void checkType(TokenId tokenId, const Value& leftValue,
                 const Value& rightValue);

  Value evaluate(TokenId tokenId, const Value& value);
  Value evaluate(TokenId tokenId, const Value& leftValue,
                 const Value& rightValue);
```

When an expression is being evaluated, its value is pushed on m_valueStack. When a variable is assigned a value, its name and the value are stored in m_valueMap. Note that, in this chapter, a value can be assigned to a variable more than once. When a function calls another function, the value map of the calling function is pushed on m_valueMapStack in order to give the called function a fresh value map, and the return address is pushed on m_returnAddressStack:

```
    QStack<Value> m_valueStack;
    QMap<QString,Value> m_valueMap;
    QStack<QMap<QString,Value>> m_valueMapStack;
    QStack<int> m_returnAddressStack;
};

#endif // EVALUATOR_H
```

The Evaluator.cpp file holds the definitions of the methods of the Evaluator class:

Evaluator.cpp:

```
    #include <CAssert>
    using namespace std;

    #include "Error.h"
    #include "Evaluator.h"
```

The constructor of the Evaluator class can be regarded as the heart of the evaluator.

The `directiveIndex` field in the constructor is the index of the current `Directive` object in the directive list. Normally, it is increased for each iteration. However, it can be assigned different values due to `if` or `while` instructions as well as function calls and returns:

```
Evaluator::Evaluator(const QList<Directive>& directiveList,
                     QList<Action>& actionList,
                     QMap<QString,Function> functionMap) {
    int directiveIndex = 0;

    while (true) {
        Directive directive = directiveList[directiveIndex];
        TokenId directiveId = directive.directiveId();
```

When a function is called, we start by looking up the function name in the function map and report a semantic error if we do not find it. Then we check that the number of actual parameters equals the number of formal parameters (the size of the name list in the `Function` object):

```
switch (directiveId) {
    case CallId: {
        QString name = directive.name();
        check(functionMap.contains(name),
              "missing function: "" + name + """);
        Function function = functionMap[name];
        check(directive.parameters() ==
              function.nameList().size(),
              "invalid number of parameters");
```

When we call the function, we push the index of the next directive on the return address stack, so that the called function can return to the correct address. We push the value map of the calling function at the value map stack, so we can retrieve it after the call. We then clear the value map so that it is fresh to be used by the called function. Finally, we set the directive index to the start address of the called function, which moves the control to the beginning of the called function. Note that we do nothing about the actual parameter expressions. They have already been evaluated, and their values are pushed at the value stack:

```
        m_returnAddressStack.push(directiveIndex + 1);
        m_valueMapStack.push(m_valueMap);
        m_valueMap.clear();
        directiveIndex = function.address();
    }
    break;
```

At the beginning of a function, we pop the value stack for each parameter and associate each parameter name with its value in the value map. Remember that the parameter expressions were evaluated before the call to the function, and that their values were pushed on the value stack. Also remember that the first parameter was pushed first and is placed below the other parameters in the stack, which is why we assign the parameters in reverse order. Finally, remember that the value map of the calling function was pushed on the value map stack, and that the value stack was cleared during the function call, so that the current value map is empty at the beginning of the function:

```
case FunctionId: {
    const Function& function = directive.function();
    const QList<QString>& nameList = function.nameList();

    for (int listIndex = ((int) nameList.size() - 1);
        listIndex >= 0; --listIndex) {
        const QString& name = nameList[listIndex];
        m_valueMap[name] = m_valueStack.pop();
    }
}
++directiveIndex;
break;
```

When returning from a function, we first check whether the return address stack is empty. If it is not empty, we perform a normal function return. We restore the value map of the calling function by popping the value map stack. We also set the directive index to the address following the function call by popping the return address stack:

```
case ReturnId:
    if (!m_returnAddressStack.empty()) {
        m_valueMap = m_valueMapStack.pop();
        directiveIndex = m_returnAddressStack.pop();
    }
```

If the return address stack is empty, however, we have a special case—we have reached the end of the `main` function. In that case, we shall not return to a calling function (there is no calling function). Instead, we shall just finish the execution of the evaluator by calling return. Remember that we are in the constructor of the `Evaluator` class, and that we return from the constructor:

```
    else {
        return;
    }
    break;
```

The IfNotGoto directive has been added by the parser when parsing the if or while instructions. We pop the value stack; if it is false we perform a jump by setting the directive index by calling the address method of the directive. Remember that we, in this chapter, have added Boolean values to the Value class:

```
case IfNotGotoId: {
    Value value = m_valueStack.pop();

    if (!value.booleanValue()) {
      directiveIndex = directive.address();
    }
```

If the value is true, we do not perform a jump; we simply increase the directive index:

```
    else {
       ++directiveIndex;
    }
  }
  break;
```

The Goto directive performs an unconditional jump; we simply set the new directive index. Since the IfNotGoto and Goto directives have been generated by the parser, we do not need to perform any type checking:

```
case GotoId:
    directiveIndex = directive.address();
    break;
```

The set directives work in a way corresponding to the parser of the previous chapter. The value of the expression has been pushed to the value stack during the evaluation of an earlier directive. We pop the value of the value stack and check that it holds the correct type. Then we add the action with the value to the action list and increase the directive index:

```
case SetPenColorId:
case SetPenStyleId:
case SetBrushColorId:
case SetBrushStyleId:
case SetFontId:
case SetHorizontalAlignmentId:
case SetVerticalAlignmentId: {
    Value value = m_valueStack.pop();
    checkType(directiveId, value);
    actionList.push_back(Action(directiveId, value));
    ++directiveIndex;
  }
```

```
        break;
```

Also, the draw directives are similar to the parser in the previous chapter. Their first and second value are popped in reverse order, since the first value was pushed first and thereby is placed below the second value on the stack. We then check that the values have correct types, add the action to the action list, and increase the directive index:

```
case DrawLineId:
case DrawRectangleId:
case DrawEllipseId:
case DrawTextId: {
    Value secondValue = m_valueStack.pop();
    Value firstValue = m_valueStack.pop();
    checkType(directiveId, firstValue, secondValue);
    actionList.push_back(Action(directiveId, firstValue,
                                secondValue));
    ++directiveIndex;
}
break;
```

The assignment directive associates a name with the value in the value map. Note that if the name already has been associated with a value, the previous value is overwritten. Also note that the value map is local to the current function, potential calling functions have their own value maps pushed on the value map stack:

```
case AssignId: {
    Value value = m_valueStack.pop();
    m_valueMap[directive.name()] = value;
    ++directiveIndex;
}
break;
```

In an expression with one value, its value is popped from the stack, its type is checked, and the resulting value of the expression is evaluated and pushed on the value stack. Finally, the directive index is increased:

```
case XCoordinateId:
case YCoordinateId: {
    Value value = m_valueStack.pop();
    checkType(directiveId, value);
    Value resultValue = evaluate(directiveId, value);
    m_valueStack.push(resultValue);
    ++directiveIndex;
}
break;
```

In an expression with two values, its first and second value are popped from the stack (in reverse order), their types are checked, and the resulting value of the expression is evaluated and pushed on the value stack. Finally, the directive index is increased:

```
case AddId:
case SubtractId:
case MultiplyId:
case DivideId:
case PointId: {
    Value rightValue = m_valueStack.pop();
    Value leftValue = m_valueStack.pop();
    checkType(directiveId, leftValue, rightValue);
    Value resultValue =
        evaluate(directiveId, leftValue, rightValue);
    m_valueStack.push(resultValue);
    ++directiveIndex;
}
break;
```

In a color expression, the red, green, and blue component values are popped from the value stack (in reverse order), their types are checked, and the resulting color is pushed on the value stack. Finally, the directive index is increased:

```
case ColorId: {
    Value blueValue = m_valueStack.pop();
    Value greenValue = m_valueStack.pop();
    Value redValue = m_valueStack.pop();
    checkColorType(redValue, greenValue, blueValue);
    QColor color(redValue.numericalValue(),
                 greenValue.numericalValue(),
                 blueValue.numericalValue());
    m_valueStack.push(Value(color));
    ++directiveIndex;
}
break;
```

In a font expression, the values of the name and size are popped from the value stack (in reverse order) and their types are checked. The resulting font is pushed on the value stack and the directive index is increased:

```
case FontId: {
    Value sizeValue = m_valueStack.pop();
    Value nameValue = m_valueStack.pop();
    checkFontType(nameValue, sizeValue,
                  boldValue, italicValue);
    QFont font(nameValue.stringValue(),
               sizeValue.numericalValue());
```

```
            m_valueStack.push(Value(font));
            ++directiveIndex;
        }
        break;
```

In the case of a name, we look up its value and push it on the value stack and increase the directive index. If there is no value associated with the name, a semantic error is reported:

```
case NameId: {
    QString name = directive.name();
    check(m_valueMap.contains(name),
        "unknown name: "" + name +""");
    m_valueStack.push(m_valueMap[name]);
    ++directiveIndex;
}
break;
```

Finally, when we have a value, we just push it on the value stack and increase the directive index:

```
case ValueId:
    m_valueStack.push(directive.value());
    ++directiveIndex;
    break;
        }
    }
}
```

The main function

Finally, the `main` function is almost identical to the previous function.

Main.cpp:

```
#include <QApplication>
#include <QMessageBox>
#include <IOStream>
using namespace std;

#include "Action.h"
#include "Error.h"
#include "Scanner.h"
#include "Parser.h"
#include "Evaluator.h"
#include "ViewerWidget.h"
```

```
int main(int argc, char *argv[]) {
  Scanner::init();
  QApplication application(argc, argv);

  try {
    QString path = "C:\Input.dsl";

    QFile file(path);
    if (!file.open(QIODevice::ReadOnly)) {
      error("Cannot open file "" + path + "" for reading.");
    }

    QString buffer(file.readAll());
    Scanner scanner(buffer);
```

The only difference is that the parser generates a sequence of directives rather than actions, as well as a function map, which is sent to the evaluator that generates the final action list that is read and executed by the viewer that displays the graphical objects:

```
    QList<Directive> directiveList;
    QMap<QString,Function> functionMap;
    Parser(scanner, directiveList, functionMap);

    QList<Action> actionList;
    Evaluator evaluator(directiveList, actionList, functionMap);

    ViewerWidget mainWidget(actionList);
    mainWidget.show();
    return application.exec();
  }
  catch (exception e) {
    QMessageBox messageBox(QMessageBox::Information,
                           QString("Error"), QString(e.what()));
    messageBox.exec();
  }
}
```

Summary

In this chapter, we have improved the DSL that we started to work on in the previous chapter. We have added selection, iteration, variables, and function calls. We have also added the evaluator, which takes the directives generated by the parser and generates the actions read and executed by the viewer. When the directives are being executed, the values of the expressions are stored on a stack, the values assigned to names are stored in a map, and the return address of function calls are stored on a stack.

This was the final chapter, I hope you have enjoyed the book!

Other Books You May Enjoy

If you enjoyed this book, you may be interested in these other books by Packt:

Beginning C++ Programming
Richard Grimes

ISBN: 978-1-78712-494-3

- Get familiar with the structure of C++ projects
- Identify the main structures in the language: functions and classes
- Feel confident about being able to identify the execution flow through the code
- Be aware of the facilities of the standard library
- Gain insights into the basic concepts of object orientation
- Know how to debug your programs
- Get acquainted with the standard C++ library

Modern C++ Programming Cookbook
Marius Bancila

ISBN: 978-1-78646-518-4

- Get to know about the new core language features and the problems they were intended to solve
- Understand the standard support for threading and concurrency and know how to put them on work for daily basic tasks
- Leverage C++'s features to get increased robustness and performance
- Explore the widely-used testing frameworks for C++ and implement various useful patterns and idioms
- Work with various types of strings and look at the various aspects of compilation
- Explore functions and callable objects with a focus on modern features
- Leverage the standard library and work with containers, algorithms, and iterators
- Use regular expressions for find and replace string operations
- Take advantage of the new filesystem library to work with files and directories
- Use the new utility additions to the standard library to solve common problems developers encounter including string_view, any, optional and variant types

Leave a review - let other readers know what you think

Please share your thoughts on this book with others by leaving a review on the site that you bought it from. If you purchased the book from Amazon, please leave us an honest review on this book's Amazon page. This is vital so that other potential readers can see and use your unbiased opinion to make purchasing decisions, we can understand what our customers think about our products, and our authors can see your feedback on the title that they have worked with Packt to create. It will only take a few minutes of your time, but is valuable to other potential customers, our authors, and Packt. Thank you!

Index

77694193R00246

Made in the USA
San Bernardino, CA
26 May 2018